A HUNDRED YEARS OF THE ASHES

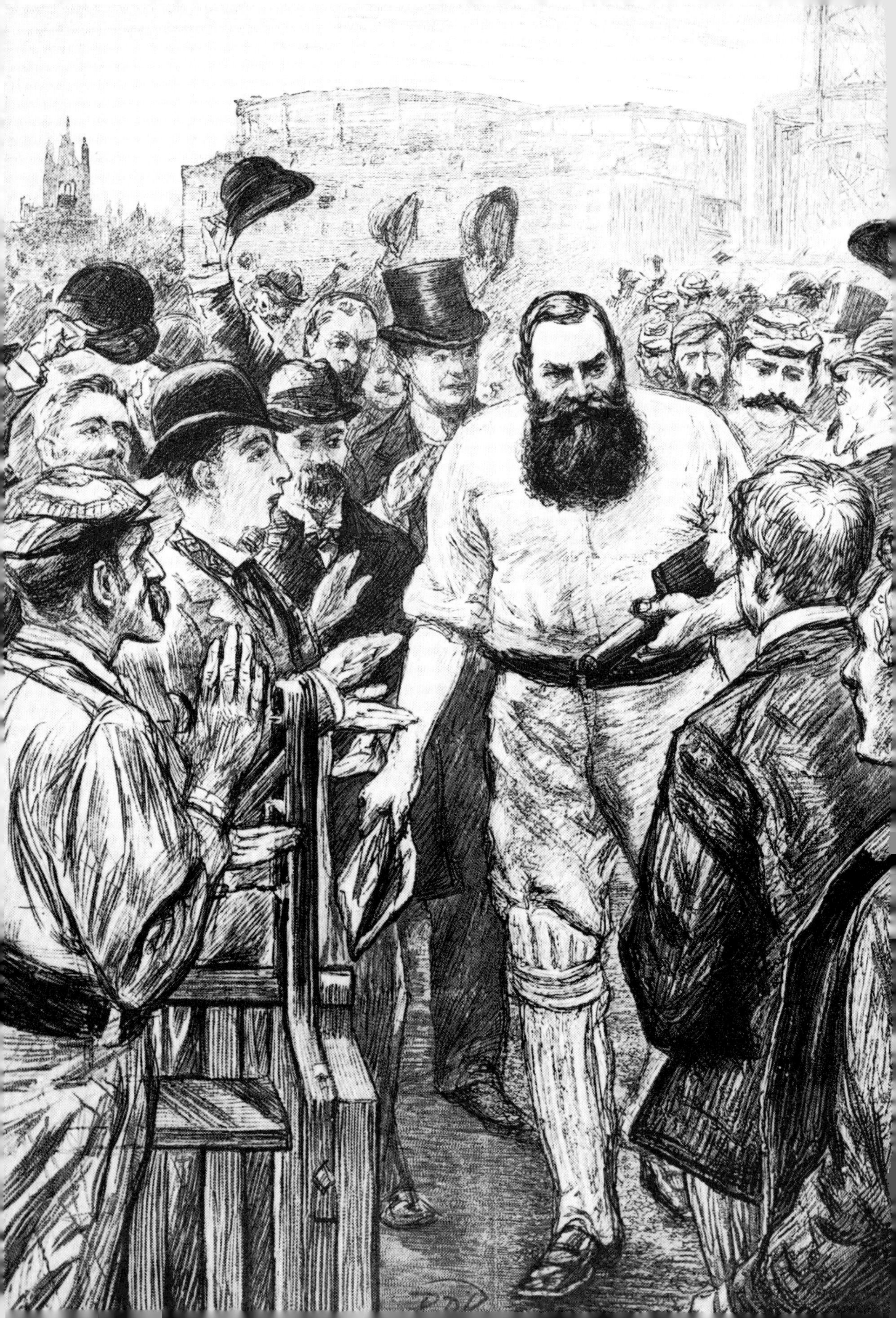

A HUNDRED YEARS OF THE ASHES

By Doug Ibbotson and Ralph Dellor

Foreword by Richie Benaud
Edited by David Frith

Rothmans Publications Limited

Published in Great Britain by
Rothmans Publications Limited,
Oxford Road, Aylesbury, Bucks.

ISBN 0 907574 03 3

Written and compiled by Doug Ibbotson
assisted by Ralph Dellor
Edited by David Frith

Designed by Tim McPhee
Design and production in association with
Book Production Consultants, Cambridge

Typeset by King's English Typesetters Ltd,
Bramley, Leeds
Printed by the Thetford Press Ltd, Thetford, Norfolk
Bound by Norton Bridge Bookbinders Ltd,
Hitchin, Herts

Photographs: Central Press Photos Ltd, Press Association Photos, Popperfoto, Flicks Photograph Library, David Frith

Front cover: *Lord Sheffield's England party for the 1891–92 tour of Australia; the urn containing the Ashes (reproduced by courtesy of the MCC, Bridgeman Art Library); and Ian Botham in 1981 during the Third Test at Headingley when he made 149 not out (Patrick Eagar).*
Frontis: *England v. Australia at The Oval, 1893. Lunch-hour on the first day. W. G. Grace (63 not out) and A. E. Stoddart (71 not out).*
Pages 10/11: *'The Ashes Match' – England v. Australia at The Oval, 1882.*
Pages 126/127: *A panoramic view of Lord's during the second Test, 1968.*

CONTENTS

FOREWORD
From Rothmans Publications

To the lover of Cricket, no perspective of the game is more evocative of its character, its drama and its development than that which has unfolded in the name of The Ashes.

Rothmans have long been associated with Cricket and are particularly pleased to be publishing this permanent celebration of the Ashes in its centenary year.

The book was conceived, and has been created, in an atmosphere of dedicated and contageous enthusiasm which is delightfully evident in the finished work.

We are grateful to Doug Ibbotson, Ralph Dellor and David Frith for their, and our, enjoyment in the research and graphic recapitulation of a classic epoch in sporting history.

FOREWORD
By Richie Benaud

FROM Botham to Spofforth is quite a span, but any reflection on the past 100 years since that 1882 Oval match brings instant appreciation of the influence of the two men in matches 99 years apart.

Botham's performances at Headingley, Edgbaston and Old Trafford in 1981 will still be talked about in 2082, and he was deservedly Man of the Series.

What, then, of Fred Spofforth 100 years ago? Musing here at The Oval on the 100th year of Ashes battles, I backtracked to 1882 and to 1880, the latter match having taken place without Spofforth, who had suffered a broken hand when hit by a wild Yorkshire fast bowler at Scarborough. Two years later he produced:

O.	M.	R.	W.
36.3	18	46	7
28	15	44	7

The figures were achieved bowling at an England victory target of only 85. Some performance!

Without Spofforth, and others, there would have been no mock obituary notice in the *Sporting Times* and no bail burned in Melbourne by the lady who later snared the Hon. Ivo Bligh. I have long wondered about that bail – and the urn – and the velvet bag. How did she manage to do all that in Melbourne and make the presentation when the third and fourth matches were both played in Sydney?

You can bet your life the young lady had no idea what she was starting; nor could she have had any idea then that, no matter how many times Australia won those Ashes, her beloved Melbourne would never see them, let alone touch them!

In 1981 we were lucky to see the most wonderful aspects of cricket. It was a marvellously exciting summer, as it must have been in 1882, when England needed only 85 to win. To be bowled out for 77 must have been an awful feeling for the batting side, one that comes to all cricketers at some stage of their careers, and Australia followed this up with another dashing victory four months later.

It was in 1899 that the great 'W.G.' played his final Test, at Trent Bridge, and made 28 and 1 – and in the same match Victor Trumper made his debut for Australia and scored 0 and 11. What timing to have such a departure and arrival.

Warwick Armstrong made his debut in 1902 on his own Melbourne Cricket Ground, where his XXXOS shirt still is on view in a glass case. In the same year, Trumper hit a brilliant century at Old Trafford. Then, in the next Test, here at The Oval, Gilbert Jessop hit that astonishing 104 in 76 minutes to win the final Test.

Armstrong was captain in Australia when J. W. H. T. Douglas led the 1920–21 side there, and almost immediately afterwards the two teams met again in England. Ten Tests in eight months against what is often argued to be the greatest Australian team of all time. What a task to offer an England captain! Almost on a par with the one offered to Ian Botham in 1980 and 1981.

The balance changed in 1926, with England regaining the Ashes at The Oval and Wilfred Rhodes, at the age of 48, routing Australia for only 125 on the final day. England's captain on that great day was Percy Chapman, and he followed up that victory by retaining the Ashes in Australia in 1928–29 by four matches to one in a series where the young Don Bradman made his debut. Like Trumper, Bradman made little impact in his first match, and he is unlikely to have been well pleased by the England victory margin in that match – 675 runs – nor by being dropped for the next Test. Were olden-day selectors as good as those of the modern era?

When Bradman came to England in 1930 under Bill Woodfull, Australia regained the Ashes at The Oval, with Bradman hitting 232. The Bodyline series gave them back to England, but they changed hands yet again at The Oval in 1934. When England ensured their return at The Oval almost 19 years later, I was in the Australian touring team, though not actually playing in the match.

This was the start of a marvellous England era. Peter May and Fred Trueman were the young players in the side, and the experienced men, Hutton, Compton, Graveney, Bailey, Evans, Laker, Lock and Bedser, made a formidable group of opponents.

There were three young Australians in the touring team that summer, Davidson, Archer and Benaud, and the thing that really hurt in the period 1951–58 was not winning anything against England. No Ashes, no series – nothing. Victories at Brisbane, 1954, and Lord's, 1956, were small fodder for enthusiastic young Australians, and even more numbing was Jim Laker's bag of 46 wickets in that 1956 series.

That period, 1953–59, provided for the England selectors a bowling choice of Trueman, Tyson, Statham, Bailey, Loader, Appleyard, Laker, Lock and Wardle. What luxury! I refuse to live in the past, but, as bowling attacks go, that list of starters is one of the most formidable known in the history of Ashes battles.

Old Trafford 1961 remains the great personal memory for me because of the way we escaped from what seemed certain defeat. It was a match something like Edgbaston 1981, though England's task in 1961 of making over 250 in the fourth innings was not at all easy.

Over the next 10 years the two countries had a series of matches where draws dominated – 17 of them in 26 games – a high percentage for undecided games. Ray Illingworth's team recovered the Ashes in 1971 and Australia produced a new captain, Ian Chappell, who, with his brother Greg, stiffened the Australian determination once again to retrieve the Ashes.

It must have been galling to the young Australian team in 1981 to have those Ashes all but in their grasp at Headingley and then to have England retain them at Old Trafford . . . and, more import, the series as well.

Many people remarked to me that things would have been different had that great Australian team of the late 1950s and early 1960s been playing. Memories become unreliable over the years, and I can tell you Australian teams of that time played just as badly and at times just as well as those 1981 Australians.

And, remarkable though it may seem in retrospect, we were, at the time, criticised just as bitterly, and praised as fulsomely, for being either inept or brillant.

Battles between England and Australia bring out a slightly sharper edge to the contest. They have been doing so for a long time now and I suppose it says much for a game that is now played at international level, having originally been built up around a handful of ashes which never see the light of day.

KENNINGTON OVAL
August 1981

PART ONE BY DOUG IBBOTSON

1981 – 1882 – 1936

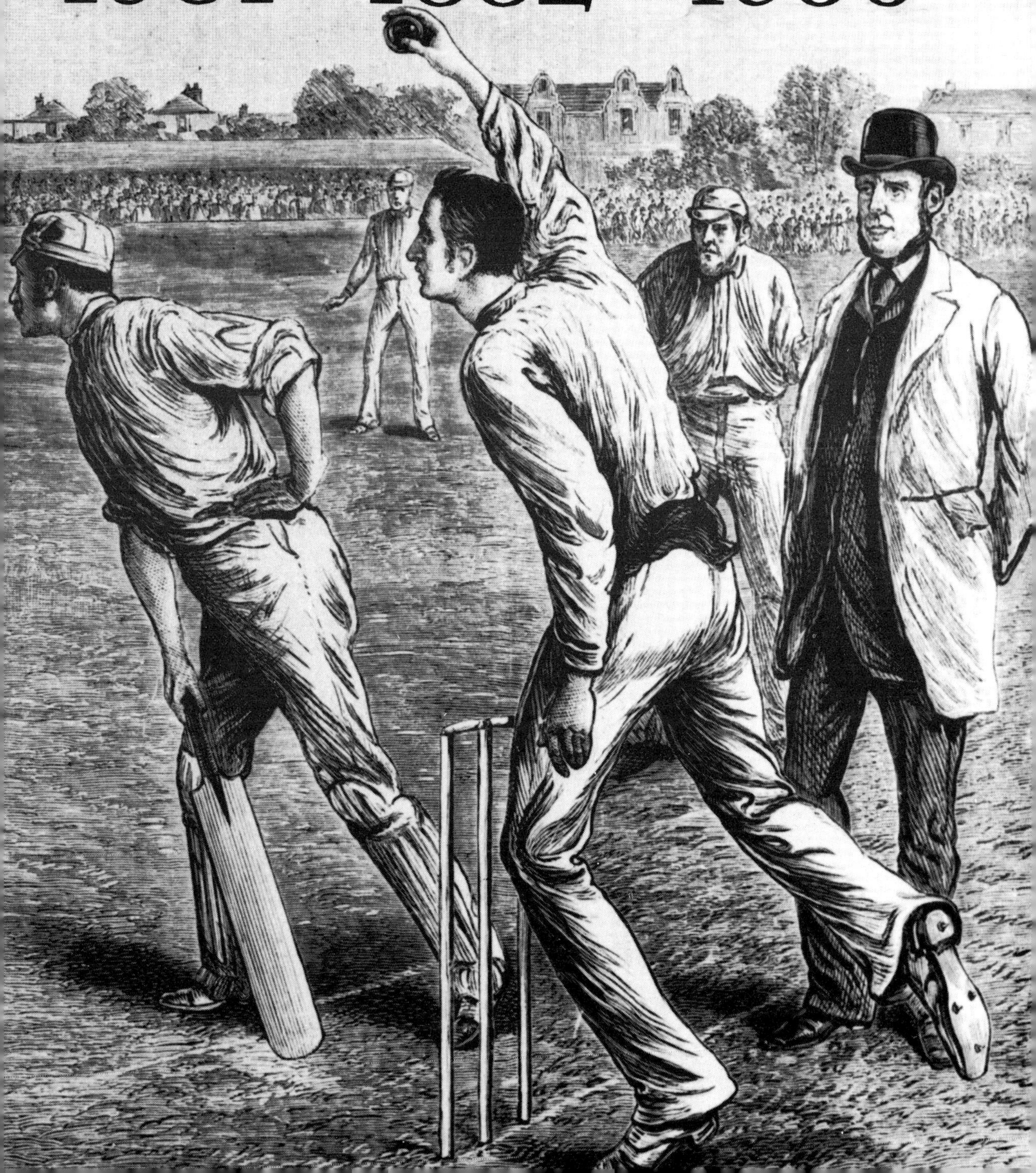

1

NINETY NINE NOT OUT

THE summer of 1981 drove a wedge between the old and new generations of Test cricket enthusiasts. To those England supporters weaned on the limited-overs game, the abject collapse of vital Australian innings was a source of excitement and vicarious pleasure. Others, not necessarily in their dotage, saw it as a travesty that epitomised an awful decline in the actual and aesthetic qualities of a sacred contest. They cast scornful eyes over the players: helmeted, vizored batsmen, arms swathed in protective bandage, shirts and trousers stuffed with purpose-made padding; fielders in floppy white hats and snappy panamas; a green bandana bearing the Australian crest. And the new breed of spectators, moved by mediocrity to excesses of delight, so patently unwilling, or unable, to understand what they were watching. Why else did they listen, on their transistor radios, to a commentary of the match before them?

Thus the elders huffed and puffed. This bunch of incompetents would not have lived with the players of the past . . . 'Except, perhaps, that fellow Botham. And, possibly, Border. Willis, of course, had his moments, and Alderman was distinctly useful. Marsh and Lillee? Well, yes: but that was only to be expected – after all, they had links with the past – and Boycott *did* score a century at The Oval . . . So did young Wellham, come to think of it . . . Even so . . .'

It has ever been thus. The history of Anglo-Australian Test cricket is founded on fable as well as fact; it is a chronicle of vicissitude and comparison. Yet, above all, from the protagonists' point of view, nothing in international sport is more important than the destiny of the Ashes, and the desolation on the face of Kim Hughes when his 1981 tourists surrendered the series was tragically eloquent.

It betrayed the bitter truth that Australia were beaten not by a superb side – which would have been tolerable – but virtually by two men who, at the lowest ebb of their form, drew from 99 years of Ashes tradition a truly phenomenal inspiration. Ian Botham and Bob Willis, to their undying glory, kept that tradition alive and, in the last resort, others from both camps followed their example. The fact remains that much of the cricket – particularly the batsmanship – was unworthy of an Ashes series.

Despite excuses offered in the convulsions of defeat, the pitches were reasonable throughout, and yet the bowlers were largely dominant. Much of England's batting reflected aberrations that go unpunished, if not unnoticed, in limited-overs cricket. But, if successive batsmen failed to acknowledge the presence of slip fielders, they almost totally eschewed the more legitimate adventures of the one-day game. Ray Bright, a spinner of modest menace, was treated with highly exaggerated respect; Mike Whitney, a seamer plucked from league cricket to meet an emergency, was viewed with rare suspicion. Capable batsmen turned pale in the crease at the more thought of an attacking stroke, and the initiative was surrendered to the ball. In this respect, much of the blanket criticism was justified, and excuses hard to find.

Perhaps England's general staleness of attitude and deed arose from the fact that, at the start of the season, they had only recently returned from

Left: *Allan Border, the backbone of Australia's batting, hits out at Bob Willis.*

an arduous tour of West Indies. Certainly several who performed well in the Caribbean suffered from early loss of form. Gower, Dilley, Gooch and, above all, Botham were cases in point.

If the immediate past were a factor, then the not-too-distant future also cast shadows on individual form. Batsmen, particularly, turned their eyes from the task in hand towards the Indian sub-continent and the forthcoming winter tour. Thus were the undoubted talents of Tavaré stifled. And, to compound the diverting complexities of past and future, Botham established, to everyone's satisfaction but his own, the reality that the leadership of England sat on his shoulders like a dead weight.

Thus, after the second Test, Mike Brearley was recalled to bring his remarkable facility for success – but, as it transpired, little individual accomplishment – to the role of captain. This meant, in effect, that some younger and possibly more productive batsman was denied a place in the side. Here, indeed, was a classic example of the Test selectors' dilemma. England were in trouble in the *current* series and Brearley had declared himself unavailable for overseas tours. In the event, the recall of Brearley, for whatever reason, heralded a change in direction which enabled England to retain the Ashes.

Australia's shortcomings and personnel problems were of a different order but, like England's, cannot justifiably be offered in excuse for indifferent overall performance. The talented fast bowler, Len Pascoe, declined to tour. Jeff Thomson was not selected and his subsequent breakdown, while playing for Middlesex, precluded his late recruitment. Thus Australia may bemoan the loss, through injury, of Geoff Lawson and Rodney Hogg. Yet, even when depleted, it was not the bowling but the batting that let them down.

None of this seemed remotely possible, however, when the series began at Trent Bridge on June 18. Australia had beaten England 2–1 in the one-day Prudential series and the men chiefly responsible, their battery of seam bowlers, appeared more formidable as the tour progressed. Conversely, England's key players were lacking form and confidence. The fast bowlers – particularly Willis and Dilley – had scarcely set the County Championship alight, and the batsmen all seemed to be suffering from a seam syndrome of West Indian origin. Furthermore, a proposal by the Test and County Cricket Board that at least 100 overs a day should be bowled throughout the series had been coolly rejected by Australia. In other words, the Australians were prepared to pin their faith on pace bowling and England would be obliged to follow suit.

Accordingly both sides went into the Trent Bridge Test without a spin bowler – an almost unprecedented step which at the end of the first day assumed a grisly justification. When stumps were drawn from this traditionally fertile pitch, 14 wickets had fallen for 218 runs.

England, put in to bat on a well-grassed pitch, were bowled out for 185 by Lillee, Hogg and Alderman who, in his first Test, took 4 for 68. Allowing for the lively bounce and movement, skilfully exploited by Australia's bowlers – and backed by highly efficient catching – it was a dismal display of batsmanship. Mike Gatting, with a serenely efficient 52, was one exception among a succession of victims who fended the rising ball to an eager arc behind the wicket. Another was Botham who, having made only a single, drove imperiously across an Alderman yorker and was bowled.

Botham's personal misery, however, was appeased in the final 100 minutes of the day when his bowlers redressed the balance by dismissing Australia's first four batsmen for only 33 runs. The last to fall, off the fifth ball of the final over, was Kim Hughes, who thereby suffered the dubious distinction of becoming Willis's 200th Test victim.

Ostensibly England started the second day with the initiative firmly in their grasp. As things transpired the same could not be said of their catching. Six chances were spilled in the course of a rain-shortened day, two of them off Border, when he was 10 and 17. These lapses, by Downton behind the wicket and Botham, high at second slip, were to prove even more critical than the rest, for Border's 63 was a vital component in Australia's rally to a total of 179. England had a slender first-innings lead.

It was not enough and the true significance of those missed catches was pointedly emphasised as the Australians gleefully proceeded to snap up the chances induced by the magnificent efforts of Lillee and Alderman. One by one the England batsmen succumbed: Gooch for 6, Boycott for 4, the crestfallen Woolmer for his second duck.

Botham briefly threatened to rally his side, but on 33 edged Lillee low and to the left of second slip. An England fielder, on prevailing form, would surely have missed it, but Border took a superb catch and England were desolate. Lillee claimed 5 for 46, Alderman 5 for 62, and Australia needed only 132 for victory.

The England bowlers strove valiantly against the odds as Dilley, with arguably his best two spells of the season, took 4 for 24, and the luckless Hendrick conceded only 33 runs off 20 overs. But Australia plodded on to reach their modest goal for the loss of six men. In many ways it was a disappointing Test, yet few would argue that Australia had earned their victory, and Terry Alderman, with an overall return of 9 for 130 in his first Test, thoroughly deserved to be on the winning side.

England's natural despondency in defeat was aggravated by the conviction of her supporters that Botham's disappointing form was not unconnected with the responsibilities of captaincy. His approach to batting betrayed a hint of desperation and his fielding was not inspired. Nevertheless the selectors persevered and Botham was recommissioned to lead a slightly modified side into the second Test at Lord's. Bob Taylor replaced Downton as wicketkeeper and spinner John Emburey was called in at the expense of Mike Hendrick. The Australians, too, brought in

Dennis Lillee – reincarnation of the Demon Spofforth?

Allan Border punishes a short ball during the Second Test.

a specialist slow bowler, Ray Bright replacing the injured Rodney Hogg.

If the Trent Bridge pitch had been less than perfect, no such complaint could be levelled at a Lord's wicket of almost flawless predictability. Hughes's decision to put England in was seen to be questionable as Gooch set about Lillee with almost disdainful ease. Boycott, however, embarking on his 100th Test match, was content to prod and push and, when Gooch departed for 44, had barely reached double figures. Indeed, when he became Lawson's second victim, Boycott had contributed only 17 to a total of 65 – in 98 minutes!

Woolmer, nursing the memory of his Nottingham 'pair', and a bruised arm from a leaping Lawson delivery, made on 13 before retiring for repairs, and David Gower had laboured 45 minutes over the run when poor light interrupted the wake. He returned, at length, to complete an uncharacteristic innings which spanned 30 overs and produced only 27 runs, in contrast to which a half-century by Gatting – his third in successive Tests against Australia – represented untold riches.

Even so, at the end of a slightly shortened day, England had mustered a mere 191 for 4, and though Willey and Emburey resumed with a fifth-wicket partnership of 97, the last six wickets fell – four of them to Lawson – for 27. One of the victims was Botham, out third ball playing across the line for nought – hardly a captain's contribution to England's disappointing 311.

If England fielded badly on that black Friday at Trent Bridge, then on the third day at Lord's the bowlers could be grateful for superb catches that dismissed Australia's three most threatening batsmen. Certainly the bowlers themselves could take little real credit from the fact that Australia were reasonably contained at 253 for 6 at close of play.

Wood, Hughes and Border all played extremely well against bowling far too liberally endowed with long-hops. Furthermore, Willis – though the more accurate of the bowlers – contributed 21 no-balls to the Australian coffers.

The first great catch, by Taylor, disposed of Wood, who had scored 44 glorious runs in an hour and looked capable of scoring many more. The ball found the inside edge of the bat and Taylor miraculously changed direction and took the catch diving to his right.

The second 'supercatch' victim was Hughes, who had reached 42 with accomplished ease when he drove Emburey hard to deep mid-off. Willis, back-pedalling furiously, thrust up his arm and plucked the ball from the air before over-balancing.

Gatting provided the third example of the match-winning – or, in this case, match-saving – chance when he threw himself to his left at second slip and took a two-handed catch when the ball appeared to have sped past him. That was the end of the bold Border who, on 64, had looked set for a century.

Though such stirring events undoubtedly frustrated Australia's more extravagant ambitions, the old firm of Lillee and Marsh ensured that England embarked on their second innings with a deficit of 34. Though Gooch departed before those arrears had been wiped off, at the end of the fourth day, England, with Boycott undefeated on 47, were 95 agreed with eight wickets in hand.

From such a position a draw was inevitable but, before England declared and invited Australia to attempt a total of 232, Ian Botham suffered the most morale-shattering moments of his sporting life. With the score at 217 for 4, the England captain faced his first ball, from Bright, swung wildly across a well-flighted delivery, and was bowled for his second duck of the match.

He walked back to the pavilion, head bowed and in obvious mental anguish. The members shuffled and stared ahead as he passed between their silent ranks and up the steps. There was not a nod of consolation, scarcely a glance of sympathy. At that point, Botham made up his mind to resign the England captaincy, not knowing that the selectors had already decided to appoint a successor.

Thus ended one of the more unfortunate selectional experiments in the history of Test cricket.

The England squad for the Second Test, at Lord's. Standing, from left: Gatting, Woolmer, Willey, Dilley, Emburey, Gooch, Gower. Sitting, from left: Taylor, Willis, Botham, Boycott, Hendrick.

Botham, young, talented and enthusiastic as he was, had no experience of captaincy – even at county level – when he was pitched into the fray against West Indies, at the time the world's most formidable opponents. There is no doubt he accepted the honour and the responsibility with a geniune personal conviction that he could do the job. He continued – publicly, at least – to express this conviction: and to deny that the pressures involved were affecting his form. Yet, to the absolute satisfaction of everyone – except, possibly Australia – forthcoming events were to resolve the debate beyond doubt.

When the third Test began at Headingley on July 16 there was no reason to suspect that the events of the next five days would not only turn the series on its head but demolish all the rational concepts and probabilities associated with Test cricket. Australia were one-up and, with the best of the Lord's stalemate under their belts, were entitled to believe they were the better of two modest sides. Accordingly they made no changes, and when Hughes won the toss for the third time he deliberated long and hard before deciding to bat under overcast skies.

Not surprisingly, the team led out by Brearley did not include Woolmer, whose lack of form had been evident in a return of only 30 runs from four innings. Less acceptable to the purists was the omission of Emburey, who was batting well when run out for 31 at Lord's – where his 46 overs had produced two wickets for 59. Nevertheless, Chris Old was preferred, and England once again were without a spin bowler. Old, like Lancashire's Brian Statham, was never the luckiest of Test bowlers. Invariably accurate, always thoughtful, he would induce in batsmen a watchful frustration that was usually capitalised upon by his more mercurial pacebowling partners. Indeed, in the first innings of this Test he was to concede only a fraction more than two runs for each of his 43 overs – but without taking a single wicket.

He was not alone, on this occasion, in suffering from dropped catches while John Dyson, accompanied by Wood, Chappell and Hughes, batted his way to a maiden Test century. Thus, at the end of a day foreshortened by rain, Australia were comfortably placed at 203 for 3.

Left: *Geoff Boycott falls for 60 – a victim of the old firm Lillee and Marsh – in the Second Test.*

Geoff Lawson – a magnificent 7 for 81 at Lord's.

The second morning also dawned beneath cloudy skies, and the negative association of showers and wide bowling restricted Australia's early progress. Dilley, having finally located the stumps, dismissed nightwatchman Bright, but Hughes and Yallop so effectively battened down the hatches, that after 30 overs, the Australian score had been advanced by only 80 runs.

Botham then induced Hughes to edge a straightforward chance to first slip, where is struck Gooch in the midriff and was missed. In the next over, Yallop edged Old and Brearley, diving at third slip, took the ball cleanly – but on the bounce. What luck there was certainly favoured the batsmen and a massive total seemed inevitable as the fifth-wicket partners took the score to 332. Then, suddenly the transfiguration of Botham began . . . .

Immediately after tea, in a devastating return to his former fire and accuracy, the dispossessed captain – dispossessed, that is, of some malignant burden – disposed of Hughes, Border, Yallop, Lawson and Marsh at a personal cost of 35 runs. It was the 15th time he had taken five or more

A familiar scenario on the final day of the Headingley Test. England's jubilation as Bob Taylor catches Lawson off Willis . . . And Australia are 75 for 5.

wickets in a Test innings, but the first since Bombay in February 1980 – his last Test before assuming the captaincy.

England's relief was short-lived for, next morning, the Australian total of 401 for 9 quickly began to assume fearsome proportions as the fast and fiery trio of Lillee, Alderman and Lawson began to work their way through the fragile English ranks. Gooch departed as he tried to hit Alderman to midwicket. The same bowler disposed of Brearley for 10, and Boycott had made only 12 when Lawson bowled him with a fizzer that came back from way outside the off stump. There was a flicker of hope as Botham, hitting hard and straight, made 50 in as many minutes, but at that point he failed to withdraw his bat from a Lillee flyer and Marsh took his 264th Test victim to overtake Alan Knott's record. Further resistance was minimal and England suffered the indignity of following on, 227 runs adrift. Even worse, Gooch was immediately out for a duck, having fallen twice in a day off only four deliveries.

The fourth day began in much the same way as the third. Lillee and Alderman, fresh from their weekend rest and sniffing an early victory, snapped up Brearley, Gower and Gatting in 65 minutes and England were 41 for 4. Willey then joined Boycott in a stand of 64, but when Botham strode to the crease 123 runs were still needed to avoid an innings defeat. Such a fate seemed even more certain when Boycott's 3½-hour vigil ended and, two runs later, Taylor's departure found England teetering on 135 for 7.

It was a situation, Botham recalled later, in which there seemed nothing to lose; an opportunity to cast all reservations to the winds and, as the Australians might say, 'Give it a go'. Nevertheless, in this or any context, the innings that followed goes into the annals as one of the most audacious in the history of Test cricket.

It began with a back-foot assault through the

covers and moved on to a sabre-like display of cutting which left the fielders flat-footed and open-mouthed. Then, as the score advanced, so did Botham's feet, and away soared the ball from a succession of massive straight-drives. Thus he reached his hundred off only 87 deliveries, and such was the ferocity of method that he moved from 39 to 103 by means of a six, 14 fours and just two singles.

Happily for England, Botham was not alone in his apparent contempt for the Australian attack. Dilley batted magnificently in contributing 56 to an eighth-wicket partnership of 117 in 80 minutes, and Old made 29 in the ninth-wicket stand of 67. The outcome of this remarkable reversal of fortune was that when Botham finally ran out of support at 149, England had established a modest but honourable lead of 129.

It should not, and would not, have been enough in any but the atmosphere of unreality which had crept over the Headingley ground. Certainly when Australia passed 50 for the loss of Wood, the contest appeared to be over. Then, just 20 minutes before lunch, Brearley switched Bob Willis to the Kirkstall Lane end. The effect was startling.

The tall, stringy bowler, often maligned as a whirlwind no-baller, prone to injury – both physical and psychological – suddenly began to bowl like a man possessed. He bowled superbly fast, on a perfect line and with brilliant control of length. It was all too much for the shell-shocked Australian batsmen. One by one they reeled and fell to the wicked Willis, whose sheer example inspired a succession of splendid supporting catches.

By lunch Chappell, Hughes and Yallop had gone in 11 balls and Australia were 58 for 4. Old intervened immediately afterwards by bowling the potentially dangerous Border for nought. Then Willis, charging down the slope with a gleam in his eye, quickly routed Marsh and Lawson. With eight wickets down, Australia still needed 55.

Lillee and Bright, no doubt with Botham's example in mind, thereupon decided to chance the arm, and in four overs a miscellany of bold, sometimes unorthodox blows produced 35 nerve-wracking runs. At this point, however, Lillee, facing Willis, failed to middle a shot off his legs and Gatting hurled himself forward at mid-on to take a stunning catch.

Bob Willis leads the England victory charge after Australia's dramatic collapse in the Third Test.

Old, in abject anguish, twice dropped Alderman off Botham, but the groans of disbelief had barely faded when Willis produced a high-speed yorker. Bright drove over it and England had won a stupendous Test match by 18 runs.

For only the second time in over 100 years of Test cricket had a side following-on emerged victorious. It was, in fact, a feat so remote that on the penultimate afternoon a firm of bookmakers cheerfully accepted £52 from a handful of 'mugs' who had backed England at 500-1. The delight of the punters who shared £26,000 can scarcely have surpassed that of Bob Willis, whose 8 for 43 elevated him with Botham among the greatest match-winners of all time.

The England selectors' decision not to change a winning formula for Edgbaston was predictable, but not universally acclaimed. For all the excitement and relief that followed the squaring of the series, no-one could pretend that everything was well with the side – particularly in respect of the batting. Gooch, for example, had reduced his average for the series to a miserable 13.6 and Boycott had accumulated only 166 in six innings. Wicketkeeper Taylor, in two Tests, had scored a total of 15 runs. Gower and Gatting had begun to look frail under pressure. . . .

On the other hand, morale and team spirit had been given a tremendous boost by the Headingley victory; the Australians, conversely, were psychologically shattered and, if things went wrong at Edgbaston, there were still two Tests to come. So, while Australia brought in Hogg for the injured Lawson and dropped Chappell in favour of Martin Kent, it was England's intention to field the same eleven. As things transpired, Dilley sustained a shoulder injury while playing for Kent and, though Hendrick was called up as a stand-by, the vacant bowling slot was given to Emburey.

A sequel to this late adjustment is not without a certain poignant irony, for Dilley was not to reappear in the series. In fact, within a couple of weeks the young pace bowler was relegated to the Kent 2nd XI, where he remained until the last match of the season. His 'shoulder injury', in fact, was the manifestation of a psychological problem which is not uncommon among the fast-bowling fraternity.

When the fourth Test began, few experts were prepared to predict a positive result. The popular belief that the game would be drawn was based on the premise that the Edgbaston wicket was a cornucopia of runs. Furthermore, a dozen batsmen of both sides would surely get their heads down and produce the traditional goods. The popular belief was to be sadly disabused. . . .

For the first time in the series, England won the toss and chose to bat – but not for long. Under a cloudless sky and on a near-perfect pitch, they were all out for 189. Far from taking sensible advantage of the idyllic conditions, England's batsmen went for runs like gluttons confronted with a mountain of delectable food. Boycott, needless to say, was a notable exception, and it was 45 minutes before his patient perusal gave way to the temptations of a wide ball from Alderman. The score was 29, and Gower, greedy for a pull at the same bowler, went without scoring at the same total.

The procession had begun, and only opener Brearley, with 48, seriously delayed the headlong chase to self-destruction. Alderman emerged with 5 for 42 as the Australians surveyed the situation with a considerable glow of satisfaction. But, again, not for long. By close of play Old had got Dyson and Border and Australia were 19 for 2.

Australian war-dance. Dennis Lillee bounds down the wicket as Mike Brearley departs, l.b.w. for 13 on the second day at Edgbaston. Skipper Kim Hughes admires the footwork.

The next morning found nightwatchman Bright in stubborn mood and, in company with Wood, he batted for an hour while the score advanced to 62. The advent of Hughes served to consolidate this start and at lunch Australia were 111 for 3. Shortly afterwards, however, Wood, who is renowned for such adventures, embarked on a suicidal single and was duly run out by Old's direct hit. Thereafter, assisted by a veritable blizzard of no-balls from a somewhat tetchy Willis, Australia cruised comfortably, if not prolifically, on until Emburey wrapped up their innings for 258, with an intelligently acquired 4 for 43.

At the end of the second day, England, 69 behind on the first innings, were still 20 in arrears for the loss of Brearley, and those who had predicted a draw were beating a hasty retreat. The odds were marginally in Australia's favour. By the time England, mindful of their first-innings indiscretions, had crawled to a disappointing 219 all out, Australia were established as near-certainties to win by a handsome margin.

The wicket was still reasonably benign and only 151 runs stood between the tourists and a 2-1 lead in the series. The loss of Wood on the third evening gave Australia little cause for alarm, and though Dyson and Hughes went cheaply the following morning the score moved steadily on to 114 for 5. The time was 3.50, Kent and Marsh were together, and only 37 runs were needed when Brearley called on a reluctant Botham. Forty minutes later Australia had plunged to defeat. The amazing Botham had done it again – this time as a bowler.

As Marsh, Bright, Lillee, Kent and Alderman reeled away from the devastating onslaught, Botham's re-incarnation as the world's most talented all-rounder was dramatically confirmed. The ifs and buts are legion. Had Botham continued as captain, how long would he have survived in the side? Could he have performed his amazing bowling feat at Edgbaston? Well, the answer to the last question is no – because, when summoned to take the ball, he felt he could not improve on the efforts of his fellow-bowlers. As captain, he would have maintained the status quo. All of which says much for the magic touch of Mike Brearley – a captain of great tactical acumen with an amazing flair for achieving the seemingly impossible.

No player in the history of the Ashes has been elevated from obscurity to Test status with such haste and in such bizarre circumstances as 22-year-old Mike Whitney of New South Wales, Fleetwood C.C. and Gloucestershire. Two days before the fifth Test was due to begin at Old Trafford, Australia, denied the services of Lawson and Hogg and in desperate need of a fast-medium bowler, took the unprecedented step of taking a player out of a County Championship match – after that match had actually started.

Whitney had been playing in the Northern League. He had also been registered by Gloucestershire – for whom he was due to play when they reported Australia's interest in the young left-arm bowler. Lord's approved the release and Whitney, watching his side bat against Hampshire, was summoned to join the Australian Test party.

Thus, the raw rookie – an apprentice maintenance engineer with Qantas Airlines – found himself at Old Trafford. By comparison, England's newest recruit, Paul Allott, was a veteran of three years' service with Lancashire, though he too came in only as a replacement, for Chris Old. England made other changes in the recall of Kent's Chris Tavaré and Alan Knott, who was thereby given the opportunity to become the first wicketkeeper from any country to make 100 dismissals against Australia. It was, as they say, a racing certainty, and the record came when he caught Kent off Emburey in Australia's first innings.

Man of the Match – Ian Botham races back to the pavilion with a victory trophy at the end of the Edgbaston Test.

His counterpart, Rodney Marsh, who had long surpassed the century of England victims, also had his sights on a personal landmark. Marsh needed 68 runs to become only the second wicket-keeper (after Knott) to make 3000 runs in all Tests. He was, in fact, to fall 20 short at Old Trafford, and did not achieve his goal until the final Test at The Oval. Three other records were established at Manchester, however, the first by Geoff Boycott, who passed Cowdrey's Test aggregate of 7624. The second came when Lillee became the first bowler from either country to take 150 wickets in Anglo-Australian Tests. But if Lillee claimed one new standard, he lost an old one to Terry Alderman, who surpassed the old campaigner's record of 31 wickets for a series in England.

All of which kept the historical statisticians happy; but, at the end of the first day's play, the historical purists were again muttering darkly about the decline and fall of the noblest game. They pointed to an England total of 175 for 9, the failure of Boycott and Gooch, each dismissed for 10, the fallibility of Botham, out for a duck, and even the tedium of Tavaré, who laboured 287 minutes for the top score of 69.

Rare aggression from Chris Tavaré as he sweeps a boundary during England's first innings at Old Trafford.

The Australians, on the other hand, were not displeased with their day's work. Young Whitney made a highly respectable start in claiming the wickets of Gower (23) and Tavaré at a personal cost of 31 runs, Alderman claimed four wickets, and Lillee three. All were assisted by a damp pitch, a lunch break extended to 85 minutes by rain, and, above all, a distinctly wet exhibition of batsmanship. Only Gatting, brisk and busy as ever, sought rather than waited for runs, but, having twice hooked Lillee with relish, fell for 32 to an even shorter delivery which lobbed off his glove to slip.

The transformation of fortunes on the second day was almost beyond belief. England, who resumed with one wicket intact, started their second innings 20 minutes before tea with a lead of 101, and at the close were 171 ahead with only Gooch out! The eventful proceedings began with 50 minutes of breathtaking entertainment as England's last pair put on 56 priceless runs. . .at least, Willis scored 11 and Allott, powered his way to an undefeated 52 – a tremendous achievement which exceeded his highest first-class score by 22. Favouring the square-drive off the back foot, the bespectacled Lancashire player made light of the Australian attack.

The Australians, though somewhat embarrassed by this tailend tantivy, were comforted by the thought that if Willis and Allott could perform so adequately, then the wicket must be a push-over for recognised batsmen. And so it seemed as Wood, with the utmost aplomb, hooked the fifth and sixth balls of Willis's first over for four and six. Within half an hour, however, the picture began to jump like an old and familiar home-movie. Dyson edged Willis to Botham: 20 for one. Three balls later Hughes was lbw: 24 for 2. Off the last ball of this third Willis over, Yallop was brilliantly taken by the diving Botham for 0: 24 for 3. And as if that were not dramatic enough, the first ball of Allott's next over had Wood lbw: 24 for 4.

Over-excited by their success, the England bowlers then proceeded to bowl a procession of long hops which Kent and Border gratefully dispatched until, in the last over before lunch, Border fell to a magnificent flying catch at fourth slip by Gower off Botham. Incredible as it

A confident shot from Graeme Wood during his opening partnership of 120 with Martin Kent at The Oval.

seemed, half the side were out in 11.4 overs for 58 – just two more runs than England's last-wicket pair had achieved.

Immediately after the interval, the debacle continued. Marsh edged Willis into the slips, Botham took a comfortable catch, and Australia were 59 for 6. Martin Kent, upright in stance and determination, then paddled the waterlogged ship slowly forward while Bright bailed manfully in the scuppers. By such means the total advanced to 104 before Kent was tempted by Emburey's spin and gave Knott his epoch-making catch at the wicket. Further resistance was short-lived and Australia, dismissed for 130, had provided a capacity crowd of 21,000 with yet another inexplicable vignette in the omnibus of Ashes cricket.

England's immediate response was marred only by the early dismissal of Gooch, who thereby surrendered his place in the forthcoming final Test. The erstwhile prolific Essex batsman had scraped only 139 runs from 10 innings in the series.

There is a recurring and misguided gallantry in England's approach to most sports which in moments of ascendency produces a kind of apologetic guilt. Thus, when they resumed on Saturday, with a lead of 171, the inevitable occurred: in the morning session, Boycott, Gower and Gatting departed for a mere 28 runs. Brearley followed after lunch and an old tradition was thereby restored as England slumped to 104 for 5. Fortunately, the bold Botham did not subscribe to such quaint conventions and promptly embarked on yet another display of mayhem.

With his foot itching on the accelerator, Botham swerved through his opening overs, twice coming close to disaster as he lofted one over cover and another to Whitney at deep mid-off. Then he really opened up. Lillee, with the new ball, fired in a couple of bouncers which Botham hooked for six, and 22 runs came off the over. He

hit Lillee for two more sixes and took a brace off Bright – one a sweep, which brought his century, and the other a thundering straight-drive. When finally brought to a halt by Whitney and Marsh, Botham had scored 118 in a sixth-wicket partnership of 149 in 105 minutes. Only Gilbert Jessop had scored a century for England off fewer balls (75 against 86) and if Jessop's feat is ever to be beaten, few would back anyone but Botham to do so.

The ultimate outcome of this astonishing innings, which whipped into its slipstream a disbelieving Tavaré (78) and an enthusiastic Knott (59), was an England lead of 505. In view of Australia's overall record with the bat, it seemed an extravagantly impossible target – particularly when Wood and Dyson departed for 24. Yet, after Hughes restored order with a confident 43, Yallop produced a high-class century and Border, in company with the 'old sweats' Marsh and Lillee, restored credibility to Australia's time-honoured fighting tradition with an undefeated 123. Nevertheless the task proved too much. England won by 103 runs. The Ashes, so often within Australia's grasp, were England's.

Despite the fact that the series had been decided, there was little sense of anti-climax as the final Test approached. Indeed on the eve of the match, as crowds queued at The Oval for tickets, Surrey announced that £182,000 had already been taken in advance sales.

Both sides introduced a batsman new to Test cricket. Australia called on Dirk Wellham, who first engaged the grudging admiration of English bowlers when he made 95 for Combined Universities against the tourists at Adelaide in 1979. Wellham certainly would have been hard-done-by had he not been selected for the final Test. Throughout the summer he had performed prolifically in county and charity matches, scoring a particularly attractive century against Northamptonshire. Essentially a middle-order batsman, he was accommodated at the expense of opener Dyson, whose place as Wood's partner was filled by Kent. It was to prove an inspirational manoeuvre.

Left: *Ian Botham in full cry and, once more, among the wicket-takers in the final Test.*

Right: *Martin Kent's military two-step – in response to a Willis missile at The Oval.*

England's new recruit was Paul Parker of Sussex, who had long been lobbied and tipped as the kind of brisk and articulate batsman England needed in the upper middle order. Unfortunately, his was not a happy debut, for he followed a duck in the first innings with only 13 in the second, and for him the shores of India receded into the mists. Other proposed changes were frustrated by injury when Old and Rodney Hogg, both scheduled to return, were forced to drop out. Hendrick came in for England at the expense of Allott, but Whitney was given a chance to capitalise on his modest success in the fifth Test.

Again personal standards were there to be established and in the first innings of this, his 30th Test, Bob Willis overhauled the record of the legendary Wilfred Rhodes, who in 41 Tests against Australia claimed 109 wickets. Botham, too, stood on the brink of joining Richie Benaud and Garfield Sobers, the only players to achieve 2000 runs and 200 wickets in all Tests. Ironically, Botham was to exceed his immediate target of eight wickets by two, but to score only 19 of the 42 runs he needed for the 2000. Nevertheless, at the end of the series, he still had 19 matches in hand to beat Benaud's double (achieved in 60 Tests) and 39 to overtake Sobers.

As for Brearley's success as a captain – unbeaten in 19 home matches – it seemed a foregone conclusion that his decision to put the Australians in, curious as it appeared to many, would be justified. And so it finally was – but only just. Indeed, at the end of the first day's play, with Australia 251 for 4, Brearley was moved to confess: 'It was a 50-50 decision. Had we batted and then bowled out for 150, it would have been a bad decision. As Australia batted and were not bowled out, you could also say it was a bad decision.'

Kim Hughes was unequivocal: 'I thought it was the best pitch I have ever played on anywhere in the world,' he said. The Australian batsmen performed, at last, with collective determination.

Thus, after Wood and Kent had set the standard with an opening partnership of 120, Border,

Left: *No second opinion for Dirk Wellham – comprehensively bowled by Willis for 24.*

Right: *Laugh-along with Lillee. The Australian pace-bowler dons an umpire's cap to supervise a sight-screen shift at The Oval.*

Above: *A century in sight for Geoff Boycott as he clips the ball away to leg. Marsh and Hughes want it back.*

Right: *Hughes takes evasive action as Paul Parker lashes out at The Oval.*

on 51, and Wellham were looking ominously comfortable. England's only solace arose in the fact that the bowling had been tidy and the fielding excellent – particularly that of the fast and enthusiastic Parker.

For the Australians, the next day was something of a return to the sub-normal as Willis and Botham went to work on a wicket which still provided little help. Each disconcerted the batsmen in his own way, Willis by summoning the extra yard of pace and Botham by bringing his great powers of swing to the well-pitched ball. Wellham departed, bowled by Willis, and the procession began. The admirable Border watched it all, phlegmatic if bemused, and emerged undefeated with 106; the first Australian to score successive centuries against England since Bill Lawry, in 1965–66. He owed much to the unlikeliest of companions in Mike Whitney, who came in at No. 11 to survive 80 minutes before scoring his four runs.

England's response was cast in a similar mould to that of the Australian innings. It began with solid assurance as Boycott set about repairing a somewhat bullet-ridden reputation. By mid-afternoon on the third day, England's score stood at a healthy 246 for 2. Then the next eight wickets fell in less than 90 minutes for 68 runs, three to Alderman and five to Lillee, who thereby finished, for the first time in his Test career, with seven wickets in an innings. One of them was Boycott, who, having redeemed himself with his 21st Test century, fell at 137 to a brilliant, leaping gully catch by Yallop. Thus ended an invaluable, if seemingly interminable, squat of 440 minutes!

In the remaining 50 minutes, Australia, already leading by 38, lost Kent and Hughes for 36; a status quo prevailed. Monday, therefore, was to prove the crucial day in the captains' calculations – particularly those of Kim Hughes.

Australia avoided the kind of batting collapse that had bedevilled the series and, after the early

Half-century specialist Mike Gatting on his way to 56 in England's second innings.

loss of Wood, Yallop and Border consolidated with a fourth-wicket partnership of 63. It was 3 p.m. before Border, having defied all attempts to dislodge him for almost 15 hours of Test cricket, finally fell to Emburey for 84. Wellham proceeded to demonstrate why he had been described by no less an authority than Sir Donald Bradman as the best Australian batsman of his generation. Wellham's endorsement of this view, with a mature and attractive century, only deepened the mystery of his exclusion from the Test side until this final match, when he became the 12th Australian to make a hundred in his first Test – having been dropped by Boycott on 99.

A charmed half-century from Marsh found Australia 344 for 9 at close of play – at which point they declared. The equation at the start of the final day read: England require 383. Time available – six hours. The likelihood of an England victory was negligible and, when Boycott and Tavaré were dismissed with 50 minutes for 18, the time had come to batten down the hatches. Gatting was determined to fire a few salvoes, however, and, blasting away, collected 46 in an hour.

After lunch the time for such adventures passed when Larkins, after a solid 130 minutes, edged a Lillee flyer to second slip. Gatting soon followed his involuntary example and the departure of Parker, whose hour of labour produced only 13 runs, reduced England to 127 for 5. It was time for a captain's innings and Brearley, lately undistinguished with the bat, embarked upon one of his finest Test innings. He was joined by Knott in a partnership which lasted almost two hours and took England through seven of the final 20 overs. Brearley fell for 51 to Lillee and the new ball, but Knott, audacious and improvising as ever, cruised on to an undefeated 70.

The Test was saved and Brearley's reputation, as a shrewd and successful captain, preserved in this his last encounter against Australia. For all that, the man of the match undoubtedly was Dennis Lillee. His overall analysis of 11 for 159 off 61.4 overs represented a tremendous effort on a wicket good enough to yield 1271 runs. Indeed, as the tall, athletic Lillee strode off the field at The Oval – probably for the last time – he might have been the reincarnation of the dark, moustached bowler who, 99 years earlier, had hastened the 'cremation' of England's cricket. A man called Spofforth.

2

CAPTAIN BLIGH'S BOUNTY

IT BEGAN as a joke; the kind of exasperated, apologetic irony the British hide behind in moments of tribulation. A mock obituary in *The Sporting Times* lamenting the death of English cricket: at The Oval on August 29, 1882. 'The Body', concluded the notice, 'will be cremated and the Ashes taken to Australia.'

It might well have been left at that; a rueful item for the scrapbook of England's captain, A. N. Hornby, whose side, needing only 85 to beat Billy Murdoch's Australians, had been bowled to a seven-run defeat by the demon Spofforth. Instead, a chance remark by Hornby's successor, the Honourable (and handsome) Ivo Bligh and a fun-loving group of Melbourne ladies conspired to materialise the myth.

Before leaving for Australia in the autumn of '82, Bligh told the guests at a farewell dinner that he hoped to recover 'those Ashes'. And, when the England side beat Murdoch's Australians at Melbourne, for a two-one lead, the ladies in question duly presented him with a small urn containing the incinerated remains of a bail. No-one questions the veracity of this event, and only the churlish historian points out that England then played, and lost, a fourth match against an Australian side not restricted to Murdoch's tourists. If this, as some claim, were part of the official series – which Bligh denied – then the Ashes, if any, should have remained in Australia. However, had such stone-faced statistics prevailed, Anglo-Australian cricket would have been denied an engaging and emotive legend that now spans 100 glorious years – in which time surprisingly little has changed. The sun shines at Sydney; it rains at Old Trafford. The dramas and controversies unfold, the crowds barrack, the supreme players emerge. The pendulum swings to and fro; the pulse and pace of the game have changed little – but today we have the 600 mph jet.

In the 1880s England and Australia were separated by a 48-day sea voyage and, for all the comfort of first-class passage on the Peninsular and Orient's new steamships, it might be imagined that intercontinental cricket tours were few and far between. On the contrary, between 1882 and 1890 five Australian sides set sail for England and five English teams went to Australia – two of them, in 1887–8, at the same time! The frenzy of activity which culminated in the double-

The Hon. Ivo Bligh – darling of the Melbourne ladies.

Frederick Robert Spofforth – the Demon Bowler.

tour fiasco was based on the premise that Test cricket was firmly established as a public attraction. While this was true, there was no corporate body to administer and co-ordinate truly representative teams.

The early commercial tours which started in 1861 were ventures organised by and for professionals such as James Lillywhite, Alfred Shaw and Arthur Shrewsbury. They constituted 'representative' sides only inasmuch as the professionals were drawn from the North, the Midlands and the South of England. While these pioneering tours were valuable in establishing the principle of international cricket, they were by no means altruistic. The touring professionals often doubled as travelling salesmen, peddling trunks of cricket equipment from town to town. They invariably sought out the best hotels, grabbed every penny, and put away champagne by the Methuselah.

This predilection for champagne, however, was not peculiar to the professionals of the era. It was almost as common a tipple as beer among the top English cricketers – or so it seemed to the Australians. One of the popular proprietory sparkling wines of the day was called 'Pommery' and there is a tenable theory that this was the source of the name 'poms' bestowed on the English by the beer-swigging Aussies.

At all events the professional Pommery-drinkers had squeezed the grape almost dry when the 1887 double-header was precipitated by rivalries between the Melbourne and Sydney cricket factions, each seeking supremacy as custodians of the Australian game. Shaw's professionals had agreed to an offer sponsored in Sydney while the Melbourne club had invited the Hon. M. B. Hawke's side to tour. Both parties subsequently toured and each beat 'Combined Australia', but neither was regarded as an official international. In order to fulfil a Test fixture, the two sides were obliged to provide a joint eleven, which duly beat an Australian XI in Sydney.

In one sense, therefore, the two touring sides were winners but, in another respect, all the protagonists were losers. The Shaw-Lillywhite-Shrewsbury trio were £2200 out of pocket and the Melbourne Cricket Club lost £4000. The game's international development owed much to these intrepid itinerants; much, too, to the personalities who, in those formative years of Anglo-Australian competition, brought cricket within the ken and compass of a vast new public.

It was said, for example, that W. G. Grace, in his heyday, was the best-known figure in England. This may have been due, in part, to that physique: a heavily-built, full-bearded man with an incongruous pipsqueak voice. He was famed and feted as the most accomplished cricketer of his times and loved by the proletariat, perhaps because, for all his medical qualification, he had not attended public school, far less university, and was never of the Marylebone elite. Grace was 34, and an automatic England choice, when that first Ashes match was played at The Oval.

Despite the fact that Australia had won two and drawn two during England's 1881–82 tour, none of the 20,000 spectators at The Oval on August 28, 1882 doubted that England would put the 'Colonials' in their place by winning the only scheduled Test of the summer. The England side was packed with illustrious names – Barlow, Grace, Hornby, Steel, Ulyett, Peate – and the

The source of all the excitement. The urn containing The Ashes, permanently lodged at Lord's.

conditions were distinctly English. It had rained for two days, and when Australia batted on a damp wicket, they lasted only 2¼ hours against left-handers Barlow and Peate. Their 63 seemed paltry, yet, when England replied, six wickets were down before they took the lead and the first-innings advantage was restricted to 38, Spofforth 7 for 46.

On the second day, after further rain, the Australian opener Hugh Massie hit 55 priceless runs in 45 minutes, a powerful audacious innings that paved the way for an Australian victory. His opening partner, Alec Bannerman, scored 13, and the captain, Billy Murdoch, made 39, but no-one else reached double figures and the total of 122 left England a target of only 85 for the match.

England seemed about to achieve a comfortable win, but the Australians, already stung by derogatory remarks, had been moved to further resentment by an unsporting incident in their second innings. The victim was young Sammy Jones, who left his crease to pat down a divot and was promptly run out by Grace. Thus, when the

'The Ashes Match' – the 1882 Oval Test. View from the Vauxhall end.

Australians took the field they prayed against hope that Spofforth could produce another masterly spell of bowling. Their prayers were answered.

Grace and Hornby opened and the score had reached only 15 when Spofforth struck twice, bowling Hornby and, next ball, Barlow. The arrival of Ulyett steadied the ship and the fifty came up before he was caught behind by the bearded Blackham, who deserves particular mention as the first of the great Test wicketkeepers. He was highly-skilled and brave, even if his 'showmanship' was not universally applauded. Genteel observers thought he brought 'an unwarranted risk of injury to the game!'

The fall of Grace's wicket for 32 produced a temporary stalemate as Lyttelton and Lucas faced 12 consecutive maidens. There was an awed hush around The Oval as a deliberate misfield brought Lyttleton against Spofforth – and a gasp of dismay as he was bowled for 12. A four from Lucas raised a mighty cheer, but his new partner, Steel, was soon caught and bowled by Spofforth: 70 for 6. Read was bowled second ball, Lucas played Spofforth onto his stumps, and, with two wickets remaining, England were still nine short. Barnes fell at the same total and only Peate and Studd were left. Hornby's decision to relegate Studd to No. 10 was heavily criticised at the time – and not without reason, for he had already scored two centuries against the Australians that summer. In the event, Studd was said to be in a high state of nerves as he waited to bat. As it happened, he did not face a ball. Peate, having hit two runs, took a mighty heave at a straight one from Boyle, and the match was over.

Spofforth's figures were 7 for 44, and his match analysis of 14 for 90 was not surpassed by an Australian 'Ashes' bowler until Bob Massie's 16 for 137 at Lord's in 1972. It was a stupendous feat of bowling, yet England might have known what to expect. Three years earlier they had seen Spofforth bowl Australia to a 10-wicket victory with match figures of 13 for 110 – including the first Test hat-trick (Royle, Mackinnon and Emmett). As a young bowler Spofforth was famed for sheer speed. As a sprinter he could cover 100 yards in less than 11 seconds, which certainly made for an impressive run-up. He also had a deadly yorker, but it was his variation of pace and angle that dominated the English batsmen of 1882. That and a smouldering determination to make England pay dearly for their arrogance. A measure of this determination is reflected in the fact that, in nervewracking crescendos of this remarkable match, he bowled his last 11 overs for only two runs and four wickets.

When Ivo Bligh's party set out aboard *Peshawar* that autumn, there was little cause for optimism that they would avenge the 'death' of English cricket. Even less when, 600 miles south of Colombo, the ship was in collision with a barque and their only fast bowler, Fred Morley, was pitched from his bunk and broke several ribs.

Australia won the first Test of 1882-83, at Melbourne, the giant Bonnor hitting 85 and 'Joey' Palmer taking 7 for 65. The next Test, however, proved a triumph for the Yorkshire allrounder Billy Bates. England were 199 for 7 when Bates hit 55 of an 88 partnership with Walter Read which pushed England to 294. He then, with his slow-medium roundarm bowling, took 7 for 28 – including a memorable hat-trick that ended with Bonnor's audacious dismissal, of which more later. Australia, all out for 114, followed on and Bates went to work again, claiming 7 for 74. England's victory by an innings made the rubber all-square; and so on to Sydney.

The match that regained the mythical – and produced the physical – Ashes echoed some of the drama and the retrospective recriminations that arose from the famous Oval Test. Again Spofforth featured in the bowling honours with 4 for 73 and 7 for 44 – his match-winning second-innings analysis in England. This time, however, he was on the losing side. And this, said some contemporary Australians, was the fault of the captain, Murdoch. One of the curiosities of the series was that the captains had the option of choosing a different wicket for each innings and, for Australia's final knock, Murdoch picked the wrong one. On the other hand, the same might be said of Bligh. England, bolstered by a stand of 116 between Read and Tylecote, had scored 247 in their first innings and led by 29. Bligh chose the same strip for the second, and fell into the hands of Spofforth, who exploited the worn, damp wicket. England managed only 123, leaving Australia a target of 153, but Murdoch's choice of wicket was even more disastrous as Barlow, the Lancashire left-arm bowler, took 7 for 40 and England won by 69 runs.

Thus were the Ashes recaptured – though Australia won that 'additional' match at Sydney three weeks later. Bligh stoutly denied that this was part of the official itinerary. In any case, the

W. G. Grace, in his day the best known figure in England.

Ashes were already, literally, in his keeping and there they stayed until his death in 1927, when they were bequeathed to Lord's. Apart from this historic contribution to the game, Bligh made little impact on the annals of Anglo-Australian cricket. The 1882–83 series marked his only appearances for England and he returned with a modest Test aggregate of 62 and an average of 10.33. Nevertheless, unlike an equally well-publicised namesake, at least he hung onto his Bounty.

One of the most remarkable members of the 1884 Australian side in England was W. E. Midwinter; not because of any outstanding ability but rather for his seemingly infinite capacity for changing sides. Midwinter, a useful all-rounder,

Australia v. England at Lord's, July 21, 22, and 23, 1884.

was born in Gloucestershire but went to Australia as a child. He returned to play for England in 1877 but, when the Australians arrived a year later, turned out for them. This was too much for W. G. Grace, who pressed him to join Gloucestershire. This done, he was selected by England for the 1881–82 tour to Australia. But now, in 1884, he was back in the Australian team.

The first Test, at Old Trafford, was drawn, and it says something of Captain Hornby's impetuosity that he was stumped in each innings. At all events, he was replaced as captain by Lord Harris for the Lord's Test, won by England by an innings, and for some of the excitement of 1882. It was notable for a splendid innings by Walter Read of Surrey. Australia established a record total of 551, (Murdoch scored 211), and in his frustration at Australia's mounting score, Lord Harris called on every man in the England side to bowl. Ironically, the most successful was wicket-keeper Lyttelton!

England were 181 for 8 when Read, angry at being so low in the order, strode truculently to the wicket. When he departed two hours later, having scored 117, the match was safe. His partner in a stand of 151 was Notts left-hander Scotton who, when last out (having opened the innings), had scored 90 in almost six hours.

Walter Read's other speciality was close-fielding, an attribute illustrated by an incident in the second Test of Bligh's victorious tour. Bates had taken the wickets of McDonnell and Giffen with successive balls. The man looming between Bates and a hat-trick was the formidable Bonnor, a fearsome striker of the ball. Bates promised to put down a fastish delivery on the leg stump in the hope that Bonnor would play slowly forward. Read volunteered to stand at silly mid-on where, under the outraged glare of Bonnor, he crouched, hands outstretched. Bates delivered the appropriate ball, which Bonnor, as if mesmerised, prodded into Read's unerring grasp.

By the mid-1880s England had taken a firm grip of the Ashes, owing, in part, to the discord in the Australian ranks. Melbourne and Sydney were constantly at loggerheads and Adelaide, too, was beginning to assert its right to a voice in affairs. In 1886 A. G. Steel led England to victory in all three Tests, by four wickets, and twice by an innings. Australia's hopes of a revival were not helped by the fact that no Tests were played in Australia for four years up to 1891–92. Meanwhile, having won the first Test of 1888, Australia were routed in the following two. This was a highly satisfactory state of affairs for W. G. Grace, Steel's successor as captain, particularly as 'the Champion', at 40, was past his prime. In fairness to the tourists, the summer of 1888 was exceptionally wet and the Australian batsmen were in all kinds of difficulty on the freakish English pitches. On the other hand, they did have, in C. T. B. Turner and J. J. Ferris, two bowlers who found conditions very much to their liking.

Despite his ever-expanding girth and diminishing prowess, Grace captained England in a further 11 Tests after 1888 and, in all, won six and lost only three. In 1890, another wet year, England won at Lord's by seven wickets (Manchester was washed out) and at The Oval by two. The

W. G. goes out to bat with A. G. Steel, the man he succeeded as England captain.

latter encounter was true to the Kennington tradition as England, needing only 95, lost eight wickets against the remarkable Ferris and Turner before scrambling home.

By the time England returned to Australia in 1891–92, the pyrrhic battles between Melbourne and Sydney had almost ceased and both the Australian team and the general atmosphere of the tour, were much the better for it. Though England lost, 2–1, it was generally agreed that this excursion, under Lord Sheffield's auspices, had been the best to date.

Sheffield's popularity in Australia was enhanced by his presentation of a shield to be contested annually by the states. In all, the noble Lord spent £16,000 against an income of £14,000. Fortunately he was a man of considerable means who, otherwise, might have pondered the fact that he was paying his 'amateur' captain W. G. Grace a fee of £3000 for the tour – plus the customary expenses. Grace could justly claim, though, that he led the tour batting averages and was still worth his considerable weight in appearance money. Nevertheless, in the first two Tests England were outplayed. In the second, Grace's tactics, hitherto regarded as Gospel, came under fire. Australia left England a winning target of 230. They began in bad light and Grace, sticking to the usual batting order, found himself, Abel and Bean back in the pavilion with only 11 on the board. Next day the wicket rolled out well and it was suggested that had W. G. sent in his tailenders the night before, the match could have been won. But Grace, to his eternal credit, always scorned the 'nightwatchman' principle. As he pointed out, if circumstances are difficult for an accomplished batsman, what's the point of sending out a straggler?

Andrew Stoddart, a dashing and popular England captain.

The Australians arrived in England in 1893 in good heart, and were soon engaged in some extraordinary batting practice when they met a Combined Oxford and Cambridge Past and Present side at Portsmouth. They batted into the third day for a staggering 843 runs, no declaration then being permitted, and for the Varsity opposition a young Indian called Ranjitsinjhi scored 44.

Ranji's great potential was noted at Lord's but there was no question of his being selected for a Test match there. It was a question of the fellow's *colour*. However, three years later the Lancashire committee asked the Australians' captain, Harry Trott, if he would object to Ranji playing against them in the England XI. Trott confirmed that the Australians would be delighted – as was the shrewd W. G.

In the meantime, tours to Australia were back in full swing under the captaincy of the dashing A. E. Stoddart of Middlesex and, in terms of public interest and classic quality of play, the 1894–95 tour established another milestone. The first Test at Sydney got the series away to a tremendous start. In those days it was agreed that all matches in Australia should be played to a finish. This dramatic encounter went into its sixth day and, incredibly, England's margin of victory was only 10 runs – after they had followed on!

It started with a record-breaking Australian total of 586, which was to stand for 30 years. England's first effort fell short by 231, but they followed on with a highly respectable 437. Even so, Australia needed only 177 to win, the wicket was in excellent condition, and, at close of play on the fifth day, they had reached 113 for 2. Sixty-four needed and eight wickets in hand. It seemed

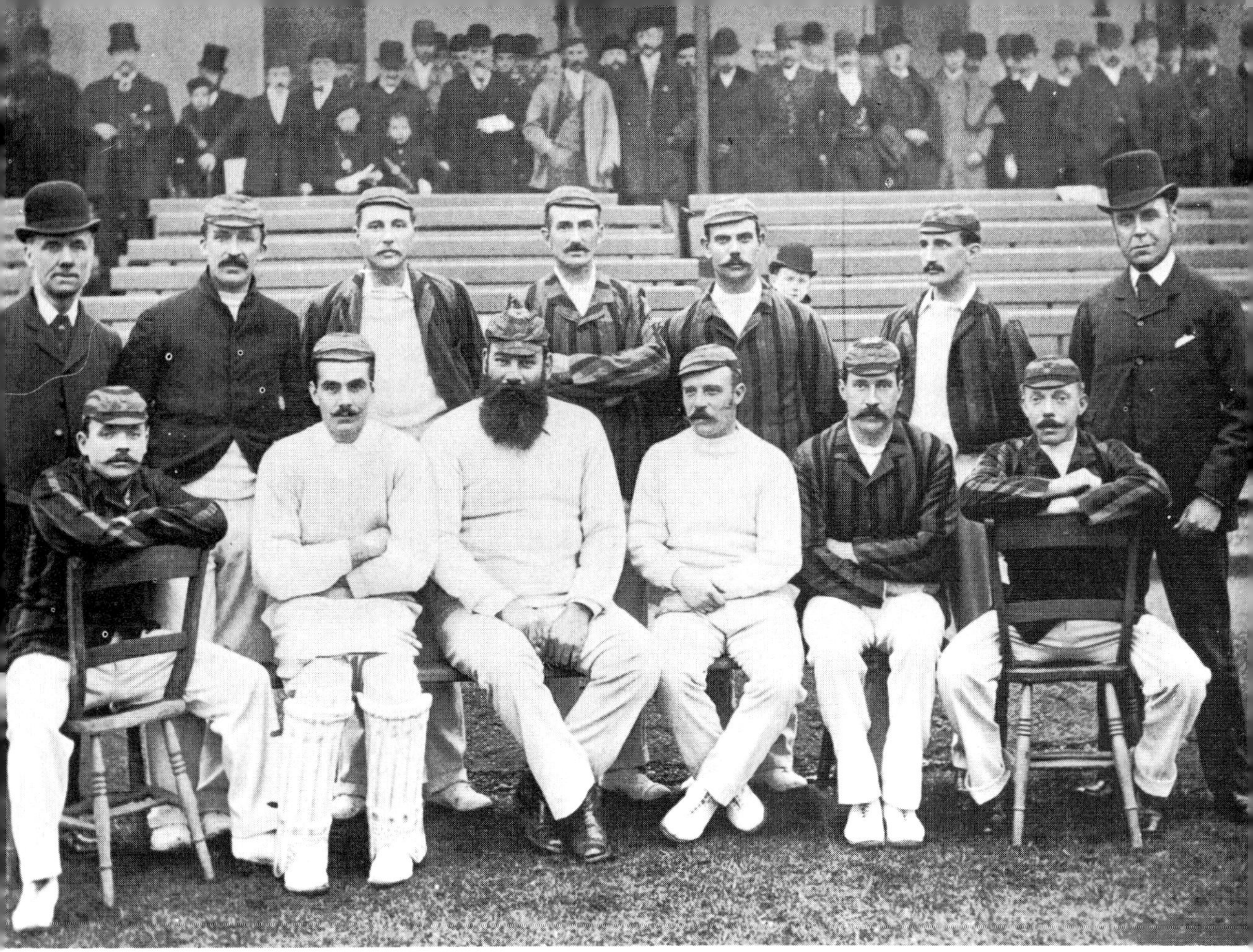

Lord Sheffield's England party for the 1891-92 tour of Australia. Back row, left to right: Carpenter (umpire), Attewell, Lohmann, M. Read, Bean, Sharpe, Thoms (umpire). Front: Briggs, MacGregor, Grace, Peel, Stoddart, Abel.

they were home and dry. But during the night it rained.

Bobby Peel, having put in a marathon stint of 53 overs in the first innings, and assuming his services would scarcely be required, took off on a bender on the fifth evening with team-mate Bill Lockwood. Both arrived late, but Australian captain Jack Blackham generously delayed the start of play. This gesture may well have contributed to Australia's impending defeat for, while Stoddart bundled Peel into a cold shower, the sun beat down on the sodden turf, turning the wicket into a dreaded 'sticky dog'. Peel wound up with six wickets and Briggs three to shoot out the Australians before lunch for 166.

England won the second Test by 94 runs, but Australia came back to win the third and fourth. All square, and the scene was set for another magnificent contest. Once again Australia got away to a good start, scoring 414 to England's 385. They followed up with a tidy 267 in their second innings, leaving England 297 to clinch the series. At 28 for 2, the odds swung heavily in Australia's favour but a stirring partnership of 210 between J. T. Brown (140) and Albert Ward (93) paved the way for an England victory. Brown's performance was particularly audacious. He scored his first fifty in 28 minutes and his whole innings came in almost even time.

Thus the rubber was won, but only just, and the feeling was that with his excellent batting line-up, two first-class spinners and a pair of great fast bowlers in Lockwood and Richardson, Stoddart's task might have been easier. A glance at the tour averages, however, shows that Lockwood took only five Test wickets at 68 each while Richardson claimed 32 for an average of 26. The answer lay in Stoddart's inability to bring the convivial, hard-drinking Lockwood to heel. The problem was, in those days, that good, bad or indifferent, a

Harry Trott sends down a leg-spinner to England's Albert Ward. Fifth Test, Melbourne, 1894–95.

player was virtually certain of his place. . . there were only 13 in the party and the reserves (in this case) were a wicketkeeper and a 'lob' bowler. One wonders why modern touring parties of 17 or so are invariably insufficient!

Ranjitsinjhi made his debut as an England cricketer in 1896, though there seemed little reason to change the side which started out at Lord's with a six-wicket victory. Cricket headquarters was crowded to overflowing as Tom Richardson (6 for 39) routed Australia for 53. England responded with 292 and, though Trott and Gregory hit 221 for the fourth wicket, Australia's second-innings 347 left England too modest a target. The selection of Ranji for the second Test at Old Trafford surprised and, some say, delighted the Australians, who regarded him as somewhat too 'artistic' for the tough arena of Test cricket. They modi'ied this view when the princely personage followed his 62 in the first innings with a majestic 154 not out.

Things looked rosy enough when England won the first Test at Sydney, where MacLaren scored a century and Ranji, weakened by illness, went in at seven and made 175! There were ominous signs, however, in Australia's second innings when Joe Darling struck a hundred and the other left-hander, Clem Hill, 96.

Hill, from South Australia, was undoubtedly one of his country's greatest left-handers, yet no-one watching him take guard for the first time would have suspected. His stance was wide and ugly, and he gripped the bat handle low down. But he picked up the flight very quickly and instantly moved into a sound position. Hill was an attacking player, yet in a crisis none was more reşolute. He was only 21 when he played what many believe to have been his finest Test innings – 188 in melbourne during that 1897–98 series.

Hill was crisp, shortish and clean-shaven, while Joe Darling, sun-tanned and heavily moustached, was slightly taller and just as powerfully built. Only in their infinite capacity for breaking the hearts of English bowlers were they entirely similar.

The Oval, 1896.

England lost the next four Tests comprehensively, largely because their bowling was not good enough. It certainly didn't trouble the brilliant Darling, and he signed off with 160 in the final Test.

Thus, whereas Stoddart's first tour to Australia had been, in every respect, a resounding success, the '97–98 expedition was far from happy – and only partially because of the results. There was more than a hint of what we have come to regard as modern cricket maladies: controversy occasioned by a player's ghosted Press articles; commercial manoeuvring by the game's promoters; gamesmanship on the field; a captain troubled by psychological problems, and the barracking of the crowd.

Ranjitsinjhi – or his goading scribe – commented bitterly on the behaviour of the crowds and, as the tour came towards its end, Stoddart undiplomatically took a similar line. It was one which was to send him home depressed and far less-loved than when he arrived. 'This system of barracking,' he said, with a degree of prophecy, 'if allowed to go on, will inevitably reduce cricket to a low level.'

Shades of Taunton on a Sunday afternoon in the 1980s?

England awaited, with some trepidation, the arrival of the 1899 Australians. It was to be the first season in which England hosted five Tests and the first time a selection committee had been appointed. The first selectors were Hawke, Grace and H. W. Bainbridge. The team chosen to play in the first Test, at Nottingham, included the 50-year-old W.G. as captain. It was to be his last appearance for England, and an unhappy one.

The match was drawn and, for England, only Ranji excelled with the bat against the hostility of Ernie Jones. Grace's contribution to an opening stand of 75 (with C. B. Fry) in the first innings, was by no means shameful. What finally caught up with the great man was his girth and it was a cruel end to a distinguished Test career that a section of the Trent Bridge crowd should jeer his clumsy fielding efforts. Grace had played his last part in the quest for the Ashes.

He was replaced as captain by MacLaren, who scored a magnificent 88 not out at Lord's but lost the match by 10 wickets. The remaining three of the series were drawn and Australia retained the Ashes: a tour of little high drama. Yet if the series saw the passing of one legend, the game was amply compensated in the arrival of three – C. B. Fry and Wilfred Rhodes of England, and Australia's Victor Trumper.

Despite Ranji's brilliant contributions, England lost the match by three wickets – though not for want of effort from the remarkable fast bowler Richardson. He bowled unchanged throughout Australia's second innings for figures of 42.3 – 16 – 76 – 6. It was typical of a man who thought little of walking seven miles to The Oval, carrying his cricket bag, then, after bowling maybe 30 overs in the day, trudging home again.

England won the series 2–1, though not before an unprecedented scandal at The Oval, where five leading professionals, Surrey's Lohmann,

Trent Bridge, 1899. The Australians return. Left to right: Kelly, Darling, Gregory, Hill, Iredale, Howell, Barlow (umpire).

Abel, Richardson and Hayward, and Gunn of Notts refused to play unless they were paid £20 – double the normal rate. This was the culmination of professional anger at the amounts being afforded to so-called amateurs.

The Surrey committee refused to give in, and three of the professionals dropped their demand. The exceptions, Gunn and Lohmann, refused to play. Lohmann never played for England again and Gunn only once – at Nottingham, three years later. If anyone doubted that W.G. was the chief source of contention, the Surrey committee made it clear enough in an official proclamation which stated that he was never paid more than £10, and that this sum was for expenses only.

At the end of the 1897 season, once more under the captaincy of Stoddart, England embarked for Australia with high hopes. The selection seemed well up to scratch and, with the phenomenal Indian prince in the side, physical and financial success was warmly anticipated. A. C. MacLaren and Stoddart stood high alongside Ranji as the potential amateur runmakers and with professionals like J. T. Hearne, Hayward, Richardson, Briggs, Hirst and Wainwright in the party, no-one foresaw the 4–1 drubbing that lay ahead. Some of the players were too fresh, some becoming slightly too stale to succeed under Australian conditions. Richardson had taken much out for himself over recent years and one of his pace-bowling partners, Hirst, was strong and willing but had little swerve or subtlety. Hayward and Wainwright, – successful on English wickets – found Australian pitches an almost insoluble problem. To add to the difficulties, the tourists suffered an extraordinary succession of illness and injury and, once again, the terms of agreement restricted the party to 13.

3

TRUMPER AND THE GOLDEN ERA

THE NAME of Victor Trumper first came to the notice of English cricketers when Stoddart's team invited a slim schoolboy to demonstrate his technique in the Sydney nets. His performance against such seasoned bowlers as Richardson, Peel and Briggs convinced observers that here was a batsman of great promise. It was an opinion to be shared by Monty Noble, a future Australian captain, who persuaded him to join his Paddington Club. There were times, however, during Trumper's teens when that promise was sorely tested by indifferent scores, but in club matches in 1897–98 he scored six centuries, at the amazing average of 204. Noble saw all these innings and remained unshaken in his belief that such talents would come to fruition in the first-class game.

Trumper was not in the original party for the 1899 tour to England, but, before the team embarked it was decided to loosen up with three matches against the Rest of Australia, and Trumper made a superb 75 in the match at Adelaide. This convinced the tour management that Trumper should accompany them – on half-pay. True to tradition, Trumper made a disastrous start to the English tour. He scored 0 and 3, against Essex, and his critics seized on these misfortunes to re-assert that the young Trumper was altogether too flashy at the expense of even cursory defence. The opinion seemed valid when, in his first Test, Trumper's stumps were shattered by Hearne before he had scored. Nevertheless, skipper Joe Darling persevered, and in the second Test, at Lord's, prodigy blossomed. His 135 not out was an innings of 'astonishing grace and freedom', and as he returned to the pavilion the crowd rose as a man to salute a supreme artist.

Though he scored no more Test centuries that summer, he scored the first 300 ever achieved by an Australian in England and was not out when Darling declared against Sussex.

As it happened, Trumper's maiden Test century at Lord's helped Australia to retain the Ashes, for all the other Tests were drawn. What surprised contemporary pundits was the rout of England's batsmen by the controversial fast bowler, Ernest Jones. Jones had accompanied the Australians in 1896 but, apart from bowling a fizzer through Grace's beard, had achieved nothing outstanding. He did, however, incur the displeasure of Sydney Pardon, the editor of *Wisden*, who wrote: 'Jones's bowling is to our mind radically unfair, as we cannot conceive a ball being fairly bowled at the pace of an express train with a bent arm.'

But, notwithstanding the royal 'we' and Ranji's subsequent complaints in Australia, here was the magnificently-built Ernie tearing England's first innings apart to the tune of 7 for 88. Certainly the rough, bluff labourer was quickly moved to anger. When asked by Lord Hawke if he had ever been to Adelaide University, he replied, 'Yes, My Lord, with a load of bloody sand!'

Almost as noteworthy as the bowling of Jones in that decisive Lord's Test of 1899 was the performance of Jackson and Jessop who, with England staggering at 66 for 6 in the first innings, featured in a partnership of 95 scored in a little over an hour. It is difficult to imagine latter-day batsmen approaching a similar crisis with such belligerent vigour.

The third Test of the series was the first ever played at Headingley and fell foul of the weather when the last day was washed out.

— FEELS FOR THE REST OF THE DAY ALMOST AS IF HE HAD PLAYED IN THE MATCH
TRUMBLE CAUGHT OUT BY A.O. JONES
"2 TO 1 ON THE BALL!"

HAYWARD AND F.S. JACKSON HITTING UP THEIR BIG SCORES.

REFRESHMENTS.
IREDALE MAKES
A CATCH THAT
END
CAPTIOUS CRITIC IN BOWLER HAT.
"THERE YARE BILL, THATS WOT WE PAYS THESE BLOOMIN' COBBIES FOR _ LIE ON THEIR BACKS AND ENJOY THEMSELVES!
J. BEGG.

Ironically, the Manchester Test was played in a heatwave, and England, once again, found themselves in a strong position when, having reached 372 in their first innings, they saw Australia slump to 57 for 7. Then came an amazing rearguard action by Noble, who made 60 not out. Australia, obliged to follow-on, were again bolstered by the defiant Noble, who scored 89, concluding a total of 8½ hours at the crease. Thus Australia were able to declare, and England were foiled.

At The Oval, England's batsmen found the pitch very much to their liking and even the demon Jones came in for a hammering. Jackson and Hayward set about the Australian attack to such effect that they achieved a record opening stand of 185 at better than a run a minute. With Ranji also in sparkling form, the total was 316 before the second wicket fell; then MacLaren and Fry hit 110 in 65 minutes for the fourth wicket. When the innings closed at 576, Jones had bowled 53 overs to take 4 164.

Lockwood's bowling figures for England – 7 for 71 – suggest an Australian rout, but he had little support and Gregory (117), Darling (71) and Worrall (55) helped steer the tourists to a respectable 352. England has neither the time nor the bowling resources to finish the job in the follow-on. At the close Australia were 30 runs ahead with five wickets standing – and the incredible Noble was 69 not out.

Thus the series went to Australia by the odd match, a bitter disappointment for England. But the 'colonials' were to confirm their supremacy by repeating the 4–1 dose of 1897–98 in 1901–02.

That winter found the Melbourne and the Marylebone clubs unable to reach agreement on terms, and when the MCC turned down the invitations, Melbourne asked Archie MacLaren to organise and manage his own selection. It was thus that Sydney Francis Barnes, a league player who occasionally turned out for MacLaren's Lancashire, was invited to join the party. The choice was to prove inspirational, for Barnes, in a Test career spanning the next 12 years, was to become one of the most successful 'good-wicket' bowlers of all time. In all Tests, including those against South Africa, Barnes took 189 wickets, averaging a wicket every 42 deliveries.

Left: *England v. Australia at The Oval, 1899.*

Though a different type of bowler to Tom Richardson he shared the same total dedication to his task. He bowled little more than medium pace but with an immaculate control which he could also bring to the variations of spin – from leg or off. Barnes pursued his skills with a professional exactness which he also demanded from his fellow players. Woe betide the fielder who would wander a yard from his allotted patch.

Barnes also pursued his skills into ripe old age. He was still playing Staffordshire League cricket at 61, when he captured 86 wickets at less than 11 each! Even at 46 he declared himself available for Johnny Douglas's 1920–21 tour of Australia and doubtless would have gone had he not demanded a free passage for his wife and family.

The first match of the '01–02 rubber, at Sydney, was a triumph for England, who batted first and, around an excellent 116 from MacLaren, built a formidable total of 464. Barnes's contribution to Australia's dismissal for 168 was 5 for 65, on a wicket of obvious quality. In the second innings, Barnes's feat was equalled by Len Braund, the Somerset leg-spinner, who took 5 for 61 as Australia fell to defeat by an innings and 124 runs.

At Melbourne, on a rain-affected pitch, Barnes steamed in again with 6 for 42 as Australia were dismissed for 112. England fared even worse, however. The great all-rounder Noble took 7 for 17 and the tourists were shot out for 61. Australia's second innings was a much more majestic affair in which Reggie Duff, batting at No. 10, embellished his first Test with a century and Hill got 99. Barnes could scarcely be held responsible for Australia's 353-run spree for he bowled 64 overs – 42 of them consecutively – for figures of 7 for 121. England were never in with a chance of scoring 405 for victory. Noble took 6 for 60, Trumble 4 for 49 and Australia won by 229 runs.

In the third Test, at Adelaide, England disastrously were to lose Barnes's services for the rest of the tour. Having taken 19 wickets at an average of 17, he twisted his knee after only seven overs and, with left-arm spinner Blythe also injured, the brunt of England's bowling fell on the shoulders of John Gunn. Nevertheless, the tourists were not badly placed at the halfway point. MacLaren and Hayward gave England a good start with 149, Quaife and Braund hit 108 for the sixth wicket,

English team going to field. Fifth Test, Melbourne, 1901–02.

and a total of 388 looked highly respectable. Indeed, when Australia fell short by 67 (Hill 98) the match seemed wide open. However, England could muster only 247 as Trumble took 6 for 74, and Australia, set 315, achieved the target with four wickets to spare. Probably the most rueful player was Hill, who, in three consecutive Test innings, had reached 99, 98 and 97 – an amazing hat-trick of frustration.

The rubber was clinched and the Ashes retained in Sydney, where Australia won comfortably by seven wickets. Noble, again, and left-arm newcomer Jack Saunders from Victoria were the architects of an English collapse. They bowled throughout for figures of 5 for 54 and 5 for 43 as England fell for 99.

Though the final Test at Melbourne had no significance in terms of the Ashes, it was the most exciting contest of the series. Australia, on a wet wicket, made only 144, and saw England take yet another first-innings lead, 45, Jessop, opening, hitting 35 of the first 50 runs *in 20 minutes*! Australia responded with 255 in their second knock and the amazingly consistent Hill made top score of 87. Requiring 211 for victory, England were faced with a difficult, lifting pitch and, in Noble and Trumble, just the men to exploit it. Even the bold Jessop had no answer to this and, despite another resolute innings of 49 from MacLaren and the dogged defiance of Tyldesley, Australia got home with 32 runs to spare.

What the outcome of the series might have been had Barnes and Blythe escaped injury is open to conjecture. There is little doubt, however, that Australia had the key players in Hill, Noble and Trumble. Hill's average of 52 speaks for itself and the fact that Noble and Trumble shared 60 of the 84 English wickets to fall is pretty conclusive. All-rounder Noble was to stamp his authority on the Ashes encounters for a decade, in which time he toured England four times.

As a captain, 'Mary Ann' favoured a somewhat Cromwellian attitude, and, at a powerful 6ft-plus, was not to be trifled with. He set a first-class example in everything he did, batting pugnaciously, fielding superbly – usually at point – and bowling immaculate off-breaks from a brisk run-up. Off the field, however, he was universally admired as a genial companion and sportsman without peer.

Trumble was a man of somewhat droll appearance. Tall and slim, he was endowed with a long nose and prominent ears. There was nothing bizarre about his bowling, however, which was medium-pace off-spin, delivered from a considerable height onto a perfect length. On a helpful wicket he turned the ball a lot. Above all he was a 'thinking' bowler, quite prepared to 'buy' the wickets of the master batsman if all else failed. Like Noble, he became a familiar and well-liked tourist in Victorian England as a member of five teams. Trumble enjoyed the rare distinction of twice performing the hat-trick against England – on both occasions at Melbourne where, in March 1904, he ended his Test career with 7 for 28.

The news of England's crushing 4–1 defeat in Australia evoked the customary inquests among her supporters. '*All would have been well had we sent the right team; No Hirst, Rhodes or Jackson – No Fry or Ranji . . .*' As far as Hirst, Jackson and Rhodes were concerned, the events of the following summer seemed to justify such speculation. All three were to perform outstandingly in one of the most gripping Test series ever staged. It has been described as the golden season of a golden era – and not because of the weather, which was wetter than average. No, the glory was provided by two richly talented teams locked in a sporting war that shifted, battle by battle, from one side to the other. In MacLaren, Fry, Ranjitsinjhi, Jackson, Tyldesley, Jessop, Braund and Rhodes, England had eight batsmen who had scored or were to score centuries against Australia. Barely outdone, the Australians boasted seven century-makers against England. Noble, Jones, Armstrong and Howell were in the vanguard of the Australian bowling while England countered with Hirst, Lockwood, Jackson, Braund and Rhodes – not to mention Jessop.

For the first time, Edgbaston and Sheffield came onto the list of Test grounds. At Birmingham the weather favoured, but finally confounded, England who declared at the end of the first day at 376 for 9, Tyddesley an impeccable 138. There had already been a heavy downpour and next morning the Australians found themselves on a sticky dog – but not for long. Darling's side were dismissed in 85 minutes for 36, the lowest score ever recorded in an Ashes match. Apart from one over from Braund to accommodate a change of ends, Rhodes and Hirst bowled throughout. In this context, Trumper's 18 rep-

Right: *Monty Noble – probably Australia's greatest all-rounder.*

resented a fine innings, but Rhodes (7 for 17) and Hirst (3 for 15) captured the headlines. Fortunately for Australia rain intervened again and, after a delayed start on the third and last day, they played out time.

Wilfred Rhodes's startling figures at Birmingham clearly owed much to the conditions yet, in a career stretching from 1898 to 1930, this modest Yorkshireman was to prove one of the truly great all-rounders. He took 4187 wickets and scored 39,797 runs, averaging 30.70. As a batsman he was to enjoy the unique distinction of sharing in record last- and first-wicket partnerships for England. The first of these was during the 1903–04 series when he went in No. 11 at Sydney and, with R. E. Foster, put on 130. Eight years later, in Melbourne, he opened with Jack Hobbs and sent England on their way with a partnership of 323. A remarkable achievement.

Yet it was as a spin bowler that Rhodes is best remembered. In these days of incessant seam, slow left-arm bowling seems to be becoming a dying art. In the age of Rhodes it was an essential part of the game's rich tapestry, and no-one wove more skilfully than he. He approached almost on tip-toe, a few unhurried steps, then, showing the batsman his right side, he would bring his left arm over with flawless rhythm that defied predetermination of the length or flight of the ball. His supreme subtlety of flight and length protected him from assault even on the shimmering pitches of Australia.

Much is illustrated by the fact that, at Sydney, on a sublime wicket and as Australia raced to 485, Rhodes bowled 40 overs and took 5 for 94. Such a performance against the likes of Trumper in full cry declaim character and brainwork almost as much as skill.

More rain; and at Lord's only 1¾ hours' play was possible. England, having lost Fry, caught at short leg, and Ranji, bowled off his pads, recovered from 0 for 2 to 102 without further loss. It was a match the Australians were not sorry to see abandoned for the weather had taken toll of key players like Noble, Darling and Saunders, all stricken by flu or tonsillitis.

Australia were back to full strength for the third Test at Bramall Lane, though it is remarkable that all the players in this first – and last – Test in Sheffield did not succumb to respiratory disorders. Set in an industrial area, the ground

England takes the field at Old Trafford, 1902. Left to right: Tate, Braund, MacLaren, Ranjitsinhji, Palairet.

was subject to great palls of black smoke that poured from neighbouring chimney stacks. Such was the selectorial whim that S. F. Barnes made his first and only appearance of the series in this match. He came into the attack after Hirst and Braund had rocked Australia with a burst of three wickets for three runs. However, from 75 for 5 the tourists recovered to 194 (Barnes 6 for 49). England, tormented by Noble (5 for 51) and Saunders (5 for 50), were dismissed for 145, whereupon Hill proceeded to add a personal 119 to Australia's lead of 49. Trumper made 62 and, despite Rhodes's 5 for 63, England were set a target of 339. The elegant MacLaren got 63 and Jessop smote a whirlwind 55, but Noble prevailed, finishing with match-winning figures of 11 for 103.

Another 'first and last' – and a decisive one – involved the selection of Fred Tate for the fourth Test at Old Trafford. Such is the cruelty of legend that England's defeat, by only three runs, was committed to the annals as 'Tate's match' – though it is better remembered for the centuries of Trumper and Jackson and the bowling of Lockwood. Tate, whose son Maurice was to achieve far happier deeds for England, made two fateful errors in the match. When Darling was only 16, Tate dropped him at deep square leg. The Australian skipper went on to make 37 out of 86 which, in view of the close finish, proved vital.

Tate's second indiscretion was as England's last batsman when, with four runs needed and the dependable Rhodes at the other end, he heaved at Saunders and was bowled. Thus Tate was blighted – but the basic cause of England's ultimate misfortune say with the autocratic Lord Hawke and the stubborn MacLaren.

Why Barnes did not retain his place is beyond comprehension. Instead, MacLaren preferred the Yorkshire all-rounder Schofield Haigh, but was over-ruled by Lord Hawke, who offered as an alternative the redoubtable Hirst. MacLaren, in a fit of perversity, rejected Hirst and chose, instead, the currently fashionable Tate. In the event, on a rain-sodden Old Trafford pitch, the England bowlers had great difficulty with slippery footholds. Trumper, on the other hand, had no such difficulty, for he raced away to a magnificent century before lunch, at which point Australia were 173 for one. The interval fortified the English spirit and, soon after, Rhodes – literally finding his feet – dismissed Trumper, Noble and Gregory. Darling, singularly unimpressed, twice hoisted Rhodes out of the ground and went on to his half-century. The first four batsmen apart, however, no other Australian exceeded five runs

C. Hill (14 not out) (left) and Trumper (103 not out) returning from lunch.

and Lockwood, in his final spell, took 5 for 8 as Australia slumped to 299 all out.

England started disastrously, losing five for 44, before Jackson and Braund pulled them round with a splendid stand of 141. Jackson battled on for 4¼ hours on a difficult pitch to reach 128 before he was last out at 262. Australia, 37 ahead, were 16 for 3 when Tate dropped the crucial chance off Darling. Even so, Lockwood's 5 for 28 found Australia all out for 86 – a modest lead of 123. Victory seemed well within England's reach as MacLaren and Palairet put on 44 for the first wicket, but the wiles of Trumble (6 for 53) and Saunders (4 for 52) proved too much for the following batsmen.

The final Test at The Oval provided Gilbert Jessop with the opportunity to produce what a contemporary critic described as 'an innings that will be famous as long as cricket is played'. It came at a time when some of the game's pundits had begun to doubt that 'The Croucher' was equal to his reputation as phenomenal attacking batsman.

Jessop was not a tall man, but he was very powerfully built, with long arms and a barrel chest. His technique was often unorthodox but sustained by a keen eye and a cat-like mobility. It was said of him that he could eliminate the time factor from a game in his ability to transform a match in half an hour. Bending low over his bat – hence the nickname – he would drive or sweep the pitched-up ball with great power and, if the ball was fractionally short, he had a devastating cut. Batsmen of more polished technique but lesser talent accused him of promoting slogging to the realms of science, but few who saw his innings in the 1902 Oval Test doubted that here was a batsman of genius.

The fact that he scored 104 in 77 minutes – including 17 fours and a five – was stunning in any context. Under the particular circumstances it was nothing short of outrageous. England, needing 263, were 48 for 5 with Trumble, as ever, in command. While Jackson batted watchfully at the other end, Jessop gave charge to the Australian spinners. His historic century was achieved off only 80 balls and Jackson's contribution to their sixth-wicket stand of 109 was a mere 18.

It would have been a tragedy had such heroics failed to achieve their intent and England were blessed to have Hirst back in the side. The

'Afternoon tea' in the Englishmen's dressing-room, 1903–04 series. Left to right: R. E. Foster, Tom Hayward, B. J. T. Bosanquet, George Hirst, Ted Arnold, Arthur Fielder, Herbert Strudwick, A. E. Relf.

experienced Yorkshireman dominated useful partnerships with Lockwood and Lilley and, in company with Rhodes, saw England home with one wicket to spare.

England's departure to Australia in the autumn of 1903 marked the beginning of a new era in the history of Ashes cricket. For the first time the party was chosen not by individual or commercial enterprise but by the Marylebone Cricket Club. The MCC also nominated the captain and, to the dismay of certain factions, Archie MacLaren – a proven batsman on Australian wickets – was overlooked in favour of the 30-year-old Pelham Warner. At all events the tour appears to have got away to a promiscuous start for it was subsequently recorded that among the passengers aboard S.S. *Orantes* was 'the lady who always wanted to sleep in some other cabin than her own.' Another young woman was reported to have 'mysteriously disappeared down an air chute'. So much for the Victorian cricket 'groupies'.

Nevertheless, more serious matters were at hand; namely the recovery of the Ashes and, at Sydney, England set about the task by winning a fascinating first Test by five wickets. It was a match of 'firsts', beginning with Monty Noble's debut as captain of Australia. He celebrated the occasion by scoring his first (and only) Test century, but, as the majestic Trumper was dismissed by Arnold's first ball in test cricket, Australia made only 285 in their first innings. A thunderstorm threatened to elevate this to a formidable total and England were 117 for 4 when Braund and 'Tip' Foster, playing his first innings for England, came together and took the side to 243 at close of play on the second day.

Next morning Foster, batting now with great

style and assurance, reached his hundred and Braund did likewise. Their stand of 192 put England ahead and when Foster was finally out, after a seven-hour innings of 287, England had established a new record Test innings of 577. More surprisingly, perhaps, the newcomer's splendid total which included 37 fours, was to stand as an individual record for 26 years. Foster's contribution could not have been more timely for, in their second innings, Trumper made a superb and undefeated 185, treating all the England bowlers – except Rhodes – with complete disdain. With Duff scoring 84 and Hill going well, the vociferous denizens of the Sydney ground had ample reason for optimism – until Hill was run out for 51.

The decision of Australian umpire Bob Crockett caused a near-riot in the members' pavilion, from whence (empty) bottles rained down on the field. Warner considered calling his men off but decided against it and order was eventually restored. Australia established a lead of 193 which, on a wearing wicket, still gave them a faint chance, but Hayward and Hirst ensured an England victory with a fifth-wicket partnership of 99.

One-up in the series, England made a painstaking start to the second Test at Melbourne. Warner and Hayward opened with a stand of 122, and when Australia set out in pursuit of England's 315, Rhodes was waiting for them on a difficult pitch. Under the circumstances the noteworthy outcome was not so much Rhodes's 7 for 56 but Trumper's peerless 74 in a total of 122. Trumble took some revenge with 5 for 34 in England's second innings – in which Tyldesley scored 62 of 103 – but Rhodes came back with 8 for 68 (Trumper 35) and Australia lost by 185 runs.

The Australians were relieved to find the sun shining on a perfect Adelaide wicket. Warner reported that it was one of the best he had ever encountered and the Australians endorsed the point by scoring 355 for 6 on the first day. After an opening stand of 129 with Duff, Trumper went on to score his third century in five Tests and Hill (88) then joined him in a partnership of 143. In reply to Australia's 388, England could manage only 245 and when a Gregory century sent the Australians on the way to a second-innings 351, they needed 495 – a target that proved to be well beyond their reach.

England's batting had failed badly in Melbourne, but one positive factor emerged in the bowling of B. J. T. Bosanquet, whose curious 'wrong'un' had sorely troubled the lesser Australian batsmen. Bosanquet had developed his then unique googly while at Oxford. Having fooled around at the nets, Bosanquet translated his findings into cricketing terms and the 'bosie' was perfected. It was a cunning weapon – provided the wicketkeeper knew what to expect and, somewhere between Melbourne and Sydney, Lilley got the message. In Australia's second innings Bosanquet wrapped up the match with final figures of 6 for 51. In this respect it might be called Bosanquet's match, but Rhodes and Arnold had already played a major role by sharing eight wickets for 61 in the first innings.

With the Ashes back in England's hands, Australia had to settle a consolatory victory in the final Test at Melbourne, where the magnificent Trumper led the charge with 88 in only 110 minutes. Braund, bowling fastish leg-breaks, finally accounted for him, and seven others, for a highly creditable 8 for 81; Australia made 247.

Arthur Fielder (left) and Bert Relf coming in at the end of England's innings at Melbourne, second Test, 1903–04.

Rhodes bowling to Duff. Second Test at Lord's, 16 June 1905.

Rain prevented play on the second day until 4 p.m. when, on a lifting pitch, England were in serious trouble against the ferocious pace of Albert 'Tibby' Cotter, whose 6 for 40, with Noble's 4 for 19, shot them out for 61. Though George Hirst then bowled Trumper for a duck and went on to take 5 for 48, the match had slipped beyond England's grasp. They fell foul of Trumble, who in this his last Test took 7 for 28 – including the hat-trick.

The first Test series under the auspices of MCC had been a success, and now the Australians began to move towards a similar set-up. The inaugural meeting of the Australian Board of Control for International Cricket was held in 1905, and six years later the Board managed to assume full control of Australian touring sides.

In the meantime, the side which arrived in England in 1905 was organised by the players themselves in association with their player-manager Frank Laver. This was the series in which three great players, Jackson, Darling and Duff, made their departure from Test cricket – each, appropriately, with a flourish. It was also the rubber in which C. B. Fry first revealed his true talents to the erstwhile sceptical Australians.

Jackson, the richly-talented Yorkshire all-rounder, was captain, and responded by winning the toss every match. Yet this was the least of his achievements, for he scored two centuries and emerged head and shoulders above the batsmen of either side with an average of 70. For good measure, he topped the England bowling figures by taking 13 wickets at 15 each, and led the side to a 2–0 success.

The tall, guard-like Jackson was the son of a cabinet minister. He attended Harrow and Cambridge and, during the Boer War, attained the rank of Colonel in – of all regiments for a Yorkshireman – the Royal *Lancasters*.

England set out at Trent Bridge to defend the Ashes against Darling's Australians, and at the end of the first innings the match was nicely balanced – England 196, Australia 221. Now the bold MacLaren – still smarting, no doubt, at his omission from the 1903–04 team – set about the Australian attack with a vengeance. With Hayward, he brought up 145 for the first wicket and went on to 140, being particularly severe on the demon Cotter, whom he hooked hard and often. Jackson, who had taken 5 for 52, now contributed an undefeated 82, and, with Tyldesley and Hayward in form, England were able to declare at 426 for 5.

Trumper, who had retired hurt in the first innings, was unable to bat when Australia batted again and only Gregory (51) and Darling (40) could withstand the wiles of Bosanquet, who claimed 8 for 107.

England's win sent them to Lord's in good heart. But thunderstorms ruined the match, which was finally washed out as a draw. At Headingley, Jackson hit 144 not out in the first innings, Tyldesley 100 in the second, and Australia, faced with a deficit of 401, were glad to hold on for another draw.

Splendid England batting, spearheaded once again by a Jackson century, proved altogether too much for the Australians at Old Trafford. In reply to 446, the tourists could muster only 366 in two attempts, though Darling hit a defiant 73 in the first innings and Duff a determined 60 in the second.

And so to the final Test at The Oval, and the emergence of Fry from the shadows to the fullness of his reputation. Charles Fry was a man of so many varied talents that he may, at times, have devoutly wished for some weird athletic or academic discipline in which he could not excel. Not only was he an England cricketer and footballer, but an athlete of international stature whose world record 23 ft 6½ ins long jump at Oxford stood for 21 years. On top of this he played rugby for Blackheath and Barbarians and still found time to win first-class honours degrees.

He scored 94 centuries, six of them in succession in 1901. He was primarily an on-side player, and so Darling set a field to stem the runs in this direction. Fry thereupon turned his magnificent drive to the off, and, in company with Jackson, put on 151 for the fourth wicket. By the time he was out, for 144, the Australians were under no illusions.

Though the English batting dominated the Test with 430 and 261 for 6 declared (Tyldesley 112 not out) the Australians emerged with much honour in a drawn match. Cotter bowled magnificently on a perfect pitch to take 7 for 148 in the first innings and Duff ended his Test career, as he had started it, with a splendid century. Darling, too, said farewell in style with a polished 57.

C. B. Fry, sportsman supreme. A world record-holder for the long-jump and winner of England cricket and soccer caps.

4

THE MASTER

IN RETROSPECT, it was a kind of irony peculiar to cricket that during the 1907–08 tour of Australia, England lost the series 4–1 but found, in John Berry Hobbs, a young player who was to prove their greatest batsman since W.G. Grace and, arguably, of all time.

Hobbs arrived on the scene at a time when bowlers were beginning to experiment with more sophiticated possibilities than mere pace, accuracy and orthodox finger-spin. Hirst and others had shown what could be done with swing, using the seam aerodynamically as well as off the pitch. Bosanquet had demonstrated the startling possibilities of the googly. The young Hobbs, tutored and partnered by Tom Hayward, followed his classic example of playing through the ball with a full swing of the bat. The new bowling demanded the options of back play to defeat the googly and late swerve. Hobbs was probably the first batsman completely to meet the challenge and, in this sense, brought a rich, new dimension to the art of batsmanship.

He was to remain at the top for 23 years, in which time, not unnaturally, he collected an impressive quota of records. His career aggregate was a massive 61,237 runs, and no other batsman has approached his 197 centuries. Fortunate in the quality of his opening partners, he figured in 166 first-wicket stands of 100 or more. In terms of centuries against Australia, he was also supreme – 12, against Hammond's nine and Sutcliffe's eight. And his Test average of 56.96 was six runs higher than his overall figure.

Hobbs's batting improved as the years went by. Before the 1914 war, his average never exceeded 58. In 1919 he averaged 60.32; in 1925, 70.32, and in 1928, when he was 45, a magnificent 82.

He embarked on his first tour in company with another bright young prospect, Kent's Ken Hutchings, whose selection was based on a meteoric 12-week success in county cricket. He was impetuous and inconsistent, yet he scored a match-winning century at Melbourne and was admired by Australian critic Jack Ryder as the best and hardest striker of a ball he had ever seen.

Jack Hobbs, the supreme batting artist, unchallenged in his day as 'The Master'.

First Test, Sydney, 1907–08. Hutchings disliked the slow bowling of Armstrong. At 91, Hutchings drove the ball back to Armstrong who held it. He can be seen here tossing the ball up.

When Noble (at 19) returned the ball to Braund, Braund collided with Hill, missing the ball. Although Hill had been in his proper position, the bowler was plainly annoyed.

Hutchings sadly was not to reach the age of cricket maturity, for he died on the Somme in 1916.

Another great talent to emerge on the 1907–08 tour was that of Jack Crawford, a tall, bespectacled all-rounder who played for Surrey as a Repton schoolboy. Having made a successful debut with 30 wickets in the series, he did not pursue his great potential as a Test cricketer. The same could not be said of Australia's new recruits, Vernon Ransford, Hanson Carter, Bill Whitty, Roger Hartigan and the incomparable Charles 'Governor General' Macartney. They, in fact, proved to be more consistent supporters of Australia's 'old guard' – Hill, Trumper, Noble and Saunders than did their England counterparts. The most successful England debutant, George Gunn, came into the side purely as a last resort. The England captain, A. O. Jones, became seriously ill shortly after arrival. As luck would have it, Gunn, the Nottingham professional, was convalescing in Australia after his own illness, and was promptly hauled into the party.

He responded by scoring a century in the first innings at Sydney and 74 in the second; but, largely through misguided team selection, his efforts were in vain. The selectors brought in reserve wicketkeeper R. A. Young as an opener – *to the exclusion of Hobbs.* The folly of this decision was all too clear in hindsight. Young scored only 16 runs, dropped three vital catches – and the Australians won by two wickets. Thereafter in the series – and for the next 23 years – Hobbs was England's undisputed opening bat.

At Melbourne, after Australia had been dismissed for a modest 266, he launched the England reply with a solid 83. Hutchings scored his dazzling century in 125 minutes, and England had a lead of 116. This was imperiously wiped off by Trumper and Noble, and the 'new boys' Macartney and Carter each scored half-centuries in helping Armstrong (77) restore the balance. England, needing 282, struggled to 243 for 9 – still 39 short. At this point the experienced Syd Barnes was joined by Kent's Arthur Fielder and, by patient application, they brought the scores level. Armstrong, in desperation, stationed seven men on the leg and bowled at Barnes's pads. Barnes drew back, pushed the ball on the off, and ran. By the time Fielder had responded the ball was in Hazlitt's hands but, instead of lobbing it gently to wicket-keeper Carter for a certain run-out, he

Braund at slip catches Ransford off Fielder for 51. Fourth Test, Melbourne, 1907–08.

shied at the stumps, missed, and England scraped home.

The third Test, at Adelaide, saw the introduction of another prodigy in Roger Hartigan of Queensland – which, in those days, was not even a first-class Shield side. It was a remarkable debut, for after three days, with England apparently coasting to victory, Hartigan joined Hill in a record eight-wicket partnership of 243 which still survives. With the temperature soaring past 100°F and Hill coming in late following a bout of 'flu, there had seemed no way Australia could mount a serious challenge. At close of play, however, the scoreboard shows Australia 397 for 7, with Hill and Hartigan each past 100. Though totally drained, Hill batted on until he was out for 160. England's faint hopes of achieving a target of 429 were not enhanced when Hobbs retired with a strain, and as they were dismissed for 183, medium-pacer O'Connor celebrated *his* first Test appearance by taking 5 for 40.

At Melbourne, in the fourth encounter, though Victor Trumper failed to score in either innings, Australia still swamped England by 308 runs. Again a combination of old and new caused the damage. Noble and Ransford laid the foundation, and in the second innings, Armstrong (133 not out), Carter and Ransford again contributed the bulk of their 385. Jack Saunders, with match figures of 9 for 104, did much to restrict England's aggregate to 291.

At Sydney, for the third successive time in the series, Australia fought back from first-innings misfortunes to put England on the rack and win. Barnes claimed 7 for 60 in an Australian innings of 137. When Hobbs and Gunn put on 134 for England's second wicket, A. O. Jones's smile grew even wider. Even when England collapsed for 281 (Gunn an undefeated 122) the possibility of losing seemed unthinkable. But Rhodes dropped Trumper off Barnes at one, and he went on to make 166; Australia reached 422 – a lead of 278 – and England fell short by 49 runs.

In view of their oustanding success of 1907–8, the Australian tourists of 1909 had every reason for confidence in their ability to hold on to the Ashes. Beneath the surface, however, there was more than a hint of resentment at the Board of control's intrusion into their affairs. The players had been permitted to choose their own manager – the rough and ready but popular Frank Laver – but Peter McAlister had been insinuated into the party as a 'treasurer' who would represent the Board at the Imperial Cricket Conference. McAlister and Laver, former club colleagues, had

not been on the best of terms since McAlister's omision from the 1905 tour – seemingly at Laver's instigation. McAlister later told the Board that Laver had taken charge of the balance sheet. For his part, Laver claimed he had kept accounts solely in the players' interests and refused to hand them over.

The Board made no issue of the impasse, but insisted on appointing future managers. When it came to organising the 1912 tour, the players once again chose Laver, whose intransigence on the matter of his accounts had made him unacceptable to the Board.

Warwick Armstrong (Australia) bowled by J. N. Crawford for 32. Fourth Test, Melbourne, 1907–08.

In the summer of 1909, such developments were merely puffs of cloud on the horizon. England emerged from the first Test, at Edgbaston, victorious by 10 wickets, thanks to the remarkable bowling of Hirst and Blythe, who claimed all the wickets – Blythe 11 for 102 and Hirst 9 for 86. One can only imagine the gasp of amazement that swept the England camp when, for the second Test, the selectors not only dropped Blythe but Fry, Jessop, Rhodes and Hayward too. Not surprisingly, the tourists romped home at Lord's by nine wickets. The match was notable for Ransford's only Test century and the one-off appearance of John King, a 38-year-old Leicestershire all-rounder, who scored 60.

The red-faced selectors tried again; this time making *six* changes. Rhodes, Jessop and Fry were re-instated and so was Barnes – recalled to play his first Test in England for seven years. He celebrated by taking 6 for 63 in Australia's second innings, but Jessop strained his back and could not bat. The outcome was another triumph for Australia by 126 runs as Cotter and the small, left-handed Macartney shared 17 wickets.

Despite a wealth of penetrative bowling by Blythe and Barnes, for England, and Laver (8 for

Noble gets four to the leg boundary off Crawford. Barnes just misses the ball at short-leg. Sydney, 1907–08.

31) for Australia, the Old Trafford Test ended in a draw, as did the final Test at The Oval. Of this last match, *Wisden* subsequently observed that the England selection once more 'touched the confines of lunacy'. On a firm and lively wicket, England went into the match without a fast bowler. When Noble won the toss for the first time, MacLaren handed the new ball to the tubby 37-year-old leg-spinner D. W. Carr, who was little-known outside club cricket. To everyone's astonishment, in his first seven overs Carr took the wickets of Gregory, Noble and Armstrong, but Trumper and Bardsley set about the newcomer with a vengeance. He finished the match with 7 for 282 and disappeared whence he came. Bardsley had a particularly fruitful match, scoring 136 and 130 – the first man to make a century in each innings of an Ashes match.

In 1911–12 the unfortunate Pelham Warner, like A. O. Jones before him, was taken ill soon after arrival and had to hand over the captaincy. The man appointed to the task was John William Henry Tyler Douglas. Douglas was not an outstanding player and his overall record as captain was mixed, but in all the years he led England – and Essex – his enthusiasm, his fighting spirit and

England v. Australia at Birmingham, 1909. A good catch by MacLaren at slip off Blythe. Batsman: Macartney (Australia), Wicketkeeper: Lilley.

the loyalty he gave and received from his players, marked him as an Englishman of the classic 'bulldog' kind.

No-one recognised his limitations more than Douglas himself. When the Australian crowds applied his initials to the jingle 'Johnny Won't Hit Today', Douglas would merely smile and admit: 'An optimist is a man who, batting with Johnny Douglas, backs up for a run.' One Melbourne member bet him that, in one hour, more trains would pass the ground than he would score runs. It is said that the trains won by 23. Nevertheless, he knew how to bring the utmost from the men around him, and in 1911–12 he had just the men to win back the Ashes.

Hobbs scored 662 runs and Rhodes had a batting average off 57.87. Barnes captured 34 wickets in the series and 32 fell to the great left-arm swing bowler Frank Foster who, some 20 years later, was to become an unwitting adviser to Douglas Jardine on the setting of leg-side fields for Larwood and Voce. This arose from Foster's own speciality, a fast, angled ball liable to cut back, and for which he often assembled six fielders in catching positions. Quite often, though, the fast breakback struck the batsman painfully on the thigh and Foster was frequently jeered by the Australian crowds. But Barnes was the man who really got under their skin. He was a master at imposing his will upon the opposition. He made it clear that he didn't play cricket for fun and that the game was going to proceed on his terms. Such a temperament was not exactly soothed when, at Sydney, Douglas put himself on to bowl with the new ball. Australia made 317 for 5 on the first day and went on to win by 146 runs: Barnes 4 for 179.

In the second Test, at Melbourne, Barnes commandeered the new hall and characteristically 'showed 'em'. In just over an hour he had disposed of Kelleway, Bardsley, Hill, Armstrong and Trumper for six runs off 11 overs. Australia were all out for 184. A J.W. Hearne century helped England to 265 and, when Foster's 6 for 91 restricted Australia to 299, Hobbs, with 126 not out, gave England an eight-wicket victory.

It was Foster's turn to destroy the Australians at Adelaide with 5 for 36, yet Bill Hitch also

Right: *J. W. H. T. Douglas, one of England's most popular and respected captains.*

Foster bowling to Trumper. Fourth Test, Melbourne, 1911–12.

Left: *Frank Woolley, the pride of Kent, a batsman of great charm and quality.*

enjoyed a moment of fame by bowling the illustrious Trumper with his first delivery. The outcome was a paltry 133, which England duly passed without losing a wicket. Hobbs was the standard-bearer, 187 out of 501 being his highest against Australia. Hill responded magnificently with 98, nightwatchman Carter scored 72, Bardsley 63, and, had not the injured Trumper been forced to bat at No. 11, Australia may well have set a challenge total. Instead, England coasted home by seven wickets.

England did not so much recover the Ashes in Melbourne as bear them imperiously away on the monumental victory of an innings and 225 runs. Douglas submitted Australia to the not-so-tender mercies of Barnes and Foster, who dismissed them for 191. There followed a record first-wicket partnership of 323, scored in only 268 minutes, by Hobbs and Rhodes, who, in almost seven hours for 179, made his only century against Australia. Rain freshened the wicket during the third night and Douglas weighed in with 5 for 46 as Australia were dismissed for 173.

The fifth Test, at Sydney, was to be Trumper's last and, not inappropriately, he bowed out with 50 in the second innings. All were overshadowed, however, by Frank Woolley who, apart from taking six excellent catches, scored 133 not out in the first innings. The great Kent all-rounder is largely remembered as a batsman of great charm and quality, but he was also a richly-talented left-arm spinner.

Woolley was a tall man with an extensive reach which allowed him to adjust to the length of a ball with an apparent minimum of movement. Certainly there was an air of leisured ease about his play which made the power and variety of his strokes all the more enthralling. His Sydney century proved to be a match-winning effort for, though Australia fought back well, they lost by 70 runs.

Australia's 4–1 drubbing proved to be the least of the Board's problems when they came to assemble a side to visit England for the Triangular Tournament of 1912, for the ramifications of the previous tour finally came home to roost. When the Board nominated G. S. Crouch as manager, Hill, Armstrong, Trumper, Ransford, Cotter and Carter rebelled, declaring that unless they were allowed to choose their own manager, they would not tour. There was no way the Board was going to accept the players' choice – Frank Laver.

In the course of the wrangling, Clem Hill and Peter McAlister became involved in a conflict of rather more fundamental proportions. At a meeting of the selection committee in Sydney, McAlister accused Hill of being 'the worst captain I have ever seen'. Hill thereupon punched him and in the course of a protracted wrestling match, McAlister was almost thrown out of the window. All good, meaty stuff for the Australian Press, but it resulted in Hill's resignation as a selector. The Board meanwhile remained adamant in its refusal to concede their choice of manager.

Thus the side that travelled to England in 1912 lacked six star 'rebels'. It scarcely mattered. The summer was so wet that the much-vaunted Tournament – England, Australia and South Africa – was a monumental failure. Of the three Tests between England and Australia, two were drawn before the first innings were completed, and England won the third after seven rain-affected days. Woolley revelled in the conditions at The Oval by taking 5 for 29 and 5 for 20.

What some have described as the Golden Age of Anglo-Australian cricket drew to a close in damp and mouldering disillusion. Before heart and unanimity could be restored to Australia's stricken ranks, half the world was engulfed in a bloody and tragic Test that was to last for four long years.

English cricket was to be sapped of much of its strength by the deprivations of the European conflict. Hobbs, Woolley and Rhodes re-emerged and Johnny Douglas resumed the captaincy, but compared with Australia, England were woefully short of fast bowlers. Foster retired after breaking a leg, and Barnes, having haggled over expenses, was out of favour, and aged 46 in 1919. Australia, on the other hand, had discovered a wealth of talent in post-war Imperial Forces sides – pace bowlers Jack Gregory and Ted McDonald,

Warwick Armstrong – 'the Big Ship' – renowned for his belligerent approach to the game. Seen here, with Johnny Douglas, on the verandah at Trent Bridge.

First Test, Sydney, 1911–12. Barnes bowled a tempting ball to Cotter who failed to half-volley it for a carpet drive enabling Barnes to catch the ball easily.

wicketkeeper Bert Oldfield, and a bright batting prospect, 'Nip' Pellew. They could also call on the proven talents of Kelleway, Bardsley, Macartney and, above all, the prodigious and powerful Armstrong.

Faced with such realities, Lord Harris – England's senior cricket administrator – resisted an early resumption of the Ashes series, but, in the autumn of 1920, England embarked once again. It was a disastrous tour. Tall and slim during his formative years, Warwick Armstrong now was heading towards the giant 22-stone proportions that made him an unforgettable spectacle. He had a haughty, sometimes bossy manner, was exceptionally strong-willed and, not unlike other Australians of his ilk, a master of the caustic comment. During the final Test at The Oval in 1921, when a draw was inevitable, he rested his front-line bowlers, retired to the deep, and began to read a newspaper. When asked what he was reading, Armstrong replied: 'I'm trying to find who we're playing.' For all that, beneath the bluff and belligerent exterior, a heart of gold was said to beat.

As a player, he performed with a weight and solidity commensurate with his size. An ungraceful bat, he was nevertheless difficult to dislodge, even when floundering against top-class spin bowling. He bowled off a run far too long, yet he could bowl for hours, and, on a helpful wicket, turn the ball sharply from leg.

This was the man who, starting at Sydney on December 17, 1920, was to lead Australia to eight successive Test victories against England. One reason for this remarkable run was the emergence of Gregory and McDonald, two fast bowlers whose complimentary skills were harnessed by Armstrong *as a pair* and, not – as had been the fashion – as individuals often operating with the new ball in tandem with a slow bowler. Gregory was the 'frightener' of the pair, bouncing the ball off the glass-hard wickets; spraying it menacingly around the bat-handle and the body, firing in the unexpected yorker. McDonald was all grace and accuracy; a fast rapier, thrusting at the perfect length and invariably on target.

Armstrong was trebly blessed in the bowling department, for in Arthur Mailey, Australia had discovered a leg-spinner of rare genius. Mailey was by no means an economical bowler. On the other hand, he had a match-winning quality,

First Test, Trent Bridge, 1921. A ball from Gregory struck Ernest Tyldesley on the head, then dropped upon the bails, putting him out.

First Test, Trent Bridge, 1921. Australian fielders in the slips trying to catch Rhodes. Holmes made 30.

taking wickets *frequently*: for every over Mailey bowled in Test cricket he conceded four runs, but for every seven overs he bowled he took a wicket. He was a puckish little man who brought to spin bowling creative imagination rather than detailed patience. What is more, he had the personality and humour to brush aside his sometimes extravagant figures which, he would claim, would have been very impressive had the spectators held their catches.

England's bowling deficiencies were cruelly exposed in the Sydney Test, where Australia made 267, Herbie Collins topscorer with 79. Jack Russell made a disastrous debut for England, playing the first ball of the innings onto his wicket, and, of England's 190, Woolley made 52 and Hobbs 49. Then, on the shimmering Bulli clay wicket, the massive Armstrong struck 158 in 3½ hours, Collins graced his first Test appearance with a century, Macartney, Bardsley and Johnny Taylor each scored half-centuries, and Australia added 581 to their lead of 77. Against the searing pace of Gregory and the wizardry of Mailey England had not the slightest hope. Though Hobbs, Hearne, Hendren and Rhodes resisted stubbornly, they were dismissed for 281 and a 377-run defeat.

If fortune favours the brave, then *mis*fortune certainly damns the faltering. England were made to suffer dreadful indignities at Melbourne. Hearne, sick, was unable to bat, but the real malady, again, was not catching. Missed chances allowed Pellew and Gregory, to hit audacious centuries, Gregory reaching his in a mere 137 minutes. The outcome was a formidable Australian total of 499. Heavy rain on the Sunday turned the wicket into a mud-pack and, despite a courageous and skilful stand of 142 by Hobbs (122) and Hendren (67), Gregory (7 for 69) ensured the follow-on, 248 runs behind. In the second innings, only Woolley's 50 was of any

Ted McDonald, more familiarly seen as Gregory's partner in a formidable Australian pace attack.

consequence and Armstrong led his side to victory with 4 for 26.

The pattern of Armstrong's triumphant march was set. England batted well to Adelaide, but Australia batted better. Thus, though England, replying to Australia's 354 (Collins 162), established a lead of 93 – thanks to Russell's 135 not out – Australia came back with a massive 582. Kelleway, Armstrong and Pellew scored centuries and Jack Gregory an undefeated 78. Hobbs earned a standing ovation for his 123 in 150 minutes, but England failed by 119 runs. On a wicket which provided a total of 1753 runs, the chirpy leg-spinner Mailey captured 10 wickets at 30.2 runs apiece – a remarkable performance.

Mailey was at it again in Melbourne with 4 for 115 and 9 for 121. Nevertheless, the 39-year-old Harry Makepeace made 117 and 54, while gritty Johnny Douglas scored a half-century in each innings. For reliability in depth, however, the Australians remained supreme. Armstrong, though suffering from malaria, hit his third century of the series in steering Australia to a lead of 105. The amazing Gregory made 77 in that innings and was 76 not out as his side cruised home by eight wickets. He carried on in the final Test at Sydney with 93, finishing the series with an average of 73.66 – on top of which he took 23 wickets and 15 catches.

When Jack Hobbs was hampered by a leg injury, his efforts in the field were cruelly jeered by the Hill. Percy Fender responded scathingly in the British Press and was, in turn, roundly barracked when the news came out. Heckling was the least of England's problems, however, for Gregory's effort, in support of Macartney's first Test century (170 in 244 minutes) was a crushing response. Australia reached 392 and, when England came back with 280, cantered to a nine-wicket victory and a crushing 5–0 triumph in the series.

Imagine, then, the mortification of the England tourists to discover that the men who had so conclusively regained the Ashes were aboard their homeward-bound ship, *Osterley*. Their apprehension was evidently shared by the England selectors who, in the 1921 series, were to call upon a total of 30 players in an effort to break the stranglehold of Armstrong's mighty team.

Among the newcomers was Ernest Tyldesley, who, in the first Test at Trent Bridge, was knocked out by a Gregory bouncer which then rolled onto his stumps. The fiery Gregory introduced himself with 6 for 58 as England crumbled for 112. Then Ted McDonald scythed through the second innings with 5 for 32 and Australia won by 10 wickets.

Desperate, the selectors invited C. B. Fry to play, but at 49 he prudently declined. Hobbs was still unfit and it fell upon the gallant Woolley to carry England's batting burden at Lord's. This he did vaingloriously, scoring 95 out of 187 and 93 out of 283. Mailey and McDonald took four wickets each in the first innings, Gregory and

McDonald four each in the second. Australia cruised to 342, and Bardlsey, who made 88, was 63 not out in the second innings as they won by eight wickets.

Two such humiliating defeats on home territory had worse effect on England's morale than losing all five in Australia. Faced with such desperate reality and the bewilderment of hastily assembled squads of players (17 are said to have reported at Lord's) the selectors decided that a change of captain was essential. Douglas, after all – however gallant and gutsy – had lost seven Tests on the trot. His successor, the Hampshire captain, the Hon. Lionel Tennyson, had been recruited for the Lord's Test with some success,

Right: *Ernest Tyldesley, knocked out by a bouncer that rolled onto his stumps.*

Below: *The Australian tourists of 1921. Back row, left to right: Smith (manager), Ryder, Gregory, Hendry, McDonald, Mailey. Middle row: Bardsley, Macartney, Armstrong, Collins, Carter. Front: Taylor, Andrews. (missing from group: Mayne, Oldfield, Pellew)*

Arthur Gilligan – appointed England's captain on the strength of his devastating form with Sussex.

Maurice Tate, a superb all-rounder who joined the England squad under the captaincy of his Sussex colleague, Gilligan.

striking a hearty and undefeated 74 in the second innings. He had the impeccable pedigree that befitted a leader of the England cricket team. Grandson of Queen Victoria's poet laureate and a baron of the line, Tennyson was duly appointed to lead the side at Headingley.

He brought with him his 34-year-old county wicketkeeper and opening bat, George Brown, also a man of stern stuff. His speciality was to deal with the fast, rising ball in a manner that later found favour with Yorkshire's Brian Close: he allowed it to whack him on the chest. Not entirely coincidentally, perhaps, Brown had previously earned a living as a warder in a lunatic asylum.

Tennyson's debut was dogged by bad luck. First he lost the toss and then, attempting to stop a fierce drive from Macartney, split his left hand so badly that he could not grip a bat. Later in the day Hobbs was taken ill with appendicitis and took no further part in the series. By late afternoon Australia, spurred on by a Macartney century and 77 from Armstrong, had totalled 407 in 296 minutes; England, in bad light, lost Woolley and Hearne.

On a cloudy morning England slumped to 67 for 5, but were restored by Douglas and the Hampshire heroes, Brown and Tennyson. The burly wicketkeeper laid the foundation with a solid 57 and added 97 with Douglas. Tennyson, his hand swathed in bandages, then bravely advanced on the Australian attack and smote it for an invaluable 63. Nevertheless, Australia led the first innings by 148 and, when they declared at 273 for 7 in the second, England – with 4½ hours remaining – needed 422. Though Brown bludgeoned his way to 46, Australia, by 219 runs, won their eighth successive Test.

At Old Trafford, the first day's play was washed out, a fact which led to a series of curious events, not the least of which was England's ability to score 363 for 4 and declare – *for the second time*. Tennyson had attempted to declare earlier but the Australian wicketkeeper, Carter, rightly pointed out that, in what had become a two-day match, no declaration could be made within 100 minutes of the end of play. In the subsequent confusion the Manchester crowd became unruly and 25 minutes were lost while Tennyson and the umpires clarified the situation. When play resumed, Armstrong, who had bowled the last over before the break, proceeded to bowl the first after it! England harboured faint hopes of a long-awaited victory as Australia stumbled to 78 for 5. Herbie Collins, however, in total contrast to the prevailing instincts of Armstrong's batsmen, dropped anchor like a waterlogged barque. He contrived to spread an innings of 40 over 289 minutes to ensure a draw.

The Oval match was also drawn, but not before the highscoring traditions of the Kennington ground had been upheld. Phil Mead scored 182 not out – then the highest for England against Australia in a home series – and Tennyson once again showed his unflinching courage. The England captain received a sickening blow over the heart when 21 but, as Pelham Warner put it, 'after a few minutes' delay, shook himself like a great collie dog and drove the fast bowler to the boundary.' Tennyson and Mead put on 121 in rapid time, mostly off the dreaded pair, McDonald and Gregory. Australia's reply to England's 403 for 8 declared was a solid 389 and, when England batted again, there was no chance of a positive result. Thus, Armstrong, who hated the restrictions of a three-day Test, signified his disinterest by lounging on the boundary and reading a newspaper. The rest took turns with the ball and Russell was handed one of the easiest centuries in Test cricket. Though Armstrong carried the Ashes back to Australia after an apparently overwhelming 3–0 triumph, the 1921 series had ended with England perceptibly on the ascendant.

Even so, the squad which embarked in the autumn of 1924 – a luxurious 17 in all – included eight who were unfamiliar to Australian conditions. Among these was the captain, Arthur Gilligan, who, with another newcomer, Maurice Tate, had established themselves as the most devastating pair of opening bowlers in the County Championship. Unhappily, towards the end of the English season Gilligan had been injured while batting and the recuperative powers of the long sea voyage were not forthcoming. Gilligan never reached full fitness or form on the tour and an extra resonsibility was thrust on his Sussex partner.

Armstrong was rash enough to declare that Tate would be a failure in Australia as 'the wickets wouldn't suit him'. He was soon obliged to reconsider his view as Tate, against New South Wales, took 7 for 74, including Macartney, Andrews and Kippax all for nought.

Johnny Taylor stumped by Strudwick off Tate. Fifth Test, Sydney, 1924–25.

Tate was a broad-shouldered, brown-faced, beaming man of somewhat rural aspect and disposition. For all that he brought to the art of seam bowling technical excellence rarely seen before or since. He could move the ball late in the air – either into or away from the batsman – with equal facility, frequently posting four slips . . . *and two short legs*. Furthermore – and regardless of Armstrong's prognosis – he could torment batsmen on any kind of wicket. He was to play in 20 consecutive Ashes matches and in 19 other Tests.

He bowled off no more that a few steps, but achieved a lively pace with a splendid swivel of the shoulders. Furthermore his stamina and spirit were such that he could bowl seemingly *ad infinitum* without flagging. So rarely did he launch a bad delivery that Collins, in this respect, at least, a more astute captain that Armstrong, remarked that a loose ball from Tate during the 1924–25 series was so startling that several batsmen were 'astonished out'. At all events, the Sussex seamer ended the series with a bag of 38 wickets at 23.18 against some of the greatest Australian batsmen of all time.

In 1924, England had also discovered a specialist opening batsman who, like Tate, was to become one of the outstanding gladiators of Ashes cricket – a stocky, sleek-haired Yorkshireman called Herbert Sutcliffe.

5

THE YORKSHIRE CONNECTION

IT MIGHT be thought of Herbert Sutcliffe that, in terms of first-class cricket, he was a late developer. But the reason he did not make his first appearance for Yorkshire until the age of 24 was entirely due to his wartime service as a commissioned officer in the Sherwood Foresters. It may well be that the disciplines during service stood Sutcliffe in good stead on battlefields of a different kind. Certainly, the quality of his batting positively vibrated with judgment and practicality. He had the perfect temperament for an opening bat, whose prime function, as he saw it, was to wear down the enemy and grind their bowlers into the dust. His aim was not to enrapture the crowds with classic elegance but to stand four square behind courage, concentration and determination and take the runs like prisoners. These were the qualities he laid before the old master, Jack Hobbs, as they embarked on their first joint crusade against Australia. It was to prove one of the greatest batting liaisons in Ashes history.

Inevitably, as England launched a great new batting talent, so did Australia in the person of Bill Ponsford. The 24-year-old Victorian who, two years earlier, had established a world record score of 429, could not have made a more testing entry to the Test arena. In the first Test, at Sydney, he came to the wicket to face Tate and later admitted that his initial 10 minutes at the crease were nothing short of a nightmare. Herbert Strudwick, who was keeping wicket, didn't believe the newcomer would survive as ball after ball beat the bat and almost grazed the stumps. Tate was continually throwing up his arms in anguish. Ponsford turned to Strudwick and shrugged: 'I've never played bowling like this before.' To which the wicketkeeper replied: 'No, it doesn't look like it!'

Ponsford's captain, Collins, was faring only slightly better, but he sensibly shielded Ponsford from Tate until the bemused Victorian could settle down. Tate felt that he never bowled better than in that pre-lunch spell, but he failed to get a wicket from 19 overs – and, for the first time in Anglo-Australian cricket, they were eight-ball overs! The luck was with Australia. Collins went on to score 114 and Ponsford persevered for a maiden Test century.

Sturdy and, at first appearance, clumsy-looking, Ponsford was nimble on his feet, especially against spin bowling. He kept bat and pad close together and had a facility for scoring ones or twos off an apparently defensive stroke. Had it not been for his subsequent fallibility against Harold Larwood and leg-theory bowling, Ponsford might well have achieved the feats and fame of Bradman. As it was, the problems presented by Larwood in 1928–29 and again in 1932–33 effectively checked his relentless pursuit of runs. Even so, over the next decade England were to see rather more of Bill Ponsford than they would have wished. By the end of the first day in Sydney, Tate had reason to fear that if Ponsford's early luck persisted, he may as well bowl donkey-drops. Instead, he stuck manfully to his task and his final analysis, as Australia reached 450, read 55.1–11–130–6.

England's reply was founded on an opening stand of 157 by Hobbs and Sutcliffe. The 'Master' made 115 and the pupil 57, but, apart from Patsy Hendren, no other batsman exceeded 13 and England trailed by 152. Australia extended their lead to a massive 603, which included a record

Right: *The most celebrated opening partners in English Test cricket – Jack Hobbs and Herbert Sutcliffe.*

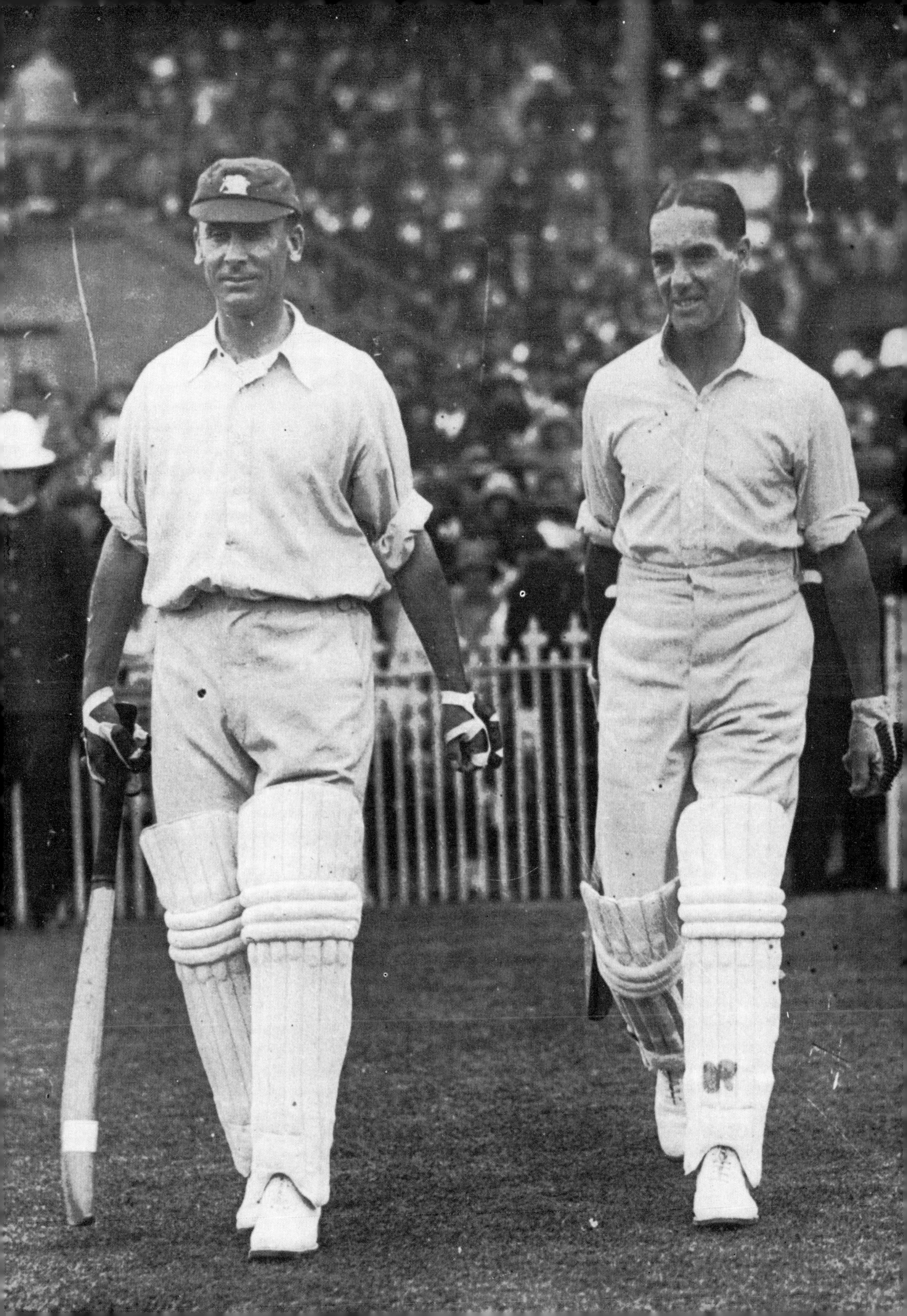

Herbie 'Horseshoe' Collins and Warren Bardsley open for Australia.

last-wicket stand of 127 between Johnny Taylor (108) and the irrepressible Mailey (46 not out). Hobbs and Sutcliffe again did England proud with a partnership of 110. This time it was Sutcliffe who made the century, in which respect he was joined by Woolley who, though suffering from a knee injury, made 123 in 2½ hours. Percy Chapman weighed in with a dogged 44 and to the delight and surprise of his colleagues 'Tich' Freeman, batting at No. 10, scored an undefeated 50. But English jubilation ended there, for they were all out for 411 and lost by 193 runs.

The second Test started only five days later in Melbourne, and 'Lucky' Collins's decision to bat again, this time on a slightly 'juicy' wicket, seemed to have misfired when the first three wickets fell for 47; but Ponsford and Taylor added 161, Ponsford going on to another century, and with Vic Richardson racing to 138 – including 4,4,4,4,2,3 off one over from Douglas, Australia cruised to a fine, fat 600. Far from being daunted, England's new opening firm scored 283 at virtually a run a minute, a chanceless partnership of the highest class which ended unexpectedly next morning when Hobbs, 154, was bowled by a full toss from Mailey. Sutcliffe went on to 176 but the rot set in and England were all out for 479.

With a deficit of 121 and an hour of play remaining, the situation appealed to Tate's challenging nature and he responded magnificently. He had Bardsley lbw and Arthur Richardson played on. Tate comprehensively bowled Ponsford with the kind of unplayable delivery that S. F. Barnes produced, pitching on leg stump and striking the top of the off. Australia were now 27 for 3 and England very much back in the game.

Next morning, Collins lived up to his 'Horseshoe' tag by offering a return catch to Tate which the unhappy bowler dropped. Still, at 168 for 8, Australia's lead was only 289 and they owed much to Taylor, whose enterprising 90 steered them to 250 and a lead of 371. The self-possessed Sutcliffe set about the task and scored his third century in four innings. By now, though, the wicket was spinning, and though England reached 254 for 4, the last six wickets fell for only 36 and Mailey marched off with 5 for 92 as Australia won by 81 runs.

Though two matches down, England were narrowing the gap in terms of performance and, at Adelaide, they came cruelly close to winning the third Test – despite losing the toss again and, more significantly, the effective services of three

Third Test, Adelaide, 1925. A. P. F. Chapman bowled by J. M. Gregory in the first innings for 26.

Third Test, Adelaide, 1925. J. S. Ryder batting during his great innings of 201, not out.

bowlers during Australia's first innings. Tate, having reduced Australia to 22 for 3 in his opening spell, was forced to retire with an infected big toe – the legacy of his marathon spells on bone-hard wickets. He was followed shortly by Freeman, who was struck on the wrist, and his captain Gilligan, who had a groin strain. The spin attack of Kilner and Woolley was pressed into marathon service, Kilner bowling 56 overs and Woolley – despite an injured knee, 43 . . . all this in an oven-like atmosphere.

The Australians made the most of the opportunity. Ryder prospered for an undefeated 201 and the last four Australian wickets added 370 while the disconsolate Tate, Freeman and Gilligan watched from the pavilion. Australia finished with 489 late in the afternoon and Gilligan rearranged his batting order to keep Hobbs and Sutcliffe in reserve. Tate opened with Whysall – despite Collins's objection that Tate had been off the field so long, but by the time Hobbs and Sutcliffe came together the following morning, England were 69 for 4. They added 90 and Hendren stayed with Hobbs for a partnership of 117, in the course of which Hobbs reached his century. In the circumstances, 365 was not unreasonable. By close of play Australia had increased their lead to 335, with seven wickets in hand. The match seemed virtually over.

Next morning, however, it rained and the marathon efforts of Kilner and Woolley were richly rewarded as last seven Australian wickets fell for 39. England's target of 375 on a tricky wicket was formidable, yet Hobbs and Sutcliffe, restored to their rightful positions and batting with great skill, put on 63 for the first wicket. Next day, Whysall (75) and Chapman (58) set a splendidly dogged example, and when the eighth wicket fell at 312 and tea was taken, the prospects of an England victory were not beyond expectation. Though rain interrupted play for 45 minutes, Gilligan and Freeman were still together at the close and England, 348 for 8, needed only 27.

Twenty-five thousand people poured into the ground next morning for the final stanza amid an atmosphere so intense that Andy Sandham actually left the ground and repaired to the nearby Cathedral. Gilligan, disturbed by his responsibility and the injury, had spent a sleepless night. So had the Australians, Collins, Taylor and Mailey, who had sat playing records till dawn in their shared flat near the ground. Thus, after the first

Clarrie Grimmett, the gnome-like tormentor of England batsmen.

Roy Kilner – fifty wearisome overs in the broiling heat of Adelaide.

over from Gregory, two of the bleary-eyed night-owls now faced each other; Mailey bowling to Gilligan. Three gentle singles accrued. Gilligan now faced Gregory. The first four deliveries passed wide of the stumps and Gilligan drove the fifth fiercely into the covers, where Andrews made a brilliant stop. The sixth slipped from Gregory's grasp and Gilligan mis-hit the slower ball to mid-off, where Vic Richardson held the catch. Thus ended Gilligan's valiant ninth-wicket partnership with Freeman, which had added 45 and taken England to within 18 runs of victory.

In Mailey's next over, Freeman's powerful drive struck the stumps at the bowler's end and robbed him of a certain four. Nevertheless, three balls later, he banged Mailey to the cover fence and only 14 were needed. Strudwick, facing Gregory, took two off the over and it was Mailey v Freeman again. The first ball went harmlessly by, wide of the stumps, but Freeman had to play the next and the Australians leapt in the air as the ball snicked to wicketkeeper Oldfield. So the epic battle, in the face of cruel misfortune, was lost – by 12 runs. Yet the hearts of the appreciative Adelaide crowd had certainly been won.

The team's popularity pursued them to Melbourne where England were to record their first victory over Australia since August 1912. The omens were good from the moment Gilligan, at last, won the toss and the incomparable Hobbs and Sutcliffe batted through the day yet again. This time the graft and skills of the openers were not wasted. Five of the remaining batsmen exceeded 40, and for once the wiles of Mailey held no anxieties. Though he claimed four wickets, he was expensive, and England cruised to 548.

After some light showers, Tate paved the way for the spinners by dismissing Collins and Ryder in one over. Taylor resisted with 86, and again with 68 when Australia followed on. But Tate, 5 for 75, bowled England to their long-awaited and well-deserved victory by an innings and 29 runs.

In the euphoria of success, England had good reason to anticipate a similar result in Sydney. Australia, on the other hand, had something up their sleeve. His name was Clarrie Grimmett, a 33-year-old leg-spinner of New Zealand origin who now played for South Australia. Grimmett had waited a long time for his chance and, as Australia proceeded towards 295, his contemporaries sensed the determination boiling within the gnomish little man. In the event, he took 5 for 45 in an England innings of 167 (Woolley 47) and 6 for 37 in the second as Australia swept to victory by 307 runs.

Gregory, Ryder and Richardson – three redoubtable musketeers of the mid-twenties.

Grimmett's remarkable debut was the chief talking point as the curtain came down on the 1924–25 series, yet no-one could deny that the prime bowling honours of the rubber belonged to Tate. He bowled roughly one-third of the total overs bowled by his side and, while the rest only took 56 wickets between them, at 46.62 apiece, Tate's 38 cost only 23.18 – and most of his victims were specialist batsmen.

The enthusiastic anticipation of the 1926 series was dismally dampened by a deluge at Trent Bridge when, after only 50 minutes of batting by Hobbs and Sutcliffe, the first Test was washed out. Happily the sun shone brilliantly at Lord's, where Arthur Carr led out an England team which included two new England bowlers, Fred Root and Harold Larwood. Root had impressed the selectors by taking 7 for 42 for the North of

Left: *Woodfull and Bardsley, prolific Australian partners during the 1926 tour.*

Above: *Arthur Carr leads out the England side for the Headingley Test of 1926.*

England against the Australians. At Lord's he bowled Collins with an inswinger, but did little else. The young Larwood claimed Macartney as his first Test victim, but otherwise gave little hint of his great potential. Indeed the whole match was dominated by the batsmen and, as MCC still persisted with the three-day Tests, this inevitably meant a draw. The 42-year-old Bardsley carried his bat through the first Australian innings, scoring 193 out of 383. Hobbs and Sutcliffe responded with an opening stand of 182, Hendren struck an undefeated 127 and England declared at 475 for 3. Charlie Macartney had reached 133 when time ran out with Australia 194 for 5.

Batsmen again held the stage at Leeds – to a great extent because the fielders failed to hold their catches. The most poignant example of this provided Macartney with the chance to play one of the most exhilarating Test innings of all time. The culprit was England's captain, Carr, and it was his second mistake of the day. Having won the toss, Carr misread the pitch and invited Australia to bat. He had a brief moment of satisfaction when Tate had Bardsley caught at slip off his first delivery. In the same over, however, Macartney edged a catch to Carr, who put it down. Car compounded his remorse by admitting that he had a premonition that Macartney was going to offer such a chance. Indeed, he was to write later: 'The memory of that missed catch is almost more than I can bear.'

Had it been held, Australia would have been 2 for 2 in the first over. Instead, Macartney, emboldened by his luck, set about the England attack with gusto. He reached his century, out of 131, in 103 minutes, and when caught at mid-on for 151, had blasted 21 boundaries. Australia, far from being 2 for 2, were 235 for 2. Even worse,

Charlie Macartney – Larwood's first Test victim, then three successive centuries.

Woodfull was to grind his way to 141 and Arthur Richardson picked up a century as Australia soared to 494.

England struggled against Grimmett and only a spirited ninth-wicket stand of 108 by the two Georges, Geary and Macaulay, rescued the innings from complete disaster. They followed on, 200 behind, and were thankful to find Hobbs and Sutcliffe back in their three-figure opening form. Sutcliffe made 94, Hobbs 88, and the match was drawn with England 254 for 3.

Rain at Old Trafford doomed the match to yet another drawn result. In the absence of Carr with tonsilitis, Hobbs led out the team on the Monday morning and thereby became England's first professional captain since the 1880s. Macartney scored his third successive Test century, Woodfull his second, and Australia made 335. England replied with 305 for 5 and set their sights on The Oval.

Provisions had been made for the fifth Test to be played to a finish and, probably suspecting this meant a tedious battle of attrition, only 16,000 spectators turned up on the first day which, ironically, was full of action. England's new captain, Percy Chapman, won the toss and batted; but by 5 p.m. Mailey had taken six wickets and England were all out for 280.

The Australians clearly did not relish the new attack of Tate and Larwood and at close of play had lost four for 60. An Australian lead seemed unlikely until Collins and Gregory, with a seventh-wicket partnership of 107, steered them towards a total of 302. Hobbs and Sutcliffe then stayed together for 49 before the close on the second evening. When they resumed, after heavy overnight rain, the wicket had turned spiteful and a cluster of short legs gathered in the sun as Arthur Richardson came on with his off-breaks. It was now that Hobbs and Sutcliffe produced one of their finest double-acts and, to the delight of a growing crowd, advanced their stand to 172.

Though Hobbs departed shortly after lunch, for 100, the foundations had been well and truly laid. Sutcliffe went on to 161 and with assorted contributions from the rest, England reached 436

Wilfred Rhodes – recalled to active Test service at the age of 48.

Jack Hobbs drives Grimmett. Andrews at cover, Oldfield wicketkeeper.

Wilfred Rhodes plays a flowing drive during the Oval Test.

– a lead of 414. As he had done in the first innings, Larwood again claimed two vital wickets, Woodful for 0, Macartney for 16, and then, amid mounting excitement, 'old man' Rhodes came into his own. Australia were all out for 125. The Oval spectators were not slow to realise that Rhodes had first played for England before Chapman, the captain, was born and he was undoubtedly the hero of the day as he walked off with 4 for 44.

Though Chapman had made no significant contribution to England's recapture of the Ashes, he was readily associated with the success by a public who took to him immediately. He stood over 6 ft tall with a mass of curly blond hair that, despite his size, gave him an almost cherubic appearance. His cheerful and debonair presence was matched by batsmanship which lacked the grace of a Woolley or the technical excellence of a Sutcliffe. Nevertheless, he had an excellent eye and co-ordination, virtues that also made him an exemplary gully fielder. Above all, he was highly popular with the players and it was no surprise when he was asked to lead England for the 1928–29 series in Australia.

He was blessed from the outset with a balanced squad. Hobbs and Sutcliffe were still going strong and Hendren was now emerging from the unaccountable nervousness that afflicted his early career. Mead, Jardine and Chapman were full of runs and even the lead bowlers, Tate and Larwood, were accomplished batsmen. In addition to this formidable line-up England brought with them one Walter Reginald Hammond.

Hammond would have faced the Australians in 1926 had not a serious sickness robbed him of the entire season. It was feared, at one point, that he may never return to the game, but in 1927 – fully restored – he made 1000 runs in May and went on to score 2969 runs for an average of 69.04. Now it was Australia's turn.

Those who had watched Hammond's burgeoning performances for Gloucerstershire were not surprised so much by his subsequent success in Australia as by the almost overnight maturity of his run-making. At home, he was all dash and impulse, forcing away off the front foot with scant regard for any untoward consequences. Vested with the honour and responsibility of facing the traditional enemy, Hammond was transformed. The fearsome power of his drive was still massively evident but, now, it grew more majestic, more deliberate, and he began to shift the balance more onto the back foot. He learned, too, the wisdom of changing gear to meet the fluctuating tempo of a match. Thus in his first series against Australia, Hammond scored 905 runs for an incredible average of 113.12.

While England had a strong side, the host selectors were suffering from the retirement of vastly experienced players like Bardsley, Macartney, Arthur Richardson, Taylor and Mailey.

Jack Hobbs, a long way down the wicket at The Oval, in 1926.

They had also seen the last of Collins, vastly under-rated as opening bat and captain.

The confidence with which England embarked on the first Test at Brisbane was not misplaced. Their first innings produced 521, of which Hendren made 169, Larwood 70, Chapman 50 and Hammond, feeling his way, 44. Australia's response was disastrous from the moment Chapman took a magnificent left-handed catch in the gully to dismiss Woodfull for nought off Larwood. The Nottingham express went on to achieve the best bowling figures of his Test career, 6 for 32, and Australia were all out for 122. The home side were in trouble in more ways than one for Gregory, injured during England's first innings, retired from the game and was shortly followed by Kelleway, who had food poisoning.

In the circumstances, and bearing in mind this was a 'timeless' Test, Chapman did not enforce the follow-on, and England were able to declare at 342 for 8 – despite Grimmett's 6 for 131. As if Australia, with only nine men and facing a total of 742, were not in enough trouble, overnight rain hastened them to humiliating defeat. Tate, Larwood and slow left-arm J. C. White (4 for 7) shared the wickets as England bowled them out for 66 to achieve a 675-run victory.

Under the circumstances it was hardly surprising that scant attention was paid to the young Australian batsman who, in his first Test, scored 18 in the first innings and one in the second. He had succeeded in running out the great Hobbs for 49, but the Australian selectors considered this hardly enough to warrant his retention and, among the Australians chosen for the second Test in Sydney, the name of Donald Bradman did not appear. It was the only time he would be dropped in a Test career spanning 20 years.

Australia's hopes received a rude setback when Ponsford's hand was broken by a Larwood flyer and he had to retire from the match. Leicester's George Geary, dismissing batsmen in a more orthodox way, took 5 for 35 and only Woodfull (68) and Oldfield (41 not out) offered much resistance. The Australian total of 253 was soon put into puny perspective as Hammond went to work. Bradman, substituting for the absent Ponsford, was one of the weary fielders who repeatedly chased the ball to the boundary as Hammond powered his way to 251 in 461 minutes. Hendren joined in with 74 and Geary 66 as England pressed remorselessly on to 636.

Australia put up a better second show as the tall, slim 'Stork' Hendry (112) and Woodfull (111) added 215 for the second wicket. At the end of the fifth day, with Ryder batting well, they had reached 329 for 4 – only 54 behind. However, Ryder mis-hit a Larwood bouncer and the remainder collapsed for a total of 397. England, needing only 16, lost makeshift openers Tate and Geary to Hendry, but White and Duckworth completed the job.

The third Test, at Melbourne, lasted seven days and proved one of the tensest of shifting encounters in Ashes history. Chapman, growing in stature both as a tactician and popular leader, had raised England's morale to a peak, while Australia, after their summary defeat in Sydney, were forced to rebuild the side. Of the team that represented Australia at The Oval in 1926 only three – Woodfull, Grimmett and Oldfield – remained. One problem was solved by the recall of Bradman, who took his chance by scoring 79 and 112.

Australia batted, though the Melbourne wicket often encourages the bowlers on the first morning, and, within minutes, the Australian openers had gone for 15. Hendry followed at 57, but Ryder and Kippax then restored the position with a gritty stand of 161. Both made centuries and paved the way for Bradman and Ted a'Beckett to push the total towards a respectable 397.

The incredible Hammond responded with another double-century which, supported by 62 from Jardine and 58 from Sutcliffe, set England on the way to a first-innings lead of 20. So there was all to play for when the Australian second innings began in perfect weather and on a pitch full of runs. Richardson again fell to Larwood – and was subsequently dropped – but Woodfull settled down to a 4½-hour century. Australia at

Pitch invasion at The Oval in 1926 – and every one wearing a hat or cap!

one stage were 143 for 4, but this was Bradman's opportunity to demonstrate not only his natural talents as an aggressive strokeplayer but great qualities of patience and massive concentration. The first of Bradman's 19 centuries against England spanned just over four hours before Geary had him caught at the wicket. Though by no means his greatest, it helped Australia to a total of 351 and a lead of 331, after a thunderstorm had hastened the fall of their tailend batsmen.

The effect of heavy rain was regarded by the old sweats as a Godsend for Australia and, when Hobbs and Sutcliffe went out in warm sunshine to open the second innings, doubts were expressed that England would reach 100. But if any two batsmen in the world could master the gluepot conditions then the 'old firm' were the men for the job. They achieved yet another 'miracle' with an opening partnership of 105 while the ball fizzed and reared about their thighs and ribs. In a sense the Australian bowlers were misguided. They surrounded the batsmen with close fielders, but Hobbs and Sutcliffe resolutely refused to play a stroke that was not absolutely necessary. Of those that were, many dispatched the ball into the vast, undefended areas of the field. The runs mounted up.

The end of Bradman's first Test innings: lbw bowled Tate 18. Brisbane, 1928–29.

'Stork' Hendry – a partnership of 215 with Woodfull at Sydney.

The stand endured for 2¼ hours until Hobbs, 49, was lbw. When Jardine was promoted to No. 3 (on Hobbs's advice) the wicket was becoming easier. By close of play on the sixth day, Jardine was 21 and Sutcliffe – though bruised from head to foot – was undefeated with 83. The Australians had missed their chance.

Next morning the wicket rolled out firm, and England pushed on – Jardine was bowled and Hammond took over and cruised to 32 before carelessly running himself out. By now the 'impossible' victory was in sight and when Sutcliffe was lbw to Grimmett for 135, only 14 runs were required. The end, however, was somewhat frenetic. Hendren was bowled, Chapman was caught going for a big hit and Tate, attempting the winning blow, was run out from deep mid-off by Bradman. But the match was won by three wickets and the Ashes safely retained.

There was no room for complacency in England's natural jubilation for, having sampled the talents of the 20-year-old Bradman, they went to Adelaide to find an even younger – and some said greater – natural genius in the Australian ranks. Archie Jackson was hailed by his many admirers as a second Trumper. Everything about his play – whether batting or fielding – bore the qualities of balance, suppleness and superb timing. Some compared his appearance at the crease with that of a ballet dancer – elegant, effortless and full of sinewy power. He watched the bowler coolly, peering from the shade of his droop-brimmed cap to meet the ball with a fluent drive or an impeccably-timed leg-glance. He had a poetic power. The slender 19-year-old prodigy was pitched into the fray against England's strongest team since the war. It might have been the beginning of a Test career to outshine even that of the immortal Bradman. Instead, within four years, Jackson was to die, the tragic victim of tuberculosis.

Hobbs and Sutcliffe gave England a three figure start, but after their departure only Hammond prospered and had not long passed 100 when he ran out of partners – most of them falling to Grimmett (5 for 102). England's 334 seemed a modest effort, yet Australia, at 19 for 3, were looking vulnerable. Young Jackson, viewing the departure of his elders with phlegmatic calm, pressed serenely on, and in company with Ryder, took the score to 145 before his captain also fell.

Like Bradman's century in the previous Test, Jackson's hundred was founded on watchful patience rather than panache. It took 250 minutes but served his side invaluably. Then, with partners fast disappearing, he accelerated to score his remaining 64 runs in an hour. Thus Australia were able to reach 369 and a modest lead of 35. Australia were delighted when the dreaded H and S were out for 21. Much depended on Hammond and the reliable 'crisis-man' Jardine, who duly obliged with a grim but glorious third-wicket stand of 262, the real value of which was not fully realised until, in its wake, England collapsed again. Hammond stuck to his task for a marathon 177 and an audacious 47 off 50 deliveries by Tate set Australia a victory target of 349.

By the end of the seventh day Australia, 260 for 6, were sick of the sight of Jack White. With Tate, Larwood and Geary nursing slight injuries, J. C.

Right: *Archie Jackson- striken by illness as he promised to outshine even the legendary Bradman.*

was called upon to bowl over after over, which he did with nagging success. Next morning the score and the situation guaranteed a full house. Bradman and Oxenham, under a blazing sun, proceeded quietly to reduce the arrears. By 1 p.m. they had reached 308, and 41 were still needed when Chapman made a superb catch at silly point to dismiss Oxenham off White. The odds were still tilting Australia's way. Bradman was batting superbly and the sturdy wicketkeeper, Oldfield, started out with unruffled confidence. Then disaster struck. Oldfield pushed a ball firmly towards Hobbs's right hand in the covers, Bradman (58) hesitated for a fatal moment and by the time he reached the crease, Duckworth, with a desperate dive, had broken the wicket.

After lunch, the Australia tail was chopped off, giving English victory by 12 runs, White ending an astonishing Test, with 13 wickets for 256 runs off 124.5 overs – a monumental performance in overwhelming heat.

There was obvious satisfaction in England's fourth successive Test victory, yet Australia, with nothing to lose, were successfully introducing talented newcomers. For the final Test, at Melbourne, they brought in three more: Tim Wall, Alan Fairfax and Percy Hornibrook.

England's changes were enforced by injury to Sutcliffe and Chapman's influenza. The replacements were Ernest Tyldesley and Maurice Leyland, making his Test debut. Leyland, a left-handed Yorkshireman, was a shrewd and humorous product of cricket's hard northern school. He was not tall, with sloping shoulders set above a broad beam but long arms and nimble feet. He could hardly have made a more auspicious start, with 137 and 53 not out, beginning a Test career that was to bring him centuries against the 'oldest enemy'.

In Chapman's absence, J. C. White won the toss and was delighted to see his batsmen amass a formidable 519. Hobbs worked his way to the last of his 12 centuries against Australia, and Leyland's 137 was supplemented by 95 from Hen-

'Nightwatchmen' openers. P. M. Hornibrook (left) and W. A. Oldfield going out to open for Australia in the fifth Test, Melbourne, 1928–29.

Maurice Leyland – Yorkshire's long-armed, pear-shaped answer to Frank Woolley.

Fifth Test, Melbourne, 1928–29. Woodfull, in Australia's second innings, just scrambles in.

dren, which included a stroke worth eight, four runs and four overthrows. Australia's dogged reply was 491, achieved at less than two runs an over. Geary got through 81 overs in taking 5 for 105 and White was into his 76th over at the end. Woodfull's 102, Bradman's 123 and a debut 65 from Fairfax ground down an England team slightly faded by a long and hard-fought tour, a growing staleness reflected in their second innings. Jardine was bowled by newcomer Wall for a duck, and Hendren and Hammond failed. Hobbs, Leyland and Tate alone passed 50, and Wall took 5 for 66 as England slumped to 257. Australia, with infinite time to get 286, opened their second innings on the seventh afternoon with 'nightwatchman' Oldfield and Hornibrook, who realised 51, and Oldfield stayed on for 2½ hours as the score mounted. There were few alarms. Young Archie Jackson scored 46 and when Bradman joined his captain at 204 for 5, Australia had the final word in the series.

As for England's tour captain, the cheerful, ebullient Percy Chapman, he returned triumphant from Australia, only to lose office before the end of the next rubber.

6

BRADMAN AND BODYLINE

DESPITE his success against Chapman's tourists, the young Don Bradman failed to gain much more than a patronising admiration from the MCC party. Tate and Fender (covering the tour) both felt that unless he kept a straighter bat, he wouldn't make many runs in England. Such monumental misjudgment might have been justified had Bradman possessed only the ordinary mortal talents. But what the initial assessment lacked was the foreknowledge that here was a man of extraordinary concentration, with exceptionally fast reflexes, and, above all, the absolute determination to elevate the art of run-scoring to an exact science.

Neville Cardus once asked Bradman for the secret of his phenomenal success. 'Concentration,' replied Bradman. 'Every ball's the first ball, whether I've just come to the wicket or I have reached 200 . . . and I never consider the possibility that anybody will ever get me out.'

To those early English critics, however, he was little more than an interesting phenomenon who frequently hit across the line and confounded the purists. In fact, a closer analysis of Bradman's technique would have revealed that the improvised shots were only 'wrong' for the ordinary player. Examined in relation to his speed of eye and foot, they were not wrong at all – as he was to confirm with galling regularity. Such was his mastery of timing and placement that one of Bradman's favourite exercises, late in an innings; was to play a bowler 'round the clock', hitting successive balls to pre-ordained segments of the field. The technique required might often have been far from elegant, but it was devastatingly effective.

Bradman was destined to become one of cricket's greatest 'cult' figures, a man who could fill a ground within minutes of walking to the crease. This became abundantly clear during his first visit to England in 1930. The bald statistics speak for themselves: in all matches he scored 2960 runs for an average of 98.66. He made 10 centuries, going on to exceed 200 six times. In the Test matches he scored, 8, 131, 254, 1, 334 (a world

Don Bradman – one of crickets greatest cult figures.

record), 14 and 232 – a total of 974 runs for an average of 139.14 – and all at the age of 21!

If an 'immature' batsman could perform such feats *on English wickets*, the destiny of the Ashes appeared to rest in Australia's hands for the next generation. This fear was fuelled by the fact that, in that 1930 series, Australia also paraded another superb young batsman in Stan McCabe. Stocky and agile, McCabe was the 'baby' of the toruing party, but by no means an innocent in the fine arts of cricket. His batting had a daring, cavalier quality which drew richly on the drive, the cut and the hook for its dazzling effectiveness. In a sense, McCabe was unlucky to come to prominence at the same time as the immortal Bradman, yet he was seldom overshadowed. He was second to Bradman in the averages in the Bodyline series, third to Bradman and Ponsford in the 1934 series, and second to Bradman in the 1936–37 Tests. His 187 not out against Larwood at Sydney in 1932 was probably his finest innings. Certainly it was his most courageous. But most regard his 232 (out of 300) in under four hours at Trent Bridge in 1938 as one of the greatest innings of all time. Certainly this was the opinion of Bradman, who implored his team-mates not to miss a single ball, remarking: 'You'll never see batting to equal this as long as you live!'

In 1930 Bradman and McCabe were newly-launched on their dazzling Test careers, while England's stars were at or beyond their zenith. Hobbs was 47, Hendren 41, fast bowler George Geary 37, and Tate 35. Not that England were alone in possessing players beyond the first flush of youth; Australia's Clarrie Grimmett was 38 – the difference being that Grimmett was a spin bowler in his prime. And, at Trent Bridge, he proved it by taking 10 wickets.

A New Zealander by birth, Grimmett – small, balding and wizened – was dubbed 'The Gnome' or, more kindly, the 'Scarlet Pimpernel'. He was certainly elfin and elusive. He approached the wicket off a short run and released the ball with a roundarm action. Mostly he delivered a slow leg-break but occasionally surprised the batsman with a wicked 'dipper', fizzing with top-spin. Though this was his second England tour, few batsmen were any nearer solving the Grimmett puzzle.

Despite the bold and balanced talents of the Australian side, England won this first Test –

Percy Chapman on the way to a typically aggressive 52 in the Nottingham Test.

Maurice Tate – an opening burst of three for seven in the Nottingham Test.

Left: *Don Bradman falls to Tate as Australia are dismissed for 144 in the first innings at Trent Bridge.*

Below left: *Little more than a hint of menace from Harold Larwood, bowling at Trent Bridge in 1930. (Ponsford the non-striker). He took only four wickets in the series at 73 runs each.*

though not without a little luck. With rain about on the first day, the Australians were hampered by a wet ball. Against tight Australian bowling, England were satisfied with a total of 270. They were even more satisfied when Australia, caught on a wet wicket, never recovered from Tate's opening burst of 3 for 7 and were all out 144.

Hobbs then completed a fine double of 78 and 74, supported by Hendren (72) and Sutcliffe (58), and England's eventual lead was 428. Australia had scored 229 for 3 when fate dealt them a cruel blow. Bradman and McCabe were looking quite capable of winning the Test when McCabe, 49, fell to a remarkable catch. The fielder was a Nottingham ground-staff man, Syd Copley, who had come on as substitute for Larwood, to enjoy his only moment of fame. Fielding at mid-on to Tate, he dived forward and snapped up a full-blooded drive that, contemporaries claimed, Larwood would never have sniffed. So ended the partnership, and the subsequent departure of Bradman, beaten by Robins's googly for 131, spelled the end of Australia's hopes.

A change of direction – Hobbs hits to leg in the same innings.

Jack Hobbs, a painstaking 78 in 3½ hours at Trent Bridge, 1930.

For the second Test at Lord's – a memorable contest – England omitted Sutcliffe, (split thumb), Tyldesley and Larwood, whose wickets in this series were to cost 73 runs each – an intriguing thought in the light of what was to come two years later. The three replacements were 'Gubby' Allen, J. C. White, and Duleepsinjhi – nephew of Ranji.

Like his uncle before him, Duleep scored a century in this, his first, Test. He, too, was a player of great elegance, who delighted the crowd – Ranji among them – with a flowing innings of 173 before lofting a catch. This was the dominant contribution to England's first innings, which realised 425. Bradman and his fellows, however, quickly put flight to any feelings of self-satisfaction.

Again, the statistics speak volumes. Woodfull and Ponsford put on 162 at the start, then Bradman and Woodfull added a further 231 in only 154 minutes. At the end of the second day Bradman was 155 not out and the Australians 404 for 2. Pressing relentlessly on, the tireless prodigy and Kippax (83) shared a stand of 192, and when Chapman caught him at extra-cover, Bradman in 339 minutes had scored 254 runs – a hundred of them in boundaries. England were left to contemplate an Australian total of 729 for 6 declared and a first-innings deficit of 304. Only a gallant

Dick Tyldesley bowling, with little success, in Nottingham. (Fairfax the non-striker, Tate at mid-on) He was dropped for the Lord's Test.

onslaught by their skipper Chapman – his 121 included four thundering sixes off Grimmett – saved England from an innings defeat. Australia easily squared the series with a seven-wicket victory.

It was, perhaps, high time someone surpassed R. E. Foster's Test record of 287. Yet none of the thousands who crammed the Headingley ground on July 11, 1930 could have foreseen the style and scale of Bradman's assault on that record. Australia immediately lost Jackson, so when Bradman strode to the wicket the ball was still new, and Tate, with a wicket under his belt, was in fine fettle. Nevertheless, against Tate and Larwood, Bradman scored 50 in 49 minutes and reached his century (out of 127) 50 minutes later. At lunch he was 105, by the tea interval 220, and, at close of play, he was 309 not out, with Australia 458 for 3.

When Bradman fell to Tate next morning, caught by Duckworth, his 334 had taken only 383 minutes, and he had found the boundary 46 times. When Bradman's record fell to Len Hutton eight years later, the Yorkshireman's 364 took more than twice as long.

Bradman's dazzling effort at Leeds to the Australians to 566 and, with the pitch beginning to wear, England were grateful for Hammond's vigilant 113 as they struggled to 391. They followed on, but rain and bad light intervened, and an otherwise historic match ended in a draw.

A similar fate befell the Old Trafford Test, which started with a long-winded partnership of 106 by Ponsford and Woodfull which sent the Australians on their way to a respectable 345. In dark and soggy conditions, England replied with 251 for 8, and the series remained all-square. If this Test was memorable for anything it was for the fact that Bradman, caught in the slips off Peebles for only 14, 'failed' in a match for the first and only time in the rubber.

He was back with a vengeance at The Oval, where England, having got away to an excellent start, were comprehensively beaten by an innings. Chapman was dropped, and England's new cap-

Right: *Woodfull and Ponsford about to put on 162 for the first wicket at Lord's.*

Left: *Cheerful smiles from Tate and Chapman as they walk out to bat in the Leeds Test.*

Right: *Bradman on the way to his record-breaking 334 in 383 minutes at Headingley.*

tain, Bob Wyatt, made his first appearance against Australia. It was not a universally popular decision, yet Wyatt, coming in at No. 7 with the score 197, immediately justified his selection by joining Sutcliffe in a stirring stand of 170. Thus, Sutcliffe's 161 was supported well enough for England to reach 405. Against an Australian side containing Bradman at his peak, it proved a paltry challenge.

Woodfull and Ponsford sounded the warning bells with an opening stand of 159 and, onto this solid pedestal climbed Bradman with a brilliant 232, his stand with the frail but brave Jackson (73) adding 243 hugely important runs. Wicket-keeper Duckworth had a wretched match, missing both openers, and Bradman when he was 82. The majesty of the Australian performance was reflected in a total of 695. Rain washed out the fifth day and, when England resumed, the left-arm spin of Hornibrook (7 for 92) was decisive.

Thus, after a 4–1 win in Australia, England were outplayed and the Ashes were lost. Without overlooking the crucial contribution of Grimmett, it was Bradman who had, physically and psychologically, dominated the series. He did it with a *series* of techniques originating from the back foot position, which he always favoured. He hooked ferociously and played a higher percentage of strokes *along the ground* than any of his contemporaries. It could be argued that his batting owed less to artistry than efficiency and, as such, lacked the aesthetic pleasure of, say Trumper's. On the other hand, in the context of his many Tests against England, in the excitement, awe and sheer compulsion of his presence at a cricket ground, the very *name*, even, brought a very special magic to the meaning of the Ashes. There prevailed in the heart of contemporary English cricket a curious blend of amazement, envy and resentment. More significantly, there prevailed, in certain quarters, a determination to find the means by which Bradman might be reduced to mere mortality, the principle being –

Right: *The end of the show! Bradman is caught by Duckworth and the marathon innings is over.*

Woodfull, extreme right, leads the Australian salute to Jack Hobbs as he arrives at the Test crease for the last time.

Left: *A thoughtful portrait of Harold Larwood – Villain or victim?*

beat Bradman and you beat Australia. In Harold Larwood and the next England captain, Douglas Jardine, were embodied the perfect catalysts for the subsequent onslaught on Australia's batsmen in what, evocatively, became known as the Body-line tour.

According to the correspondent of the *Morning Post*, it was Yorkshire's Bill Bowes who first tested the theory at The Oval in 1930, 'bowling several very short-pitched balls,' the writer indignantly declared, 'with five men on the on side.' Larwood, however, writing his version of the historic affair, claimed categorically that fast leg theory 'was born in the Test match at Kennington Oval in August 1930, *unknown* to anybody but myself.' Larwood goes on: 'A spot of rain had fallen. The ball was "popping". My great friend Archie Jackson stood up to me, getting pinked once or twice in the process, and he never flinched. With Bradman it was *different*. It was because of that

Douglas Jardine – an almost pathological dislike of Australians.

difference I determined, then and there, that if I was again honoured with an invitation to go to Australia, I would not forget that difference.'

Whatever else that statement says, it smacks of belligerent intent and, in Jardine, Bradman was to find a captain whose general dislike of Australians was almost pathological. This is borne out by Sir Pelham Warner, who managed the ill-fated tour. In a letter to a friend in 1934, Warner wrote: 'Jardine is a queer fellow. When he sees a cricket ground with an Australian on it, he goes mad!' So we have the world's fastest bowler with a contentious plan, a captain with a bee in his bonnet and a manager-and-gentleman who is to be permanently embarrassed by the dramas that befell this tour.

Whatever anyone else thought of fast leg theory – and it was almost universally condemned – Larwood remained adamant that it was a legitimate and non-malicious device. Indeed, he claimed that the only malicious aspect of the whole affair was the name 'Bodyline', coined by '*a cute Australian journalist for the express purpose of obscuring the issue. The mere use of the word Body was meant to damn me, and damn me it did.*' Jardine was the prime mover in its relentless use. He had *three* other fast bowlers in his locker – a virtually unheard-of circumstance in those days, when two was the average. Bill Voce was to prove Larwood's chief ally. Bowes did not play a significant part on the tour – apart from bowling Bradman for a duck – and G. O. 'Gubby' Allen declined to subscribe to leg theory.

One of the most interesting aspects of Larwood's ability arises in the fact that he was not at all in the physical mould of the archetypal pace bowler. In his prime, Larwood weighed only 10 st 8 lb and stood a mere 5 ft 8 ins. He was well-proportioned, but it was the strength of *inner determination* allied to a belligerent gallop and classic action that gave him his awesome pace. In his heyday, the Nottingham artisan was invariably frustrated by inert and immaculate wickets fashioned to accommodate the talents of master-batsman, and none more so than his own Trent Bridge.

In 1932 he topped the national averages with 162 wickets at only 12.86 each – statistics that should be placed at the head of any assessment of Larwood's status in the history of the game. Instead, the most-quoted figures are those he

Bob Wyatt batting in the final Test, at The Oval, where he shared a stand of 170 with Sutcliffe.

Larwood, stern-faced and square-shouldered, follows up a thunderbolt.

returned during the Jardine tour. His 33 wickets were taken at an average of 19.51, which makes for an interesting comparison with the performance of other fast bowlers on Australian Test wickets – Richardson, average 30; Gregory, 31; McDonald, 65; Jones, 27; Cotter, 30.

Left-armer Voce was much more the orthodox fast bowler, taller than Larwood, and better operating with a normal field. Furthermore, Voce swung the ball, which Larwood, who relied on sheer pace, could not. As is so often the case with 'pairs' of fast bowlers, one sows while the other reaps.

The news that Bradman was not to play in the first Test at Sydney in 1932 evoked mixed feelings among the England ranks. The Don was not fully fit. Larwood declared himself disappointed on the grounds that their mission was to beat *all* Australia, which a team without Bradman, palpably was not. Nevertheless, the fast leg theory was tried and proved highly effective. Larwood (10) and Voce (6) were the match-winners as Australia went down by 10 wickets.

McCabe here played the so-called Bodyline attack to such great effect that he was undefeated in the first innings with a glorious 187 out of 360. His ability to deal with Larwood and Voce was re-confirmed throughout the series. In 10 innings, McCabe lost his wicket only once to Larwood and twice to Voce.

England had three centurymakers in the first test: Sutcliffe (194), Hammond (112) and the Nawab of Patandi, who compiled a painstaking 102.

Though Bradman was back for the Melbourne Test, his contribution was 'only' 103; yet Australia won by 111 runs, Fingleton having made a gutsy 83 in the first innings. There were further ironies in the fact that Bradman, cheered all the way to the wicket, was out first ball, snicking a delivery from Bowes onto his stumps. It was the only wicket Bowes took in the series, and Bradman's undefeated knock in the second innings was his only century. It was hailed, though, as a sign that Bradman had conquered leg-theory bowling and that he and McCabe were now ready to put England to flight. Certainly the English batsmen had disappointed in the face of some excellent leg-spin bowling by Bill O'Reilly, who has match figures of 10 for 129.

Nevertheless, Jardine and Larwood went to Adelaide unshaken in their belief that, given a livelier wicket than the one at Melbourne, fast leg theory would prove decisive. Just how decisive was to be chronicled throughout the cricketing world under such evocative banners as 'The Battle of Adelaide'.

An unpleasant atmosphere prevailed long before the match began. Vast numbers of Australians flocked to the net practices expressly, it seemed, to cheer their own heroes and to deride and barrack the English . . . this despite the fact that Australia had squared the series one-all and Bradman had scored a century, suggesting that

Bodyline bowling was 'rubbish'. Jardine, against whom most of the abuse was directed, greeted it with icy disdain, but, following his representations to the Australian Board of Control, the ground was closed to the public for the final net session.

Shortly after the start of play, the barrackers were again in full voice, jeering and cheering as England were in all kinds of trouble. Four wickets were down for 30, with Sutcliffe, Jardine, Hammond and Ames back in the pavilion. The situation was restored by Leyland (83) and Wyatt (78), who added 156 – but not before another controversy had arisen. Leyland, noting that the spinner Ironmonger was getting more turn than might have been expected on the first day, enquired if he were using resin to assist the spin. Woodfull was called in and the matter resolved. Yet, it later came to light that Ironmonger was in the habit of impregnating his handkerchief – quite innocently – with eucalyptus oil to ward off flies. Leather and eucalyptus make tacky companions.

Leg theory in practice. Woodfull ducks a rising ball from Larwood as the onside vultures wait to swoop.

Bradman's first Test duck against England – bowled by Bill Bowes in the Melbourne Test of 1933.

Further contributions from Paynter (77), and Verity (45) brought England a creditable total of 341.

After Australia had lost Woodfull, Fingleton, Bradman and McCabe for 51, and Richardson at 131, Ponsford and Oldfield were pulling the innings together when Oldfield was hit by Larwood. It was a short, rising delivery. Oldfield got into line and tried to hit it to leg but the ball struck him a sickening blow on the right side of the forehead.Oldfield went down and all hell broke loose. In the ensuing furore, Woodfull, who was also struck – on the body – in that same Test, was moved to remark to Warner that, of the two teams, one was trying to play cricket, the other was not. Kippax, who was twice dismissed by Larwood in the first Test (for 8 and 19) and was not to reappear in the series, said he would accept that Larwood was attacking the leg stump – 'if the leg stump is two feet wide and six feet tall!' Compared with other comments of the day, these were mild.

Australia were dismissed for 222, England batted with depth and resolution for a second-innings total of 412 and a lead of 531. Despite a courageous undefeated 73 by Woodfull, who carried his bat, and a stirring 66 from Bradman, Australia could muster only 193 and were beaten by 338. By then the first broadside of the diplomatic war had already been fired.

On January 18, 1933, the day *before* the Test ended, the Australian Board dispatched a cable to Lord's protesting at the Bodyline tactics, and suggesting they were 'unsportsmanlike'.

If the Australian Board hoped for a conciliatory reply, the first sentence of MCC's cable of January 23 quickly disabused them: 'We at Marylebone Cricket Club, deplore your cable.' The Captain, team and managers were supported, and while the injuries to Oldfield and Woodfull were regretted, the only suggestion was that a proposal to alter the Laws would be duly considered. If the Australians wished to cancel the rest of the tour, Marylebone would consent – 'but with great reluctance'.

Whether chastened more by the imperious tone of the MCC reply or the thought of losing the revenue from the remaining Tests, the Australian

Left: *Herbert Sutcliffe strides out to bat in 'The Battle of Adelaide'.*

Bert Oldfield – pole-axed by a ball from Larwood.

Board's second cable of January 30 was far milder in tone: the original opposition to the idea of Bodyline bowling was reiterated, and it was stated that a special study committee had been set up.

Back came MCC's second reply, slightly more patronising, but still bearing a whiff of asperity.

The final cable from the Australian Board, dated February 8, started with the words MCC wanted: 'We do not regard the sportsmanship of your team as being in question.' Bearing in mind the first cable, this was something of a climb-down.

The decisive Test was the first ever played on Brisbane's Woolloongabba ground, and is also associated with a crucial and brave innings from Eddie Paynter. The little Lancastrian, who had displaced Pataudi at Adelaide, started the match with a sore throat and, when England set out in pursuit of Australia's first-innings 340, was in hospital with tonsillitis. Jardine was not amused and chastised the unfortunate batsman for not having declared his condition before the game began. However, with England battling, Paynter left his sick-bed and at the fall of the sixth wicket (for 216), with only Verity, Mitchell and Larwood to come, he made his way to the crease to join Allen. Despite his weakness and a high temperature, Paynter put together a marvellous innings of 83 to steer England to a lead of 16.

With the curiosity of human nature, Paynter's valour had a salutory effect upon the atmosphere. Woodfull paid the little man all courtesy and respect during his gallant innings, and the Brisbane crowd cheered, according to Larwood, 'almost as if Bradman had made the 83'.

Australia could muster only 175 second time round and England, bolstered by a bold 86 from Leyland, won the match by six wickets, Paynter's final six-hit winning the Ashes.

Probably the greatest irony of the 1932–33 series was that in the last Test, at Sydney, while Verity spun his way to success with eight wickets for 95, Larwood, who was never to represent his country again, came within two runs of scoring a century. Australia compiled a formidable 435, and when, near the close of the second day's play, England were 153 for 2, Jardine sent in Larwood as nightwatchman. Resuming next morning, the Notts express went on to hit 98 in 135 minutes before being caught by Ironmonger, the worst field in the Australian side.

England, with Hammond's 101 also to thank, took a lead of 19, and Australia scored only 182 in the second innings, Vic Richardson completing a 'pair'. England knocked off the runs to win by eight wickets and Australia had been beaten 4–1 at home for the second time in four years.

Jardine returned home to public acclaim and, unlike Larwood, was to play for (and captain) England again – but not against the Australians. Larwood was entitled to be disillusioned. He had done what he was directed to do and, in the face of tremendous abuse, done it well. Furthermore, he said he would do it again. And that was where the Establishment failed him. He refused to give an assurance that he would not use fast leg theory against the 1934 Australians and was left out of the county side to meet Woodfull's men. In November of that same year, fast leg theory was outlawed, which act, one might have assumed, would lead batsmen into elysian fields of everlasting peace and tranquillity. It didn't, of course.

7

VERILY VERITY

AS FAR as the moderates were concerned, by the time the Australians arrived in England in April, 1934, the great leg theory scandal had been laid to rest. There was tacit agreement among the 17 counties that the captains would not countenance any such form of bowling. Unfortunately, the Notts captain, Arthur Carr, while cheerfully accepting the directive, refused to concede that the bowling of Larwood and Voce fell into this category! Sides visiting Trent Bridge at the onset of the 1934 season found themselves subjected to the 'Bodyline' barrage. Meawhile, Jardine had been quoted as saying that he had 'neither the intention nor the desire to play cricket against the Australians this season' – a remark avidly seized upon by the Press.

As it was, Woodfull's Australians, though spared the physical threat of the Nottingham pace-men, were confronted by a very fast and formidable replacement in the Essex amateur Kenneth Farnes. Compared with Larwood, Farnes was a giant, standing 6ft 5ins and weight 15½ stone. His lofty delivery, accentuated by a final, downward flick of the wrist, made the ball lift sharply from the pitch, even in relatively docile conditions. He bowled off only 11 paces, yet approached Larwood's speed of delivery and, because of the economy of his run-up, was capable of long, unflagging spells. It was no fault of his that England lost the first Test, for he was to complete the match with excellent figures of 10 for 179. But the ironic truth was that England, who had plundered the Ashes with blistering pace, were spun to 238-run defeat by the tantalising skills of Grimmett and O'Reilly . . . and with only 10 minutes of the match remaining.

A disturbing aspect for England was the confirmation of Australia's batting depth. Apart from all-too-familiar faces like Woodfull, Ponsford, McCabe, and Bradman, two newcomers, Arthur Chipperfield and Bill Brown, made impressive debuts in the first Test. Chipperfield was a surprising choice, yet he went into action like a veteran and scored 99 in the first innings before falling to Farnes off the third ball after lunch. It was the major contribution to an Australian total of 374, and England, bedevilled by Grimmett (5

Arthur Chipperfield, a surprise Test choice who went into action with 99.

Sutcliffe smartly snapped up by Chipperfield at Trent Bridge.

for 81) and O'Reilly (4 for 75), fell 106 runs short. Hendren made 79, Sutcliffe 62, and Geary 53 but the remainder of England's much-vaunted batting failed to shine. They fared even worse in the second innings after McCabe (88) and Brown (73) had enabled Australia to declare at 273 for 8. This time O'Reilly routed them almost single-handed, taking 7 for 54.

There could be no better single example of O'Reilly's stature among the world's greatest spin bowlers. It was typical of a big-hearted man – jovial only *off* the field – who, in an era of high-class batsmanship and on wickets prepared and pampered to perfection, took 102 England wickets at a cost of 25.36 each.

O'Reilly's skills were difficult to determine from afar. There was no prodigious turn and, despite his height of 6 ft 3 ins, little extraordinary bounce. His run, though unusually long for a spin bowler, betrayed nothing, and the action, long arms going like flails, looked neither smooth nor subtle. From a spectator's point of view the only real evidence of his extraordinary capability was the way the ball hustled off the pitch. It was on the 'unreadable' that O'Reilly relied. The leg-break, the wrong 'un, the top-spinner – they all came the same, or so it appeared. And they were delivered by a man with a glint in his eye and a cynical snort for any response that betrayed a batsman's luck or discomfort.

Wyatt, who had missed the first Test with a thumb injury (C. F. Walters had deputised), was restored to the captaincy for the second encounter, at Lord's, and England's fortunes changed dramatically for the better. Indeed, it was to become the first time England had won an Ashes match at headquarters since 1896, and the chief architect of the success was Hedley Verity. In common with O'Reilly, Verity was a big man who brought the utmost dedication to the bowling craft; but unlike his Australian contemporary his technique and his temper were of gentle pace.

England were 182 for 5. At this point, however, Ames (120) joined Leyland (109) in a stirring

Bill O'Reilly – one of the world's greatest spin-bowlers. Six feet three inches of animated resentment.

partnership and England pressed on to 440. Australia started well against a disappointing attack. Farnes had a heel injury and, like Bowes, who bowled too many long-hops, was in poor form. Only Verity, of the immaculate length and thoughtful variation of flight, prevented Australia from taking complete command. As it was, at close of play on Saturday, they were not displeased with a score of 192 for 2.

During a weekend of heavy rain, it cannot have been far from Australian minds that Verity had twice taken all 10 wickets in an innings (against Warwickshire and Nottinghamshire) in Championship cricket. They certainly had cause for such reflection by Monday evening for, at ten-to-six, they had lost the Test by an innings and 38 runs, and Verity's match figures were 15 for 104, a performance which excelled even that of fellow-Yorkshireman Rhodes, who, at Melbourne 30 years earlier, had claimed 15 for 124. In fairness to Rhodes, however, the England fielding at Lord's was infinitely superior – particularly at slip and silly point, where Hammond and Hendren were superb.

Brilliantly as Verity bowled, some of the Australians were not entirely blameless in their departure. The great Bradman was a case in point, caught for 13 rashly attempting to hit a good-length, turning ball out of sight. Skipper Woodfull, who alone had batted with characteristic phlegm for 43, is said to have given the young Don a withering look as he returned to the pavilion. But perspicacity and patience under normal conditions is one thing; a bowler of Verity's class on a sticky dog is quite another and Australia's humiliation could be ascribed to bad luck as well as bad judgment.

After Lord's, the Australians – the batsmen, at least – found conditions at Old Trafford entirely to their liking. The weather was good, the wicket gentle as a lamb. They also discovered among the spectators the former England wicketkeeper, George Duckworth, who looked like the victim of a nasty accident. Heavily-bandaged, arm in a sling, and limping, he explained that his injuries

Hedley Verity, immaculate and incisive with fifteen wickets for 104 in the Lord's Test.

Chipperfield is missed by Hammond at slip in the Nottingham Test. Wicket-keeper Leslie Ames prays in vain.

had been incurred during Lancashire's match at Trent Bridge . . . Larwood and Voce were still at it!

No batsman had anything to fear at Old Trafford – except Bradman and Chipperfield, who suffered more than most from a throat infection that assailed the Australian party. This, no doubt, accounted for their comparative failure in a drawn match of 1300 runs, taken for the loss of only 20 wickets. It was 4 p.m. on the second day before Wyatt declared the England innings closed at 627 for 9, after the amazing O'Reilly, in one blistering early spell, had brought an anxious frown to their faces. Cyril Walters had made 52 out of 68 when the ball was found to be out of shape. A replacement was handed to O'Reilly who immediately claimed three wickets in four balls. Walters was caught at short leg, Wyatt was bowled by the next, and Hammond, after inside-edging a four, was also bowled. Hendren and Sutcliffe responded boldly, adding 77, and thereafter the batsmen were in command. A glorious partnership of 191 between Hendren (132) and Leyland (153) was followed by another of 142 between Hendren and Ames (72). Allen hit a typically forceful 62, Verity made an excellent 60 not out, and England cherished hopes that Australia could be bowled into a follow-on situation. These hopes might have been realised had England taken their chances, for Woodfull, dropped before he had scored, went on to 73, and Brown's 72 helped McCabe put on 196 for the second wicket. It was McCabe's brilliant 137, however, that dashed England's aspirations. Australia made 491 and though England declared for a second time, at 123 for 0, it was merely a token gesture.

In the first three Tests, Bradman had failed to reach a half-century. But English satisfaction was violently crushed at Headingley, where the fully fit maestro put together a superb 304 to match his 334 on the same ground four years earlier. It contained two sixes and 43 fours, and overshadowed all but Ponsford's superb supporting 181.

Who said leg theory was dead? Ponsford is hit by Clark during the fifth Test at The Oval 1934. Note the five men on the leg side.

Frank Woolley, then aged 47, is England's emergency wicket-keeper.

England earlier had fumbled and fiddled against a varied Australian attack and were all out for 200, Walters top scorer with 44. When Bowes, just before close of play, dismissed Brown, Oldfield and Woodfull for two runs, the match seemed interestingly balanced. Next morning, however, Bradman and Ponsford had a partnership of 388 which flourished until ten-to-six, when Ponsford trod on his stumps in attempting to hook Verity. This started a slide, and Australia finished with 584, of which Bradman and Ponsford had scored 485.

Bradman's innings lasted 430 minutes, twice as long as any other innings he had played that season, and though he left the field smiling broadly, he was so exhausted that his team-mates had to undress him and lift him bodily onto the massage table. He was not a man to seek records or individual acclaim and his sole pleasure at that time lay in the knowledge that he had put his side in a strong position. Nevertheless, that second triple-century remains unique in the annals of Test history. Furthermore, it was scored in a four-day Test and at a personal striking rate of 42 runs an hour.

England, faced with a huge deficit, were encouraged by the rejuvenation of Hammond, who in previous matches had been suffering from a back strain which clearly affected his form. Now he was batting with all his old assurance, and it was a tragedy when Walters called him for a suicidal single and he was run out. When rain halted play on the third evening, England were still 196 runs behind with half the side out. There were more showers on the final morning, and just before 1 p.m. the heavens opened and no further play was possible. A great lake on the Headingley square reflected the England score as 229 for 6, Leyland 49 not out. It also reflected the home side's good fortune in escaping near-certain defeat and keeping the series all-square.

As the Oval match was to be played to a finish it was a matter of winner take all. Injury problems caused England's selectors to respond in startling fashion: they recalled the 47-year-old Frank Woolley, who had been batting exceptionally well in the Championship and, as a left-hander, might be expected to emulate Leyland in dealing with the skills of O'Reilly and Grimmett.

Right: *Bill Voce, having bowled in the Australians' first innings against Notts, was then diplomatically withdrawn. Here he packs his bags to leave the ground. Members subsequently resigned and a section of the crowd barracked the Australian team.*

However, Woolley had not played in a Test against Australia since 1930, and had never seen O'Reilly, let alone faced his bowling. As many people feared, it was to prove an unhappy batting return. To compound Woolley's misery, he spent the entire Australian second innings behind the stumps as an unaccustomed and unpractised substitute for the absent Ames.

After losing the toss, England soon found themselves at the mercy of Australia's twin-cylinder scoring machine, Bradman and Ponsford. In the course of the day they exceeded their 'dress-rehearsal' at Headingley to establish a world-record second-wicket Test partnership of 451 – and they did it at full throttle. Bradman hit one six and 32 fours in an innings of 244 which offered not the slightest chance until nearly 6.30 when, hooking at Bowes, he was caught at the wicket. Ponsford, in his last Test, enjoyed a lot of luck and offered six chances in a 460-minute innings of 266. Nevertheless, it was a thrilling climax to a distinguished Test career and when he finally departed, hit wicket against Allen, Australia had 574 runs on the board. While retrieving one of Bradmen's blistering boundaries from the crowd, Herbert Sutcliffe leaned over the fence and ruefully enquired: 'Anyone got any suggestions?' Had he put the question to Jardine, he would have got a positive reply.

The following Australian batsmen made merry and when England went in at 4.55 on the second day, they faced an awesome total of 701. The dour, deliberate Sutcliffe and the stylish Walters responded with an opening stand of 104, but individual back-up centuries were required and only Leyland (110) obliged. His third Test century contained one six, 15 fours and lasted 2¾ hours. He was well supported by Ames, and England might have mounted a significant response had not the wicketkeeper suddenly been transfixed by lumbago and forced to retire. Grimmett, O'Reilly and pace bowler Hans Ebeling did their job and Australia went out to bat again with a lead of 380.

Though Bowes (5 for 55) and Clark (5 for 98) bowled mightily in an attempt to keep the Australians in check, Bradman and McCabe put on 150 in 95 minutes and England were faced with a staggering 708. They caved in. Grimmett claimed

Frank Woolley, in the unaccustomed role of wicketkeeper, fails to run out Ebeling at The Oval.

The end of Wally Hammond – caught by Bert Oldfield in the final Test.

5 for 64 and only Hammond, 43, showed any real form or fight as Australia stormed to victory by 562. Bradman, Ponsford and McCabe brought their aggregate runs for the series to a staggering 1810. Grimmett (25 wickets) and O'Reilly (28) had been models of consistency; and, unlike England, Australia held their catches. Reflecting on the final selection for the 1936–37 tour of Australia, one of the committee, 'Plum' Warner, admitted that too much emphasis was laid on the 'blooding' of young talents for the future, and he lamented particularly the omission of Eddie Paynter – one of the great and gutsy successes of the 1932–33 tour. Yet there seemed scant cause for anxiety by the end of the first Test, at Brisbane. Allen won the toss and put his batsmen in to make the acquaintance of Ernie McCormick, a 6ft Victorian with a reputation for bowling as quickly as Larwood. That may have been so, but there was an extravagance of good-humoured histrionics about McCormick's approach to bowling that would not have found favour with the dour Nottingham man. His run-up, for example, was inordinately long – some 30-odd paces – and liable to come apart in the middle as he lost count. Ths inevitably resulted in a no-ball.

His action was high and smooth and his body-swing quite prodigious. Because he was frequently liable to stray from line and length, batsmen were always in with a chance to score fairly rapidly. McCormick's first delivery of the series, to Stan Worthington, was just what Bradman, his captain, would have ordered. It pitched short and rose very fast towards the batsman's left shoulder. Worthington hooked instinctively, but inaccurately, and the ball flew high into the air. Oldfield stood transfixed for a moment then moved forward to take the catch. England one-down off the first ball. In the same over, newcomer Fagg (Sutcliffe was now an ex-Test player) was struck amidships and the next delivery flew past his head. Barnett, having viewed the proceedings with stoic calm, decided that, against such startling – if speculative – speed, attack was a legitimate form of defence, and when his turn came, he cut and edged McCormick for three fours in rapid succession. Fagg, encouraged, then attempted to leg-glance McCormick and was magnificently caught by Oldfield. Enter Hammond – and exit, first ball, fending another McCormick flyer to short leg.

England were 20 for 3, but fate then dealt Australia a cruel counter-blow. McCormick, having bowled only three more overs, was stricken with lumbago and could bowl no more in the match. England's spirits immediately began to improve, Barnett belted leg-spinner Frank Ward over the long-off boundary, and the fourth-wicket pair embarked on a restorative partnership of 99, the dependable Leyland going on to a splendid 126. Despite the unfailing skills of O'Reilly – rewarded with 5 for 102 – Hardstaff (43), Robins (38) and skipper Allen (35) lifted England to a comforting 358.

Jack Fingleton, shrewd, patient and stubborn, was typical of the kind of men who opened for Australia between the two wars. Steadfast rather than showy, he pitted his skills against Voce, who bowled magnificently. The Nottinghamshire 'penitent', having abandoned the contentious leg theory, now concentrated on moving the ball away from the bat and, in this way, had Bradman caught at slip for a modest 38. It was left to

Health
No TOTAL. No 8
0 701 42
WICKETS 10
BOWLER 8
CAUGHT
BOWLER 11
LAST PLAYER 7
LAST WICKET FELL AT 701

G. O. 'Gubby' Allen – a fine fast bowler and captain of the 1936–37 England party.

Fingleton (100) and McCabe (51) to steer Australia to the respectability of 234, while Voce took the bowling honours with 6 for 41.

While fellow spinner O'Reilly bowled astringently at the other end, Ward began to work his way through the England second-innings – Barnett, Fagg, Hammond, Leyland, Handstaff. Allen then played one of his finest innings, using his feet and his bat without apology and fighting his way to an invaluable 68. Although Ward finished with 6 for 102, England advanced their lead to 380.

The wicket was beginning to wear as Australia embarked on the challenge on the fourth evening, and, in poor light, Voce bowled Fingleton first ball. Overnight rain turned the pitch into a trampoline from which the ball reared and twisted alarmingly. Allen's second delivery found the edge of Badcock's bat and Fagg took the slip catch. In the faint but unlikely hope that the pitch would simmer down, the next man in was not Bradman but the phlegmatic Oldfield. However, when Allen dismissed Sievers in his second over, there was nothing for it but to call out the Don. Within two deliveries he too was gone, snapped up by Fagg off Allen for a duck: Australia 7 for 4.

McCabe went at 16 and Robinson four runs later, both rashly attempting aggressive leg-side strokes to balls that rose acutely. And so they came and went, only Chipperfield – undefeated with 26 – showing the extreme resolution the situation demanded as Australia were dismissed for 58. On this 'sticky dog', all the wickets were taken by the seamers, Allen (5 for 36) and Voce (4 for 16). Verity, who had welcomed the rain like manna, was not required to bowl a single over!

Victory by 322 runs sent England to Sydney in buoyant mood. Bradman the batsman had made a poor start to the series and Bradman the captain had not exactly spurred his side onto valiant

Left: *Australia's record score during the Oval Test of 1934.*

deeds. Yet it was the weather that played him false, and he was to prove equally unfortunate in the second Test, at Sydney, where Allen won the toss and Hammond made a majestic return to form.

The unpredictable McCormick was back for Australia, spraying the ball down the leg side so frequently that the first decent delivery to move away to the off so surprised Fagg that he nicked it to slip. This brought in Hammond to Barnett, audacious as ever, proceeded to a chancy half-century and his departure, bowled by a Ward googly at 118, brought a temporary lull.

O'Reilly and Ward gave little away on an unhelpful wicket and Leyland was content to watch Hammond proceed solidly towards his century. He was 147 at the close. Next day the Gloucestershire gladiator continued to reap a remarkable crop of runs from the Sydney wicket, and when England declared at 426 for 6, Hammond had batted for 458 minutes, hit 27 fours, and reached 231 not out. It gave him a Sydney Test sequence of 251, 112, 101, 75 not out and 231 not out – an astonishing 'ground average' of 256.

Ernie McCormick – no-balled eight times in one over!

Charlie Barnett, stepping into Sutcliffe's shoes.

England's declaration was tactical. It had rained heavily overnight and Allen lost no time in letting Voce loose on the unlucky Australians. Though the wicket was lively, lack of application, allied to exaggerated suspicion, played a major part in the their downfall. Leo O'Brien hung out his bat to Voce's seventh delivery and was taken at slip for nought, by Jim Sims. Bradman fended the next ball off his left hip and Allen gleefully snapped up the catch at short leg. In Voce's next over, McCabe needlessly thrust at a ball outside the off stump, Sims swooped, and Australia were three wickets down for one run. Chipperfield briefly threatened to repeat his gallantry at Brisbane before he, too, played an unworthy flick at Allen to give Sims his third clip catch. Fingleton had survived to greet Verity with a fiercely-driven four, but attempting a similar shot off Voce, he also fell to an edged catch. Had it not been for a swashbuckling 37 from O'Reilly, Australia would have fared even worse than in their second innings at Brisbane. As it was, they mustered only 80 while Voce and Allen rejoiced in the respective returns of 4 for 10 and 3 for 19.

The pitch was duly rolled and Fingleton and O'Brien began the follow-on in a mood of somewhat shamefaced solidity. When they had accumulated 38 – 15 of them in an over from leg-spinner Sims – Hammond appeared, in the role of brisk seam bowler, to dismiss O'Brien. Fingleton and Bradman saw out the day without further alarms, and, with the score at 145 for one, there were doubts that England had been wise to send the Australians in again. Next morning these doubts began to loom like grim suspicions as Fingleton and Bradman batted serenely on against an attack which could scarcely raise the ball waist-high. Allen began to look worried and it was an almost desperate gesture when he tossed the ball to Sims. His prayers were answered when Sims's fourth delivery pitched leg and hit off, ending Fingleton's vigil for 73.

Verity soon bowled Bradman after an innings of 82 which spanned almost three hours, and McCabe moved from apparent mourning into majesty, the sixth wicket produced 92 runs quickly. The end came from McCabe seven short of his century when he tried to hook a delivery from Voce which kept low.

Australia failed by 22 runs to stave off the innings defeat, and England, to their delight – and, it might be said, surprise – found themselves two-up in the series.

At the start of the third Test, in Melbourne, it seemed that fortune would continue to smile on the England team. At the end of the first day, Australia were struggling, with six top batsmen out for 181. When rain stopped play just before 5 p.m. almost 90,000 Australians shambled home, convinced that the Ashes were lost.

Next day, play was delayed until after lunch when, in his first over, Voce had McCabe (63) caught in the slips 63 with a ball that leapt wickedly from the damp and devilish pitch. O'Reilly, after a brief black-comedy of an innings, fell to a similar ball from Hammond, and Ward was soon stumped. Oldfield survived with a gallant 27, but Bradman had seen enough and declared the Australian innings closed at 200 for 9.

Now it was England's turn for torment. McCabe, Sievers and O'Reilly had only to serve up the ball and the fiendish Melbourne mud did the rest. Hammond batted bravely for 32 before falling to a brilliant catch by Darling off a defensive prod. Leyland managed 17 and Barnett 11. No other batsman reached double figures and, at 76 for 9, Allen declared – intent on striking back in the last 40 minutes of the day. Bradman countered by reversing his batting order and the men who marched out to face Voce and Allen

Hedley Verity – only seven runs off 56 deliveries.

were O'Reilly and 'Chuck' Fleetwood-Smith. There was barely time for Voce to dismiss O'Reilly for a duck when further rain ended play for the day.

After a fine Sunday the pitch rolled out perfectly and, though Fleetwood-Smith departed for 0, tailender Ward managed 18 as Australia settled down to increase their already useful lead. Rigg struck a pleasant 47, Brown made 20, and when Bradman joined Fingleton for the sixth

The Don flows on – 270 in the extraordinary Melbourne Test of 1937.

wicket his side were 221 ahead. Showers returned to interrupt the partnership from time to time and to torment the England bowlers with a wet ball. Bradman hit Voce for 13 in five deliveries and served notice that he was about to make amends for recent failures. In 364 minutes, he and Fingleton savaged 346 runs from England attack and, had it not been for the excellence of Verity, might had added a hundred more. At one stage, when the partnership was well-founded and fluent, Verity conceded only seven runs of 56 balls.

The Don's 270 and Fingleton's 136 pushed Australia to a final total of 564 – and an unassailable lead of 688. Though the wicket was playing comfortably, the most England could hope for was the kind of performance which might sober Australia's bowlers and send them to Adelaide with just the slightest hangover. To a degree, this was achieved as Leyland, 111 not out, Robins 61 and Hammond 51 made cheerfully confident contributions to a final 323. Thus, Sievers, who had claimed 5 for 21 in the first innings, returned only one for 39 in the second, and the best performance was that of Fleetwood-Smith, 5 for 124.

Fleetwood-Smith was firmly established in the top gallery of Australian spinners. Essentially a back-of-the-hand bowler, he developed his prodigious spinning style to accommodate a schoolboy arm injury. He had the ability to turn the ball on the hardest wicket, at near medium-pace. His 'natural' ball, the off-break to the right-hander, was supplemented by a 'wrong'un', and in the 1936–37 series he finished with 19 wickets at 24.36 each – to complement O'Reilly's 25 at 22.2. On the other hand, his 14 wickets in the 1938 series were to prove highly expensive, largely because of Hammond's mastery.

If ever this mastery were sorely needed however, it was at Adelaide, where England were given, and let slip, a golden opportunity to clinch the series. Though Australia won the toss, they batted indifferently, only McCabe (88) and Chipperfield (57 not out) prospering. England then started well and at the end of the second afternoon had scored 174 for 2, with Barnett 92 and Leyland 35. Next morning, Leyland soon went, and Barnett advanced to 129. Thereafter, though Ames made an aggressive 52, England could make little headway and were all out for 330 – a lead of only 42.

With Bradman back in business, it was nowhere near enough. A brilliant 212 by the Australian captain – McCabe the second-highest scorer with 55 – sent his side on the way to 433, and England were chasing 392 runs. At the end of the fifth day, with Hammond and Leyland together, the target had been reduced to 244, with seven wickets intact.

Next morning found Fleetwood-Smith at the height of his powers. He bowled Hammond, had Leyland taken at slip, and, though Wyatt (50) and Hardstaff (43) showed speculative defiance, the left-arm impresario spun Australia to victory with 6 for 110. Thus, for the first time since the 1894–95 tour, a series was tantalisingly balanced at two-all.

It seemed the entire population of Australia flocked to see the deciding match at Melbourne.

Their first mighty roar of approval confirmed that Bradman had won the toss and Australia would bat. Three weeks' inactivity through injury had left Allen a little rusty. The first hint of this came in the fourth over when Fingleton glanced Farnes straight to him. The England captain (born in Sydney), normally an impeccable fielder, missed this catch and, later, a similar chance off McCabe who, 11 at the time, went on to score 112. Indeed, Allen had a most disappointing match personally. He conceded 72 runs off 12 overs for no wicket and scored 0 and 7. It was far less than Allen deserved, for few captains of either camp have earned much respect and popularity. Cheerful and optimistic, he led a somewhat weak but willing party nearly 9000 miles around Australia and achieved far more than even the most optimistic Englishman had hoped for. At Melbourne, however, the truth of Australia's latent supremacy was to be ruthlessly revealed.

The partnership between Bradman and McCabe was to set the seal on the rubber. When McCabe finally departed, Australia were 303 for 3. Bradman went out to score 169, Badcock made 118 and young Ross Gregory a stylish 80. The outcome was a daunting 604, in which context Farnes' 6 for 96 – reaped in sweltering heat from a perfect batting wicket – was a magnificent achievement.

England's openers, Barnett and Worthington, embarked on their task like men on piecework and an over apiece from McCormick and Lawrie Nash yielded 25 audacious runs. It was too riotous a pace by far and Barnett was soon gone. Worthington was settling when he went back to pull Fleetwood-Smith and trod on his wicket for 44. England's desperate need was a partnership between Hardstaff and Hammond to match that of Bradman and McCabe, but at the end of the third day Hammond was gone. So, too, was Leyland, and England were 184 for 4.

Next morning, on a rain-affected pitch, O'Reilly and Nash were too much for the lower-order batsmen. Hardstaff battled on for a commendable 83, but the last five wickets fell for three runs and England were forced to follow-on, 364 behind. By close of play another undistinguished batting performance had reduced the tottering tourists to 165 for 8. Next morning, Voce and Farnes were instantly dismissed. It had been a miserable display, and Allen, addressing the crowd after the defeat, expressed a sadness and a disappointment with which even his adversaries could sympathise.

The Australian batsmen, headed by Bradman with an average of 90, had heavily outscored those of England, whose best was Hammond, 58.50. Sievers, O'Reilly, Fleetwood-Smith and McCormick all bowled well for Australia while only Voce and Farnes excelled for England. Sims (3 for 244) had proved bitterly expensive, Verity (10 for 455) disappointing, and even Allen (17 for 526) below his best. Above all the failures of Fagg, Worthington, Fishlock, Sims and others confirmed 'Plum' Warner's candid admission that the England selectors were not without blame.

8

HUTTON ARRIVES

ONE OF England's major shortcomings in the 1936–37 series was the inability to produce an opening stand of any consequence. How wistfully must Allen have cast back his mind to the heroic deeds of Hobbs and Sutcliffe. As the England selectors cast their eyes around the countries in the spring of 1938, the man with the best credentials appeared to be a 21-year-old Yorkshireman, Leonard Hutton, who had been 'blooded' against New Zealand the previous year.

The association of Hutton and Sutcliffe in the selectors' minds was not confined to wishful thinking. The legendary England opener had played a major role in Hutton's development from a promising 13-year-old schoolboy through club and colts cricket and into the Yorkshire ranks. There, under the shrewd and seasoned guidance of George Hirst, Hutton matured in the mould of his mentor. But he also had another idol in Hammond, who among other things inspired him to perfec tthe off-drive which was to become his magnificent hallmark.

Having settled the issue of an opening bat (and they could not have dreamed how successfully), Warner and his fellow-selectors turned their attention to other matters, notably the excellent form of two young Middlesex players, Denis Compton and Bill Edrich, who were duly enlisted for the first Test. Both were attacking batsmen and, in the absence of Voce, Allen and Bowes, the lively, sling-shot deliveries of Edrich might prove useful. A far more interesting choice in the bowling department was Kent's Doug Wright, whose performances had already impressed a shrewd Australian 'spy' in the person of Don Bradman. Wright, of the loping run and kangaroo leap, unleashed leg-breaks and googlies at almost inde-

That kid's got class! And he went on to prove it. A sea-side snapshot of the seven-year-old Len Hutton.

Right: *Hutton, as a young colt, walks from the pavilion to open the Yorkshire innings with Herbert Sutcliffe for the first time.*

cent pace, confronting the batsmen with near-insoluble problems. When *not* in full control, he was inclined to confront the batsmen witha choice of fours or sixes. At all events he was seen as England's answer to Fleetwood-Smith.

The inclusion of Reg Sinfield in the England side, and the recall of Paynter, presented the Australians with a side difference in six respects from the one they had routed in Melbourne 16 months earlier. Australia were content to intorudce two new faces, wicketkeeper Ben Barnett and a diminitive, cheekyfaced young batsman, Lindsay Hassett.

The Trent Bridge wicket was in perfect condition, and by lunch, the England selectors were purring like contented tabbies. Barnett, in his most cheerfully agressive mood, was 98, Hutton 61, and England 169 for no wicket. Barnett was missed twice, a difficult chance at backwood point, and then at mid-off, where Bradman should have held a drive off O'Reilly. Hutton was the ideal partner, presenting a straight bat in defence and timing his off-drives and cuts to perfection. Only once was he at risk, when he stabbed a ball from O'Reilly onto his wicket . . . without dislodging the bails.

Barnett reached his century off the first ball after lunch, and when he was bowled by McCormick for 126, England had produced their first double-century opening stand against Australia in a home series. It was achieved in only 172 minutes and, less than half an hour later, Hutton was raising his cap to acknowledge the crowd's appreciation of a fine century.

After the cheap dismissals of Edrich and Hammond, another massive partnership was launched by Paynter and the 20-year-old Compton, the left-handed Paynter, exceptionally fast on his feet, relying less on technique or artistry than sheer application, and a remarkable sense of occasion, Compton, carefree of aspect, playing all the orthodox strokes with panache and improvising with equal facility.

At the close of the first day, England were 422 for 4, and when the partnership ended with

Right: *The flying McCormick attempts to explode England's first innings at Trent Bridge.*

Australia's Ben Barnett in action at Nottingham.

Compton's dismissal – caught at deep square leg for 102 – the pair had put on 206 in a mere 138 minutes. Paynter went on to an undefeated 216 and, at 3.15 on the second day, England declared at 658 for 8. The bowling figures made sickly reading for Australians: Fleetwood-Smith 4 for 153, O'Reilly 3 for 164, McCormick 1 for 108, Ward and McCabe conceding 142 and 64 respectively without success.

The Australian counter-attack started badly, and the phlegmatic Fingleton was not amused to be bowled for 9 while tilting at the windmilling Wright. Though Brown and Bradman steadied the ship, both were out when seemingly set and, next morning the decline continued. Six wickets were down when Hammond made a contentious tactical decision. It was 12.40 p.m. Farnes had been rested and may well have made further inroads before lunch had he been handed the new ball. Hammond held back, however, and allowed McCabe to embark on one of the most remarkable rescue acts in the history of the Ashes. Of his four remaining 'partners' only Ben Barnett, with 22, reached double figures, yet, when last out, McCabe had scored 232 and the Australian total was 411.

This was the innings which so impressed Bradman that he marshalled the entire team onto the Australian balcony to watch it. The stand with Barnett realised 69, the eighth wicket added 56, the ninth 15, and the last 77. McCabe's planning and execution were magnificent. Shielding his tailend partners, he launched a most furious offensive, Wright coming in for a fearful hammering and conceding 44 runs off three overs. McCabe's second hundred took only 84 minutes and the final acceleration of his stupendous innings brought him 72 runs in less than half an hour – in which time Fleetwood-Smith scored two. McCabe had hit 34 fours and a six when he was caught at cover off Verity.

The dismissal raises another question-mark for

O'Reilly strikes again. This Trent Bridge victim is Hammond, bowled for 26.

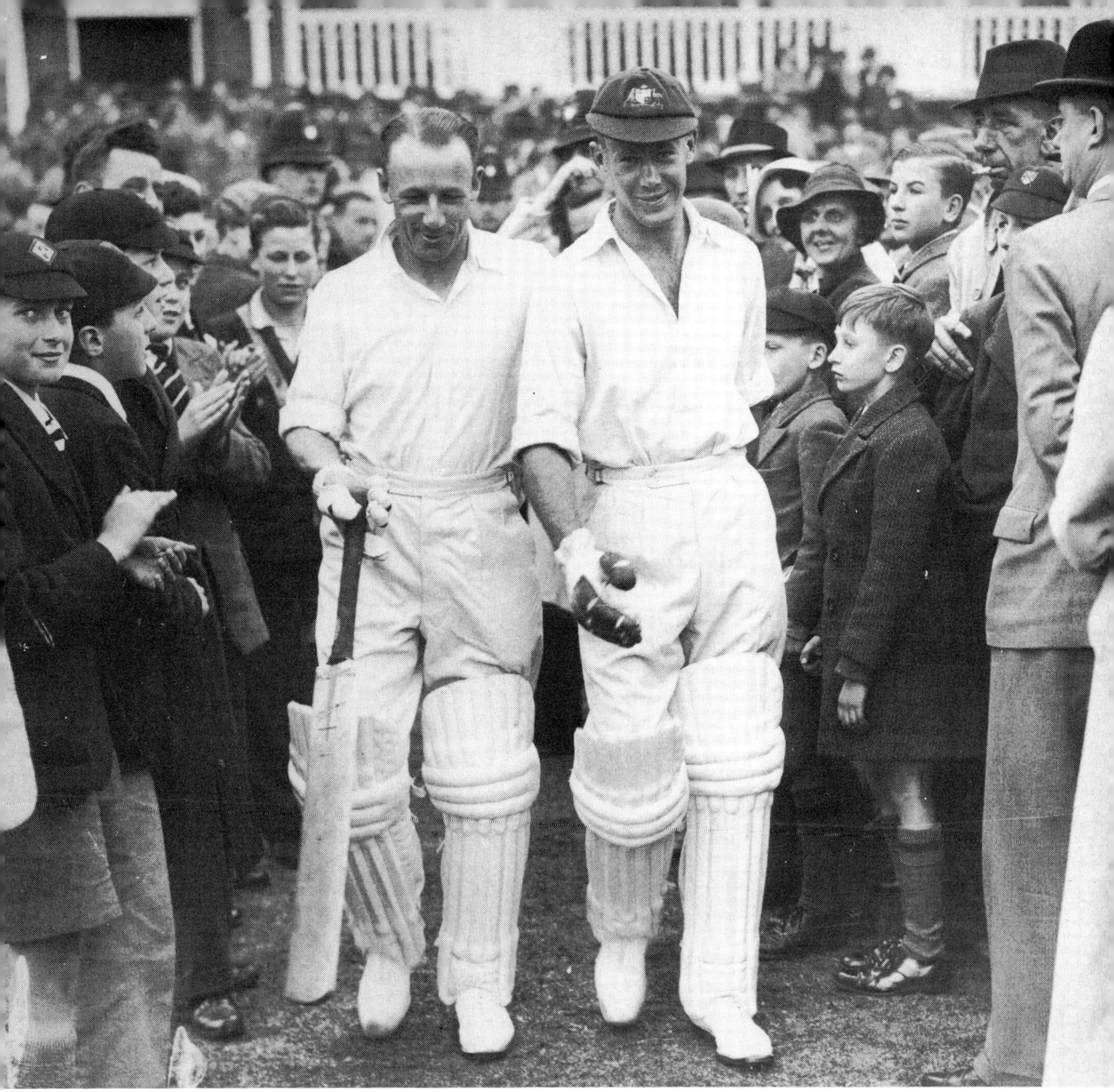

Bradman and Bill Brown on their way to the crease at Trent Bridge. Both were dismissed – caught at the wicket.

it came when Verity had bowled only 45 balls in the entire innings. If Hammond was saving England's supreme left-arm bowler for the follow-on, the economics went sadly astray. As for England's answer to Fleetwood-Smith? Well, that proved to be engagingly apposite , for Wright's analysis of 4 for 153 exactly matched that of his Australian counterpart.

Batting again, Australia were comfortably launched by 89 by Fingleton and Brown, who went on to score a grimly patient 133. Bradman, too, was in his most determined mood, and unbeaten with 144 of Australia's 427 for 6.

The draw gave England little satisfaction in the traditional sense, yet there was much to enthuse about, Hutton and Compton having more than justified their inclusion.

Hammond again won the toss at Lord's but this time England found themselves on a lively pitch upon which McCormick bowled at his fastest and best. The ball swung and lifted awkwardly and in less than an hour, Hutton, Barnett and the unhappy Edrich were back on the pavilion for 31 runs – dismissed by McCormick in 25 balls at a personal cost of 15. It was a time for seasoned campaigners to launch a defiant counter-attack and none was better equipped for this than Hammond and Paynter. In three hours of vintage batting, the pair added a record 222, Hammond reaching his century in 146 minutes. He was unruffled by McCormick, coolly commanding against the accurate O'Reilly, and ruthless in pursuit of Fleetwood-Smith, whom he drove to the boundary hard and often. Paynter, less fluent, batted with characterstic enterprise and was unlucky to fall for 99. Compton failed, but at the close England had soared to 409 for 5, Hammond 210 not out.

When play resumed on the Saturday a record 33,800 spectators were crammed into Lord's. Despite the fact he was limping badly – the legacy of a short run – Hammond went on to 240 before falling to an off-cutter from McCormick. He had batted for 367 chanceless minutes to achieve his fourth test double-century, and the highest score by an England captain against Australia. Ames scored a delightful 83 and England, after their traumatic start, were blessed with 494.

If England cherished any hopes of pushing Australia towards a follow-on, they reckoned without the gutsy determination of Bill Brown, whose strokes unfolded from immaculate defence like flowers in a rock-garden. Fingleton, fidgeting before the wondrous uncertainties of Wright, finally flicked him to Hammond in the slip, Bradman, cheered all the way to the wicket, soon played on to Verity: but Brown went on . . . and on. He was strong on the back food and scored prolifically off his legs, where he was well-served by some indifferent bowling. He drove well and square-cut splendidly – observed by the amazing cyclops eye of the new 'television apparatus' installed for the first time on the Lord's fire-escape.

Brown proceeded past his century, but McCabe, whose glorious hooks and cuts

Denis Compton acknowledges the applause for his magnificent century at Nottingham.

Bill Brown drives defiantly, supervised by Les Ames.

threatened a replay of Nottingham, fell to a brilliant gully catch by Verity for 38. Hassett 'arrived' with an attractive 56 and, though Badcock went for nought in the same Wellard over, Barnett and Brown (140 not) were together at the close.

At 308 for 7, England might yet have enforced the follow-on, but O'Reilly was missed by Paynter at long-on, and proceeded to thrash the luckless Verity for two sixes. With Brown still in unshakeable form, 85 were added in 42 minutes, and England's chance was lost. Australia reached 422 and the splendid Brown withdrew, unbowed, with a five, 22 fours and a total of 206, having carried his bat through the innings.

When England went in again to extend their lead of 72, the pitch was hard underneath but soft on top. The ball flew nastily, and the openers were soon gone. Conditions were no better next day and half the side were out for 76. It was a critical situation, but Compton joined Paynter to play what Bradman later described as the best innings of the series – a generous tribute in view of McCabe's superb effort.

The young maestro met the fast-rising deliveries of McCormick with unflinching assurance, drove handsomely and hooked anything pitched short. Paynter also batted well, until run out for 43. Wellard seized the opportunity to score a rapid 38, which included an on-drive into the grandstand balcony, and England were safe. When Hammond declared at 242 for 8, Compton was 76 not out. Australia's target was 315 in 2¾ hours and, on a responsive wicket, England must have fancied their chances of getting them out – even with Paynter deputising for the injured Ames behind the stumps. When Fingleton, Brown and McCabe went cheaply, the prospects improved – but Bradman was still there, and heading for his 14th hundred against England. It was achieved with typical determination and took him past Jack Hobbs's Anglo-Australian record aggregate of 3636 runs. Hassett rounded off a satisfactory Test with 42 but the unfortunate Badcock collected a 'pair'. Neither had England's Bill Edrich covered himself with glory – yet he was among the possibles chosen for Old Trafford. In the event, the issue was academic for it was raining in Manchester when the two sides

What was all that about? A bemused Badcock is bowled by Doug Wright in the First Test.

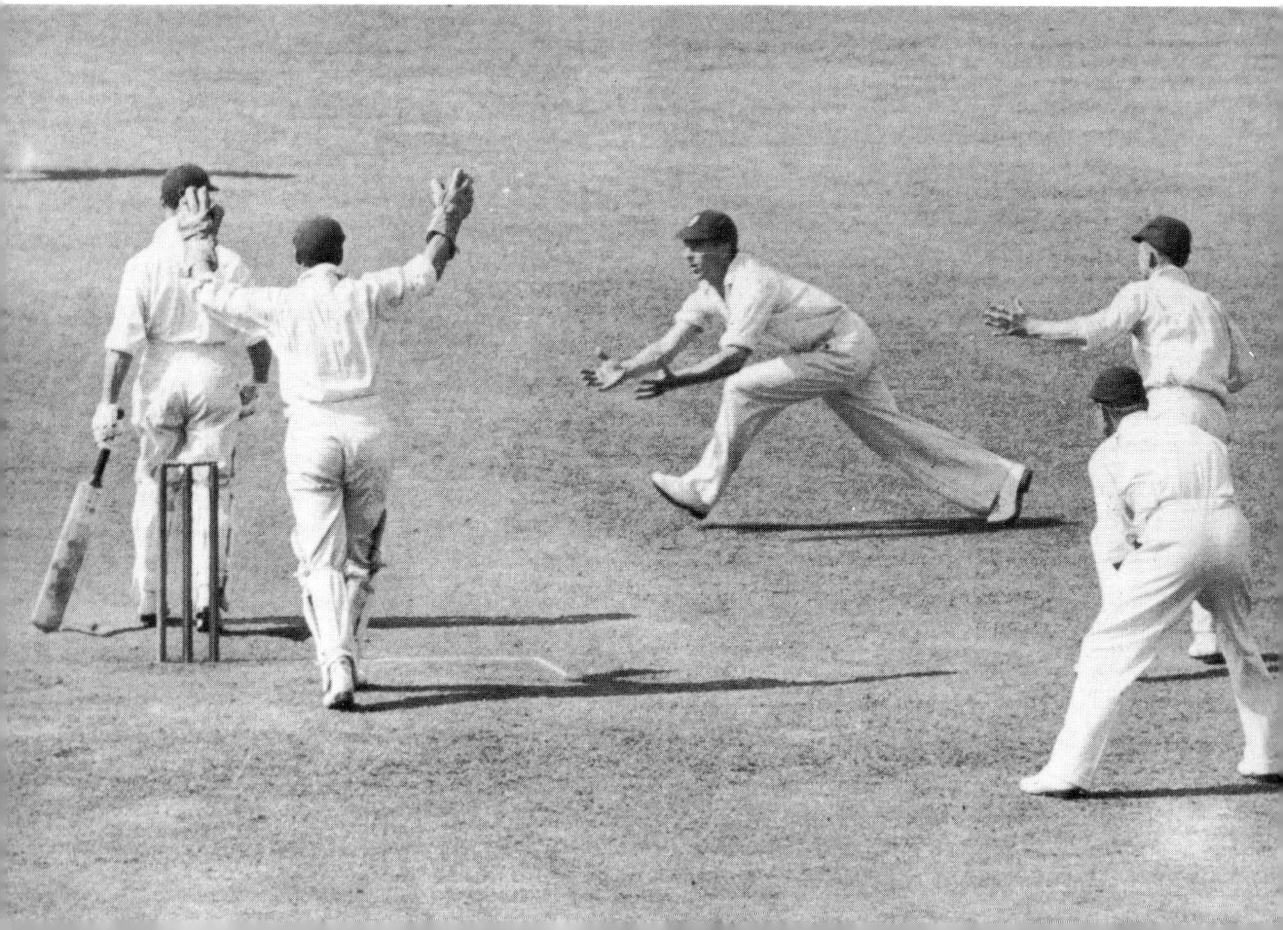

Left: *Stan McCabe reaches a hundred during the Trent Bridge innings that astonished even the great Bradman.*

Below left: *Lindsay Hassett fails again, snapped up by Compton at point, Trent Bridge, 1938.*

arrived, and it rained non-stop for the next five days.

A week before the fourth – now the third – Test at Headingley, a County Championship match at Lord's played a fateful part in England's selection. Warner and Co. had already made their choice, which included the Yorkshiremen Hutton, Leyland and Paul Gibb – a talented batsman-/wicketkeeper who would replace the injured Ames. The match against Middlesex, however, removed all three. Hutton sustained a broken finger, Leyland a fractured thumb, and Gibb, ducking into a flyer, was hit on the head and concussed. Thus, the England side at Headigley had what Warner described as a 'fearful tail' which started with Middlesex wicketkeeper Fred Price and was followed by Verity, Wright, Farnes and Bowes. When Hammond won the toss, in damp, overcast conditions, the Australians were not in the least depressed by his decision to bat.

Edrich was first to go, bowled by a beauty from O'Reilly for 12; Hardstaff was run out for 4, and by lunch, England had struggled to 62. Thereafter Hammond sailed bravely into McCormick, hitting him for four through the covers and then driving a glorious six over long-off. But at 88, Barnett (C.J.) flicked at McCormick and was caught by Barnett (B.A.) for a laborious 30. Hammond pressed on to 76 and was then bowled by O'Reilly, and when Paynter was brilliantly stumped by Barnett off Fleetwood-Smith, the 'fearful tail' was exposed. The total of 223 (O'Reilly 5 for 66) was regarded as hopelessly inadequate. As things transpired, it could have proved a match-winning score – except for the redoubtable Don Bradman.

Australia were 32 for 1 that evening, and at the start of the second day the light was abysmal. Fingleton, trying to force Verity wide of mid-on, missed the ball completely and was bowled. Now the flashing of cameras heralded the arrival of Bradman and, from the outset of his innings, he batted like a man with cat's eyes and ultra-sonic reflexes. Ben Barnett relied cheerfully on blind faith in reaching a valuable 57, but thereafter the Don was virtually on his own. He batted three hours for a defiant 103 – his third century in five innings and his 15th against England. None was to prove more valuable.

Arthur Wood, Yorkshire's jovial wicket-keeper, an eleventh-hour replacement for Ames at The Oval.

England began again on the beautifully warm and sunny morning of the third day. Gloom of every kind was shortly to follow. It began with Barnett nudging a short one from McCormick to his namesake behind the wicket. Hardstaff fell to superb O'Reilly leg-break that clipped the off stump. Hammond, wildly cheered to the wicket by a capacity crowd, fell first ball to Bradman's carefully-laid trap – brilliantly caught at short leg off O'Reilly. Paynter survived the hat-trick, but next over Edrich became the third victim to fall at 73, stumped for 28 off Fleetwood-Smith. No-one else reached 20 and, just before lunch, England were all out for 123, ten wickets having fallen in

Cause and effect. Oval groundsman 'Bosser' Martin and the roller that helped produce a record-breaking England score.

the morning session for 74. Allowing for the intelligent use of a wearing pitch by O'Reilly (5 for 56) and Fleetwood-Smith (4 for 34), the English batting had been abysmal.

If England, with a lead of only 104, were to hold out any hope of victory it lay in the heady possibility that Wright could produce a miracle on a helpful pitch. Given a slightly larger reserve of runs, this might have become a reality. Wright was always a gamble, and so Hammond introduced the Kent spinner in two belated sessions to bowl only five overs. His figures of 3 for 26 suggest the gamble might have been worth taking; but no-one could blame Hammond when Australia eased home by five wickets.

Bradman's first innings century ranks as one of the finest. Jack Hobbs, who reported it for a paper, commented that 'Bradman was in such form that he could have played by candlelight.' It was a performance avidly analysed and appreciated by a crowd of 36,000, few of whom realised that, apart from its outstanding quality, the innings established new records. Trumper's 11 centuries on the 1902 tour were overtaken, and Bradman passed 5000 runs in Test cricket in the second innings and at the youngest age (29).

The Ashes had slipped away from England

again, and they turned now to the problem of choosing a side to restore some honour at The Oval. Injuries to Ames and Wright complicated the issue which was restored by a late call to Yorkshire wicketkeeper Arthur Wood and the decision to include Leyland at the expense of a bowler. The selectors were relieved that Hutton was fit again, but their decision to drop Barnett after four indifferent innings and to retain Edrich after five seemed inexplicable except that Edrich, in Hammond's words, was 'good in bits and pieces and likely to obtain a wicket or two'.

It was scheduled as a 'timeless Test' and, as Australia were to discover to their cost, the young Hutton had all the time in the world on a wicket that had been outrageously over-prepared in the batsmen's favour.

The Australians, faced with a procession of misfortunes, earned the highest praise for their dogged determination to fight every inch of the way. They were handicapped by the absence of McCormick, their only 'shock' bowler, who, even on a pitch that groundsman 'Bosser' Martin boasted 'would last until Christmas', might, steaming through half-a-dozen new-ball overs, conceivably have spiked England's foundations. Instead, the opening attack was entrusted to Waite and McCabe who, on the Oval's perfect plateau, could call upon little more than faith, hope and perserverance, even the great OReilly was reduced to a mortal trundler as England ground remorselessly on, hour after hour.

Such were Fingleton's exertions in the field that he was stricken first by cramp and then a badly-pulled muscle, which prevented him from batting in either innings. Even worse, Bradman, taking his share of the bowling toil, twisted his leg and was carried from the field with a fractured shin-bone. What might have been had Bradman won the toss on August 20, 1938 is anyone's guess. But that fateful flick of the coin went Hammond's way and the amazing 'Hutton Test' began.

Australia's only first-day success was the dismissal of Edrich, lbw to O'Reilly with the score at 29. By close of play Hutton and Leyland (in his 39th year) and taken the score to 347. Both had offered stumping chances – Hutton, when 40, off Fleetwood-Smith, Leyland, at 63, off O'Reilly. Waite also missed a chance to run out Leyland when he broke the wicket before gathering the ball. These incidents apart, the performance of

A tragic moment for Australia. Bradman is carried off after injuring his foot during England's mammoth innings.

Maurice Leyland – always at his best against Australia.

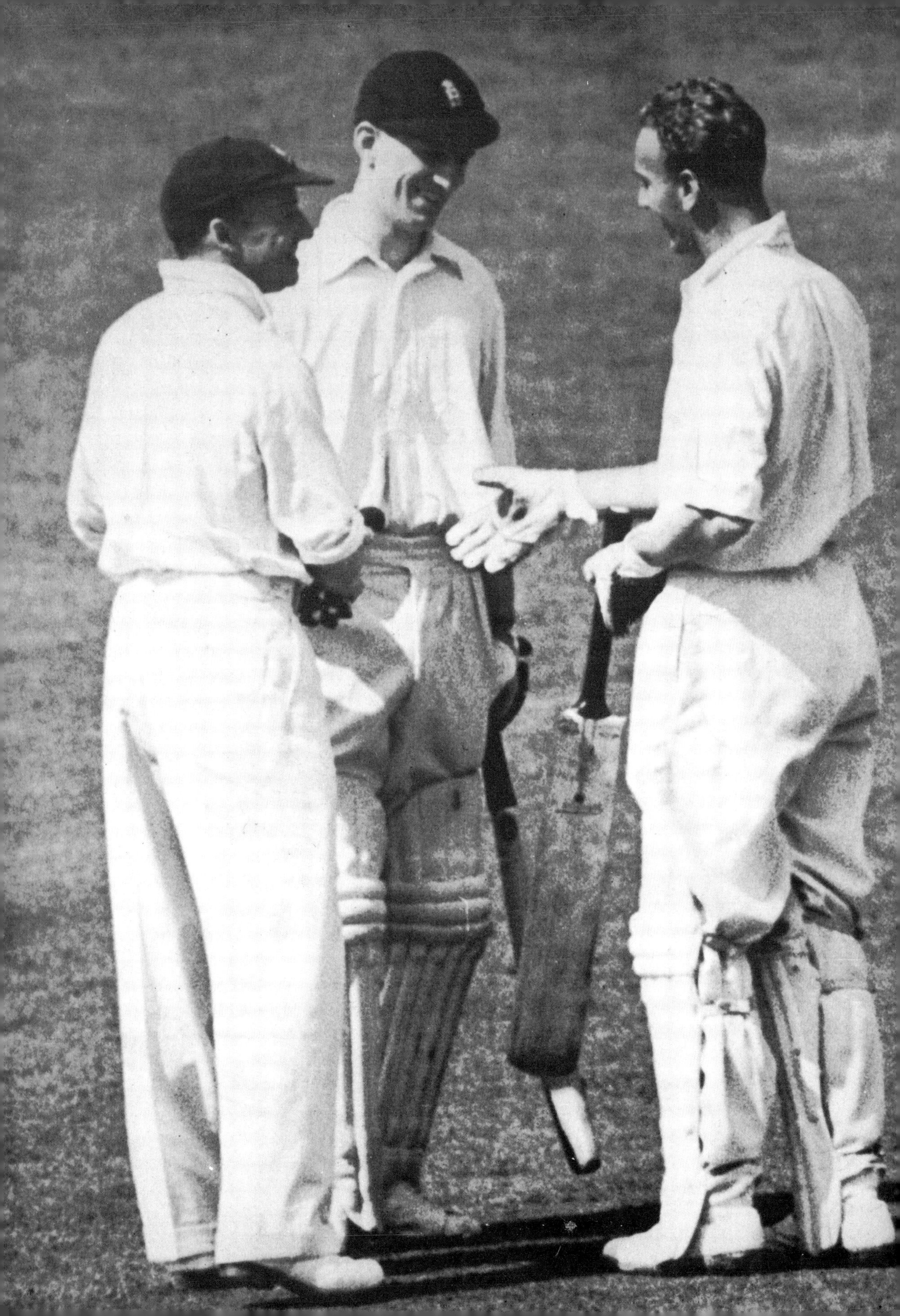

Left: *The moment of triumph for Len Hutton. Bradman and Hardstaff congratulate him on establishing a new Test record of 364.*

the two Yorkshiremen had been flawless. Hutton's flowing off-drives, late cuts and beautifully-timed strokes off his legs were complemented by an immaculately straight defensive bat which endorsed everything his mentor, Herbert Sutcliffe, had prophesied. Leyland, always at his best against Australia, also drove magnificently with a bat that seemed as broad as a barn door.

The pair had established a record partnership of 382 next day when Hutton drove a ball from O'Reilly to extra-cover. Hassett recovered quickly and flung the ball back accurately. Bradman, hurtling in from mid-on, caught it, whipped off the bails and Leyland (187) was out by yards. This one incident typified the Australian spirit throughout.

The breaking of the mammoth partnership brought only temporary joy for the footsore fielders: Hammond joined Hutton and immediately took three fours off Fleetwood-Smith. At the interval, England were 434 for 2. Australia took the new ball and in the next hour the flow of runs was restricted to 43. In that time Hutton reached 200, and though Hammond fell lbw to Fleetwood-Smith, Australian hearts sank as Fingleton limped of the field.

Then came encouragement as Paynter departed for nought, deceived by O'Reilly, and after bad light and rain held up play, Compton managed only a single before he played over a ball from Waite and was bowled. Thus England had slipped from 546 for 2 to 555 for 8. But Australian hopes of a further breakthrough were dashed by the arrival of Hardstaff in top form. At close of play Hutton, after 11 hours at the crease, was 300, his Notts partner 40, and the total an awesome 634 for 5.

When the third day dawned bright and clear, the thousands who flocked to The Oval were primarily interested in the 22-year-old Yorkshireman's pursuit of Bradman's record 334. But the day's early runs had to be grafted from an astringent attack backed by enthusiastic fielders. Gradually Hutton inched towards the target and a delightful cut to the boundary off Fleetwood-Smith gave him the record. The crowd erupted and, as hats went up in the air all over England, the first man to shake Hutton's hand was the generously smiling Bradman.

Hutton had increased the record score by 30 when he finally surrendered to fatigue and mishit a drive to cover, where Hassett took a simple catch. His 364, which lasted 13 hours 17 minutes, was made up of 35 fours, 15 threes, 18 twos and 143 singles.

England might have been content to declare at that point. But on they went. Hardstaff scored 169 not out, Wood 53, and, to compound Australia's misery, as the score soared past 800, Bradman sustained his fateful injury. In the absence of two major batsmen, Australia were never in with a chance of avoiding the follow-on. In a first innings of 201, only Brown (69), Hassett (42) and Barnes (41) made scores as Bowes, with 5 for 49, blasted his way through their ranks. The second innings was even more abysmal as Farnes (4 for 63), Bowes (2 for 25) and Verity (2 for 15) dismissed them for 123 to give England a massive if somewhat hollow victory by an innings and 579 runs. Australia, however, had retained the Ashes and events emanating from the Third Reich were to preclude any further England challenge for eight years.

PART TWO BY RALPH DELLOR

1946–1979

9

AUSTRALIA SUPREME

IN 1945 the world struggled to regain its equilibrium, and cricket was as keen as every other area of life to revert to what had been accepted as normal in 1939. But the consequences of those six war years were pronounced. England had lost players of the calibre of Ken Farnes, a pilot officer in the RAF, and Hedley Verity who, as Captain Verity of the Green Howards, died from wounds in a prisoner of war camp after the action at Monte Cassino.

Bill Voce – from battle-dress to whites, and into action again.

No sooner had hostilities ceased than a series of 'Victory Tests' against the Australian Services XI was arranged and, reflecting the spirit of the times, it finished all-square at two matches each. There were some very good cricketers in that Australian side, men like Carmody and Pepper, yet only two of their number were to appear in the 1946–47 series when the Ashes contest was resumed: Lindsay Hassett and Keith Miller.

The 1946–47 English touring party which set out for Australia on board *Stirling Castle* did not undergo ideal preparation for an encounter with such strong opposition.

Even its best was unlikely to have proved good enough for Australia.

Food was still rationed in England and the contrast between ration queues and replete shipboard tables did little to ensure that they arrived at Freemantle at their best fighting weights. Voce and Pollard had to get special permission to exchange khaki battledress for cricketing whites, while Hutton's whole technique had to change as a result of a war-time injury. A fall in an army gymnasium had broken his left arm: the setting was less than perfect; and for the rest of his career his left arm was shorter than his right. He had to modify his grip, and when it is considered that all the best batsmen have relied on a strong top hand, Hutton's handicap can be appreciated. His re-emergence as a force in Test cricket after the war was quite an achievement: bearing in mind his injury it was nothing short of remarkable. Compton and Edrich, too, were back in harness, their careers foreshortened but not destroyed by the war; while Hammond, at 43, was past his zenith.

Two men have popularly been blamed for

Keith Miller teamed up with Ray Lindwall for the first time in the Brisbane Test. His 7 for 60 heralded a long and fruitful association.

Ray Lindwall, the straight man of the double-act.

England's defeats in Australia in 1946–47. Adolf Hitler was one, Wally Hammond the other. In matches outside the Tests Hammond averaged 77.50, and his powers as a slip fielder appeared undiminished. But he could not reproduce that form where it mattered – in the Test arena – and so a strategy founded on the runs he was likely to score was doomed.

If Hammond's lack of Test runs was pertinent, his attitude off the field did little to bolster the spirit of the touring party. They travelled much by train around Australia, but while long train journeys were undertaken by the team across monotonous miles of the continent, the captain and the manager, Major Rupert Howard, took themselves off in a Jaguar car. It was not the way to dispel a reputation for aloofness.

There was some doubt before the series began whether Don Bradman would come back to the highest level of cricket. It was thought by some that his appetite for the game had gone and that the years had diminished his powers of reaction and concentration. They were wide of the mark. He scored 680 runs at an average of 97.14 in this series and 508 more in 1948 at an average of 72.57 to demonstrate that all his faculties were still razor-sharp.

MCC were unbeaten in the first-class matches leading up to the first test at Brisbane. Hutton and Cyril Washbrook had both scored two centuries, Hammond had taken 208 off the Western Australian attack, and Compton too had reached three figures.

That made it all the more unpalatable that Brisbane, where England had a 100 per cent record in Tests, provided a 'sticky dog' and England were twice bowled out for under 200. Australia, in the meantime, scored 645 to win by the staggering margin of an innings and 332 runs after Bradman (187) and Hassett (128) had put on 276 for the third wicket. Later in the batting order came a young man making his Test debut – Keith Miller. He made 79 before taking the new ball with Ray Lindwall and finishing with 7 for 60. It was the start of a legendary Test career

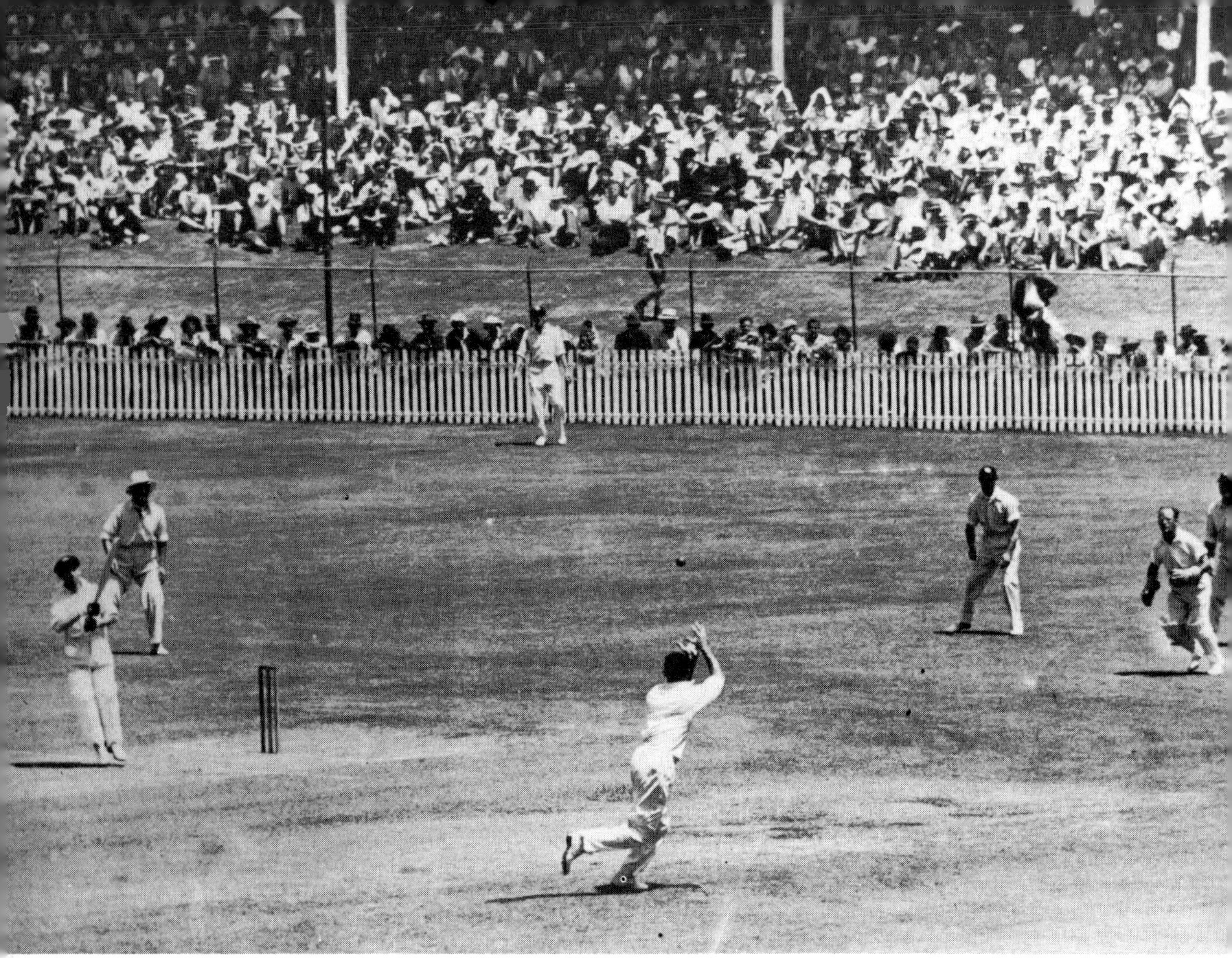

Above: *A narrow escape for Bradman early in his century innings. He pulls a ball into the hands of Edrich – who fails to hold the chance.*

Opposite: *Two for Toshack. Barnes about to catch Compton for 15 . . . And Hardstaff, comprehensively bowled.*

during which he scored 2958 runs at an average of 36.97, held 38 catches, and took 170 wickets at only 22.97 apiece.

Keith Miller, though, was not the sort of cricketer whose influence on the game can be measured merely in statistics. He was a character of individual temperament, a magnificent athelete, and a genuine all-rounder, beloved by crowds wherever he went. Well-built, with the looks of a film-star, he was topped off with a mass of black hair which he would order into place with a toss of the head as he walked back to his mark. He was a man of moods, at his most dangerous if he had over-indulged the previous night. There are stories of Miller arriving by taxi, minutes before play was due to start, still in his dinner-jacket, having failed to make it back to the hotel on the previous evening. Changing into whites, he would then give batsmen of the highest calibre the most torrid half-hour of their careers until he had worked the excesses out of his system.

He had learned all about English conditions while stationed in the UK as an RAAF pilot during the war. This made his seamers valuable even when the ball was not swinging and, furthermore, he could slip in the quickish leg-break or googly to confuse the batsman.

Miller was a potential match-winner, and England's Doug Wright went into this series with the same label. But, though he performed creditably, he did not manage to win a game for his country. Miller was one of Wright's five victims in the first Test, but they cost him 167 runs in 43.6 overs. He got just one at Sydney in the second Test and that cost 169 runs off 46 overs as Australia won by an innings and 33 runs.

At Brisbane England had suffered the worst of the conditions and could point to a disputed umpiring decision as excuses for defeat. When Bradman, on 28, played a ball from Voce to Ikin

Voce and Hutton dive for a snick by Miller at Brisbane.

Sid 'Bagger' Barnes – always ready to make the most of an opportunity, both on and off the field.

at slip, the umpire answered the appeal with 'Not out'. Bradman scored another 159 runs and cast aside thoughts of retiring. In the next Test, at Sydney, he and Sid Barnes each scored 234 and put on 405 for the fifth wicket – another Test record.

Sidney 'Bagger' Barnes was in some ways a man ahead of his time. Had he been around in the days when cricketers can and do make large amounts of money from commercial activities he would have been in his element. He was not a mean man, and helped several less fortunate friends out of difficulty, but he did believe in making the utmost of what financial opportunities came his way. On the 1948 tour it was Barnes who had the idea of making a film of the tour. He even inquired from the cameraman whether he had successfully recorded the ball hit by Dick Pollard which felled him at short leg. He spent ten days in hospital after that blow, but it did not prevent him from specialising in the close catching positions, much to the consternation of the English authorities who considered his proximity to the batsman unsporting.

Barnes was one of the three Australians whose career straddled the war. A fractured wrist on the way over for the 1938 tour meant that his batting style tended to be a little one-sided. After the war, he tightened up on his technique to the extent that when he became set he was very difficult to dislodge. He had an impish sense of humour. It was he who convinced the England players, during the tropical storm at Brisbane, that the hailstones about an inch in diameter were small compared with some he had seen, and promptly lobbed chunks of man-made ice past the England dressing-room window. It was Barnes who, on the 1948 tour of England, captured a dog that had strayed onto the field and presented it to umpire Skelding with the words, 'Now all you need is a white stick.'

Paul Gibb played his last Test at Brisbane in 1946. At Sydney his successor Godfrey Evans kept wicket throughout the Australian innings of 659 for 8 declared without conceding a bye. His opposite number in the series was Don Tallon who, though a genuine wicketkeeper/batsman, seldom produced his best batting form in Tests. With the lineup that preceded him, he did not get too many opportunities!

Tallon the wicketkeeper made a tremendous contribution to Australian sides of this era, and spectators now had the opportunity to see two of the very best. Like Evans, Tallon appreciated the value of diving to reach balls that otherwise might

Hutton, caught first ball by Sid Barnes off Miller in the second innings at Brisbane.

Post-war enthusiasm. Melbourne fans, long starved of Test cricket, line up for tickets in Collins Street. Some even waited in queues for tickets to admit them to other queues!

have been out of reach; but he was safe before spectacular. He was also one of the game's great appealers. As the Australians say, he would not die wondering, for at the slightest provocation would let out a raucous appeal. He claimed 20 of his 58 Test dismissals in this series and played an innings in the third Test at Melbourne that prevented England getting back into the rubber.

In the first innings Colin McCool had scored 104 not out. When Australia batted again only Arthur Morris with 155 managed to master the English attack, and 341 for 7 looked a vulnerable score. Tallon and Lindwall then joined forces, and the pair who shared so many wickets became a batting partnership of consequence. Tallon scored 92, Lindwall 100, and they put on 154 in just 88 minutes. Whereas a total of 375 might have been feasible, there was no way the tourists could reach a final target of 551 in seven hours despite an inspired innings of 112 by Washbrook.

Washbrook is bowled by Bruce Dooland after scoring an inspired 112 in Melbourne.

Washbrook could be counted as one of the English successes of the tour, and enjoyed with Hutton three consecutive opening stands of three figures, to establish himself as the Yorkshireman's opening partner. A fine cutter and hooker, he had great resilience and character and he loved nothing better than batting against Australia. It was then that he was seen at his most determined, his jaw set a little firmer, his cap at a slightly more rakish angle.

If Washbrook and Hutton could usually be relied upon to get the England innings off to a respectable start, then Australia could counter with Barnes and Morris. Barnes did not appear in the fourth Test, at Adelaide because of fibrositis. But Morris more than made up for his partner's absence with scores of 122 and 124 not out.

Morris burst upon first-class cricket during the war with a century in each innings of his debut match for New South Wales against Queensland. His impact on the Test scene was hardly less dramatic with six centuries in his first 10 Tests against England. A delightful person, Morris was also one of the most effective opening batsmen Australia has ever produced and his performances might have gained even greater historical recognition had he not been a contemporary of

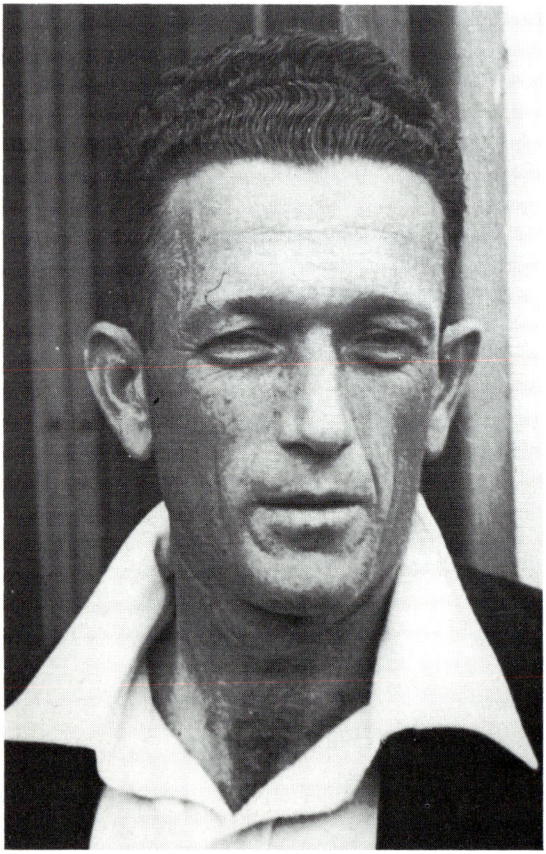

Don Tallon, one of the game's great appealers.

Bradman. Strangely for an opening batsman, he was also outstanding when facing spin, using his feet to great effect; his weakness was found to be a swinging delivery pitching aroung leg stump. Only Bradman scored more heavily in this 1946–47 series and in 1948 Morris averaged 87. In the 1950–51 series, after five failures, he thundered back by scoring 206 in his next Test innings at Adelaide. He remained an integral part of Australian Test teams until 1955.

The fourth Test of 1946–47 ended in a draw favouring Australia. Compton emulated Morris with a century in each innings, Miller scored his first Test century, and Bradman was bowled by Bedser for a duck in the first innings. The Ashes were already Australia's before the fifth Test in Sydney, when the physical exertions of a long, losing tour began to tell on England. Hammond had to give in to fibrositis and handed the captaincy to Norman Yardley. Hardstaff's knee injury prevented him from appearing, and Hutton went sick during the first innings and took no further part in the match, though he had 122 on the board. Australia won by five wickets, with Lindwall taking 7 for 63 in England's first innings and McCool 5 for 44 in the second. England too had a seven-wicket man in Doug Wright.

Wright finished the series as England's most successful bowler in terms of wickets with 51 on the tour and 23 in Tests, but the costs were high at 33 and 43 respectively.

In every department Australia's players had been better than their English counterparts. They had been better prepared, and they were playing at home. The thought was that when they were to meet again in 1948 there would be a more equal battle.

It is said that the 1948 team was the strongest Australia has produced. It had no obvious weakness, and the results speak for themselves. The Ashes were retained by the time the third Test ended in a draw, and Australia won the four other matches by impressive margins. The first was at Trent Bridge. Compton scored 184 in England's second innings, spread over three days, and interrupted by the elements no fewer than 11 times. England, however, had been bowled out for 165 in the first innings and Bradman and Hassett

Cyril Washbrook plays a shot through the slips at Brisbane.

Read all about it. The Melbourne scoreboard at the end of the third Test, Adelaide.

made hundreds in Australia's first to set up a position which Bill Johnston exploited to the full with nine wickets in the match.

Most people, recalling the 1948 series, will talk in glowing terms about the batting of Bradman and Morris, or with awe about the fast bowling partnership of Lindwall and Miller. They tend to overlook the support the pace bowlers received from the man who filled the role of the third seamer, and provided variety to the attack. Bill Johnston's deliveries, bowled left-arm at a pace well to the quick side of medium, accounted for 102 batsmen on the tour, while he took 27 wickets (at 23.33) in the Tests exactly to match the haul by Ray Lindwall. Whereas Lindwall would come gliding in over a smooth approach, Johnston had a run of under a dozen yards which was anything but aesthetically pleasing. What was lacking in grace, however, was found in effect, for he reached a century of Test wickets in just over four years, which, at the time, set a new record. He used his height to the full and, making the ball swing late into the right-hand batsman, was no easy proposition for any but those with the very soundest technique.

His figures at Trent Bridge were 5 for 36 off 25 overs, reducing England to 74 for 8 before a touch of respectability came from the unlikely source of Jim Laker's bat. The Surrey off-spinner scored 63, but it was not enough to affect the eventual

Alec Bedser – got Bradman out for a duck in the Adelaide Test.

Bradman, out for a duck, bowled Bedser at Adelaide. Personnel, left to right: Bradman, Compton, Edrich, Ikin, Hammond, Evans and Yardley.

result – only to delay it as Johnston bowled another 59 overs in the second innings to finish with 4 for 147. Those who thought the English defeats of 1946–47 could be quickly avenged had to revise their thoughts.

Australia's strength was underlined at Lord's in the second Test, where Australia won by 409 runs despite the fact that Miller, injured, could not bowl. Johnston shared the new ball with Lindwall, who took eight wickets in the match, and left-arm medium-pacer Ernie Toshack took 5 for 40 in the second innings, which subsided almost without opposition. There was nothing to match the centuries of Morris in the first innings and Barnes in the second.

Hutton scored only 20 and 13 at Lord's, and although technically he was perhaps better-equipped than any other Englishman, the selectors saw fit to leave him out for the third Test, at Old Trafford. Gloucestershire's George Emmett was chosen to partner Washbrook, but it was Compton who put England into a winning position with a brave 145 not out. When he had scored only four Compton went for a hook, got a top edge into the face, and retired hurt until the fall of the fourth wicket. For the first time in 15 Tests (in which he had batted) against England, Bradman failed to score at least a fifty. However, no play was possible on the fourth day and England's 142-run advantage from the first innings was of little avail. Though Yardley declared on the fifth morning the draw was inevitable.

By avoiding defeat at Old Trafford, albeit helped by rain, England enjoyed a boost to their confidence. They won the toss at Headingley and the runs came. Hutton scored a determined 81, Washbrook and Edrich both hit centuries, and even nightwatchman Bedser joined in with 79. At 68 for 3, Australia were in trouble. Then Miller was joined in a century partnership by a 19-year-old left-hander making his debut against England. His name was Neil Harvey.

Harvey was to become one of the great left-handers in Test cricket. He played in more Tests than any other Australian and was second only to Bradman in terms of runs and centuries scored for his country. Harvey had a tremendous repertoire of strokes, and delighted in using them. His footwork was quite exquisite, so that the bowler might deliver a ball he considered to be of a useful length only to find the batsman turning it into a half-volley, duly cracked through the covers. Furthermore, such unwarranted punishment was not reserved for spinners.

As a cover-point he set new standards of excellence, anticipating the direction of the shot and swooping to send a return from below the shoulder that found the top of the stumps with unerring accuracy.

Harvey's century at Leeds was very nearly matched by Sam Loxton, who hit five sixes before being bowled by Yardley, seven runs short. England declared at 365 for 8, in their second innings, giving Australia the last day to score 404 on a turning pitch. Compton's spin was introduced into the attack, and he caught-and-bowled Hassett with the score 57. There was no further success until Arthur Morris fell for 182 . . . 301 runs later.

Bradman was still there with 173 when the winning run was scored. This century was his last in Test matches and his fourth in six innings at Headingley. At the time, the 404 was the highest by any side in the fourth innings to win a Test, and it remained so until 1976, when India scored 406 for 4 to beat West Indies. Any confidence England had gained from the Old Trafford draw was shattered by their experience in Leeds.

The fifth Test at The Oval was dominated by Lindwall and Morris – and to some extent by Bradman and Hollies. Lindwall destroyed England's hopes with one of the great bowling spells of Test cricket. His figures were 16.1–5–20–6, followed up by another three wickets in the second innings to give Australia victory by an innings and 149 runs.

Morris played a magnificent innings of 196, run out, accounting for more than half the Australian total of 389, and putting on 117 for the first wicket with Barnes before Evans caught Barnes off the Warwickshire leg-spinner, Eric Hollies. That wicket was the prelude to an historic occasion, for it brought Donald Bradman to the wicket for his last Test appearance: cheered by the crowd and England players alike from pavilion to the middle. Some say Bradman had tears in his eyes as he took guard, but he played his first ball from Hollies, a leg-break, with familiar ease. The next ball was a googly; Bradman touched it, and was bowled. He left the scene with a career average in Tests of 99.94. Just four more runs would have given him a round 100.

Above left: *Keith Miller makes an amazing slip catch to dismiss Hardstaff off Johnston, Trent Bridge 1948.*

Left: *The 1948 Australians before their opening match at Worcester: Standing, left to right: I. W. Johnson, A. R. Morris, E. R. H. Toshack, K. R. Miller, D. Tallon, R. R. Lindwall, R. N. Harvey. Seated, left to right: W. A. Brown, A. L. Hassett, D. G. Bradman, C. L. McCool, S. G. Barnes.*

Ian Johnson bowling in the First Test at Trent Bridge.

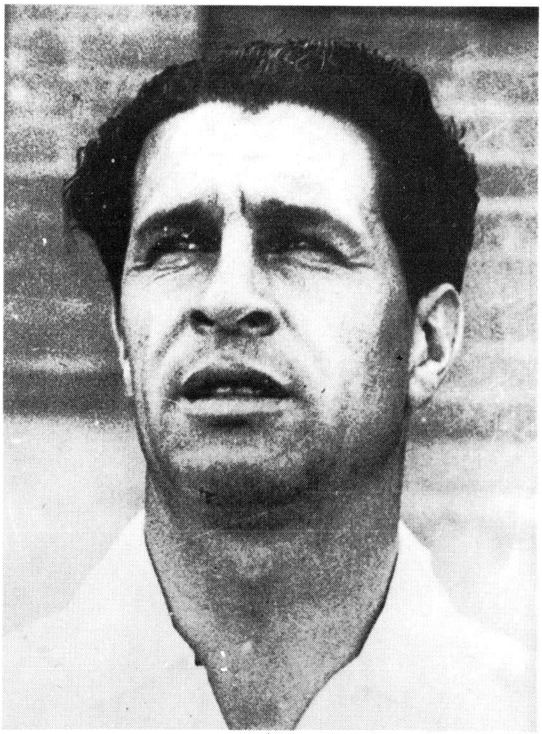

Ernie Toshack – 5 for 40 at Lord's.

Left: *Compton hit in the face attempting to hook Lindwall at Old Trafford.*

Right: *The traditional scramble for stumps at the end of the Old Trafford Test.*

Hollies won a place in the legend of cricket by bowling Bradman with that ball, but it was Lindwall who won the match for Australia. England could muster only 52 in their first innings, their second-lowest total in Tests.

Lindwall did not fulfil the usual requirements of a fast bowler. Less than 6ft tall, he did not even use the height he had, for his arm was not vertical when it came over. But he was fast, very accurate, and had the ability to make the ball swing at the crucial stage in its flight. He can be counted among the very finest, if not the fastest, seam bowler the game has produced. He was certainly not short of pace, and his fastest ball was not far short of the quickest in the game, but his forte was control and variation. He would use a bouncer infrequently – as it is best used – as a surprise weapon.

Lindwall's cricket began in the suburban backstreets, bowling at a kerosene can, but he was to form, with Miller, one of cricket's greatest partnerships. He was the perfect foil for Miller, undemonstrative and apparently unemotional, but every bit as good, if not better, at his job. Lindwall took 228 Test wickets at 23 each, and he took them, in general, on good pitches and against good batsmen. No mean batsman himself, he made two Test centuries.

On his retirement from cricket Lindwall became a florist, but few batsmen received bouquets on that first day at The Oval in 1948. England faced a deficit of 337 as they started their second innings and were unable to make Australia bat again.

Hutton, who scored 30 of the 52 in the first innings, made 64 out of 188 in the second. Australia were triumphant once again, and England could no longer offer excuses about the war years. The Australians had been a superb team in every sense. Before England could hold sensible hopes of regaining the Ashes there had to be a considerable shift in the balance of talent.

Left: *After departing for repairs, Compton presses on towards a valiant 145 runs having, on this occasion, jettisoned his bat.*

Right: *Don Bradman, in his last Test match, is bowled by Eric Hollies for a duck.*

10

A TURNING POINT

THE resumption of hostilities in 1950–51 was entrusted to an 'old sweat', Freddie Brown, who had returned to the game not with Surrey, his former county, but with Northamptonshire, and led them to such effect that he was awarded the captaincy of the tour. Brown had much strength of character, but he knew that the side he led into the field for the first Test at Brisbane on December 1, 1950 would be stretched to the limit. Furthermore, there was no dramatic decline in the power of Australia. Barnes was now wielding a wicked pen in the Press-box. Bradman too had gone, of course, but if anybody could rise to the psychological challenge of replacing him, and fill the cricketing gap, it was Neil Harvey.

Harvey scored 74 in the first innings at The Gabba, but the English bowlers had the satisfaction of dismissing Australia for 228 on the type of pitch on which they might have expected to toil much longer. In fact it was the England batsmen who were doomed to struggle. The second day was washed out, as was the third morning, so England began their first innings after lunch on a typical Brisbane 'sticky'. It was a remarkable afternoon's cricket. Twenty wickets fell; there were two declarations; yet only 130 runs were scored.

At one point England were 49 for 1, but, at 68 for 7, Brown declared to get the Australians in while the wicket was at its most treacherous. It was an imaginative ploy and could easily have been outrageously successful had not the first-innings margin been so great.

England had to bat again sooner than Brown had anticipated, for Hassett alas knew a thing or two about imaginative captaincy. When Bailey and Bedser accounted for seven Australian batsmen for 32 runs, Hassett handed back the 'poisoned chalice' to Brown by declaring and setting England 193 to win. Brown's key was Hutton, and he was witheld from the action while pawns were sacrificed. The order was changed about so that potential match-winners could be preserved until conditions improved. Bailey and Bedser, nine and ten in the first innings, went in at four and five; Hutton, Compton and Brown were at eight, nine and ten and did not appear until the last day. By then, six pawns had been lost for 30 runs and England were still 163 adrift.

The fifth morning belonged to Hutton. He played an innings numerically unremarkable: 62 not out in a losing side. But in terms of technical excellence, to say nothing of courage, he displayed a standard of perfection seldom matched.

Arthur Morris takes a vicious swing at a no-ball from Doug Wright on the first day of the Brisbane Test, 1950–51.

Bafflement at Brisbane. Compton looks for the ball as it scoots off an impossible wicket and flies over the slips.

Compton could offer no support, but Brown made a brave 17, and Wright scored just two of the 45 runs added for the last wicket. Hutton was undefeated, Australia won by 70 runs, and 'mystery spinner' Jack Iverson, in his first Test, had taken 4 for 43.

Iverson enjoyed an extraordinary rise to this level of cricket and his demise was equally swift. He was an innovator, though the style of spin bowling he pioneered found few imitators, and only John Gleeson reached Test standard by following it. Iverson played little cricket until he was 30, but then found he could impart great spin to the ball by flicking it with a bent second finger, breaking either way with no discernible change of action. In his early days he caused havoc among the best batsmen.

Iverson played an important role in the second Test of the 1950–51 series. Bailey and Bedser dismissed Australia at Melbourne for 194 but England, plagued by the mystery man (4 for 37) were restricted to a lead of only three. The match was interrupted for two days to accommodate Sunday and Christmas Day, but by that time Australia had been dismissed again for 181 and England, needing only 179, had an outstanding chance of squaring the series. Instead, Lindwall and Johnston bowled superbly and Australia went two-up by a margin of 28 runs.

Brown won the toss for England in Sydney for the third Test, and after the rain of Brisbane and humidity of Melbourne the better batting conditions were mirrored in the scores. England reached 290 – Hutton 62 and Brown 79 – but, more significantly, Bailey had his thumb broken by Lindwall, while, in being run out, Wright tore a tendon in his leg. This meant that England were reduced to just three front-line bowlers, one of whom, John Warr, was making his Test debut. Compton was not fully fit, having missed the second Test with a knee injury, so Brown had to bowl 44 eight-ball overs, Bedser one fewer, and Warr 36 as Australia amassed 426, founded on a

magnificent 145 not out from Miller. Iverson took 6 for 27 as Australia won by an innings and 13 runs to retain the Ashes.

The fourth Test, at Adelaide, was memorable for individual performances, good and bad, and Compton took over the England captaincy on the fifth day after Brown had been injured in a motoring accident. He did not inherit Brown's ability to play a captain's innings, making a duck in the second innings. By then, England's cause was lost. Morris was the cornerstone of Australia's first-innings 371 with a magnificent double-century before he became off-spinner Tattersall's first Test wicket. England's first innings closed 99 runs short, and ended as it had begun, with Hutton at the wicket. He scored an undefeated 156 to become the only Englishman to carry his bat twice through completed Test innings.

When Australia batted again they declared at 403 for 8, with a lead of 502. Miller was out for 99, and Jim Burke, in his first Test, scored 101 not out. Warr had Ian Johnson caught behind and thereby claimed his only Test wicket, at a cost of 281 runs! When, in 1980, he spoke at a function to mark the centenary of the first Test in England, Warr noted wrily how many great names from the

A marvellous throw by Washbrook shatters Harvey's wicket as he backs up too far at Melbourne.

Reg. Simpson, on his way to a birthday century, is narrowly missed by Miller off Iverson.

past had made the trip and how Johnson, his only victim in Test cricket, was absent! Australia went on to their fourth successive victory of the series.

England had met with bad fortune, injuries, and a superior side. But these were not auguries for what was to happen in Melbourne in the final match of the tour. Australia for once achieved only one substantial partnership, between Morris and Hassett, and were out for 217, Bedser and Brown each taking five wickets. England's lead of 103 then owed much to Reg Simpson, aided by Hutton, with whom he shared a second-wicket stand of 131. Tall and correct, Simpson continued to dominate the bowling while others fell, much in the same way another Notts batsman, Derek Randall, was to do in the Centenary Test on the same ground in 1977. Simpson was still there when No. 11 Tattersall went to the wicket – and hung on while Simpson savagely accumulated 64 to celebrate his 31st birthday with his only century against Australia. After Bedser had taken 5 for 59 in the second innings, England needed only 95 to win. Hutton scored an undefeated 60 and England were home by eight wickets.

Bedser's haul during the series was 30 wickets at 16 apiece. He was immensely strong and liked nothing better than to bowl long spells. His economical action meant that he could maintain his medium-fast pace without losing the control that became his hallmark. His large hands and high action were in many ways reminiscent of Maurice Tate, and he was one of the few bowlers worthy of such comparison, with accurate inswing and his major weapon, the leg-cutter. In normal conditions this could be dangerous, but when the pitch encouraged it there was no batsman who would bet against falling to it. Such skill and a willing attitude found adequate reward in 236 Test wickets in a career most of which saw him as England's major attacking force.

It was Bedser who did as much as anyone to win that first English victory over Australia for 13 years, ending Australia's run of 25 Tests without defeat. And it was Bedser who was to play an integral part in shifting the balance of cricketing power away from the Antipodes. At the time, England's victory in Melbourne could have been dismissed as a fluke result against a side lacking full motivation. In the light of what was to happen over the next eight years it can be seen as a real turning point. Australia had been predominant since the war, but the final match of the 1950–51 series marked the precise moment when that predominance was to become England's for the next three series.

Australian captain, Hassett, applauds as England win the Fifth Test. Others scramble for stumps.

Hassett was still captain of Australia, in the Coronation Year of 1953, but Brown had handed the England leadership to Hutton – the first time this century that a professional had held the post.

Hassett scored a century in the first innings at Trent Bridge, in a first Test badly affected by the weather. It was anticipated that either Bedser or the weather would decide this opening encounter and despite a magnificent effort from the former, the latter had the almost inevitable last word. Bedser took 7 for 55 in the first innings as Australia slumped from 237 for 3 to 249 all out. In the second innings they failed to get any kind of foothold and were all out for 123 (Bedser 7 for 44), leaving England 229 to win. At the close of the third day they were 42 for 1, but the fourth day was washed out and the fifth would not begin until 4.30 p.m. Though another 78 runs were added, there was no question of a positive result.

Batting at No. 6 for England was the 23-year-old Peter May. He scored only 9 in this his first

A victory smile from England skipper, Freddie Brown, after the Melbourne Test.

encounter with Australia, but he was to develop into one of the finest classical batsmen England has produced. May's early cricket was nourished at Charterhouse and Cambridge, where immaculate batting pitches encouraged an immaculate style. Driving back through the 'V', May personified timing, gaining power in his shots with an apparently effortless ease. Pictures of May at his best would grace any coaching manual, for his elegant strokeplay has seldom been surpassed. It took him time to master the needs of England–Australia Tests, but once he had done so his record was superb. He made three centuries at critical times and averaged 46 in 21 Tests. In all he played 66 times for his country – 41 as captain – and scored 4537 runs, often under pressure and always with style. Despite his amateur background, May was highly professional in his approach to captaincy. A charming, cultured exterior concealed a man who was, according to some who played under him, a hard and relentless skipper.

A career in the City beckoned, and May retired prematurely from first-class cricket. Had he decided to continue for another half-dozen years he could have established records to support his greatness. But those who saw him play can rely on memory-pictures rather than statistics to confirm what an outstanding batsman he was.

May was not in the side for the second Test at Lord's, where once again Hassett won the toss. The Australian captain opened the innings and scored a century for the second successive match, while Alan Davidson, playing in his second Test, scored 76. Hutton answered Hassett's century with one of his own, and Tom Graveney hit 78 before becoming one of Lindwall's five victims. Strangely, Graveney did not achieve many of his higher Test innings against the Australians, and scored his only Ashes century at Sydney in 1954. Nevertheless, he was a valuable member of the England side in the ensuing battles and captained the team at Headingley in 1968.

The one epithet invariably applied to Graveney's batting is *elegant.* First with Gloucestershire and then Worcestershire, he played his county cricket with style and evident enjoyment. Unlike some, he took that enjoyment into Test cricket. Graveney moving onto the front foot to drive was one of cricket's aesthetic experiences, for the mastery of his timing could send the ball accelerating past mid-off with an effortless swing of the bat. His career in first-class cricket lasted 23 years, in which time he scored 47,793 runs, with 122 centuries, average 44.91. In Tests his average was similar.

At Lord's in 1953 Graveney still had the major span of a distinguished career ahead of him. His partnership of 168 with Hutton helped England to a first-innings lead of 26. Miller scored the third century of the match during Australia's second innings and England's victory target was 343. Hutton, Kenyon, Graveney and Compton were all back in the pavilion with 73 on the board, and all hopes of victory were gone when Trevor Bailey joined Willie Watson in one of the most famous rearguard actions.

Against the pace of Lindwall and Miller, the

Above right: *England's new captain, Len Hutton, strikes out at Trent Bridge.*

Right: *The England team lines up at Trent Bridge for the First Test of the 1953 series. Back row, left to right: D. Kenyon, R. Tattersall, P. B. H. May, T. W. Graveney, J. H. Wardle, T. E. Bailey, Front row, left to right: T. G. Evans, A. V. Bedser, L. Hutton (Capt), D. C. S. Compton and R. T. Simpson.*

Too late – Davidson reels backwards as he is stumped by Evans off Laker for 15.

Arthur Morris anxiously plays Bedser in Australia's first innings at The Oval. Godfrey Evans smiles ruefully.

leg-spin of Ring and Benaud, they held their ground from 12.40 p.m. on that final day until 5.50. In that time, though only 163 were scored, Watson made a century on his debut against Australia and Bailey accumulated 71 in the role he loved best. Both finally fell to Ring, but by now the Australians had been denied.

Manchester's reputation for rain was amply endorsed when less than 14 hours of play were possible. Harvey scored a century in Australia's 318 and Bedser, almost inevitably took five wickets. England trailed by 42 on first innings and, with so much time lost, a definite result was never likely – though Australia slumped to 35 for 8 against Bedser and the spin of Wardle and Laker in the final session.

Hassett's toss success continued at Headingley, but this time he went against all accepted convention and put England in. It had a particular irony for Hutton, who lost his wicket before a run had been scored – and on his home ground. The pattern for the innings was set, for England struggled to 167 all out; Lindwall 5 for 54 and Graveney 55. Australia built a lead of 99, despite the heroic Bedser's 6 for 95, the last of which broke Grimmett's record 216 Test victims. England managed respectability in their second innings yet were only 177 runs in front with nearly two hours of play remaining. A certain dilatoriness on England's part ensured that Australia had made only 147 for 4 when stumps were drawn.

So the teams went back to London for the final Test, at The Oval, with four matches drawn and four tosses won by Australia. Hassett won this toss too, and, with the pitch likely to take spin towards the end of a six-day Test, reverted to tradition. For Australia, Johnston was recalled in place of Benaud, while England brought back May for Watson and replaced Simpson with a young fast bowler new to the Ashes contest. Freddie Trueman was to have a considerable bearing on the outcome of this and many another Ashes match.

He had made his England debut the previous year against India, and took 24 wickets in three matches, terrifying his victims with sheer, blistering pace. He was not tall for a fast bowler, but his strong frame was well muscled, his action impeccable. A smooth approach gradually accelerated until he met the crease with an explosive sideways action. Early on, pace was his main asset – yet it could be a liability. If he received any sort of punishment, Trueman's instinctive reaction would be to try to bowl even faster, at the expense of control. His bouncer could strike dread into the bravest heart, and often it would be followed by the obligatory glare.

Though maturity did not dampen the fire of Trueman's pace, it enabled him to eliminate the extravagant and wasteful delivery. Instead he introduced subtle skills into his repertoire: the fast away-swinger was one speciality. Later, he introduced other variations, easing back the velocity, and seaming the ball all over the place. As a character, he was considerably larger than life, while his bowling figures confirm him as a cricketer of the greatest dimensions. His immortality was assured when he became the first man to 300 Test wickets.

A taste of his own medicine. Trueman bowled by Johnston at The Oval.

In the first Australian innings at The Oval in 1953, Trueman took 4 for 86 as Australia were dismissed for 275. Bedser's three wickets brought his total for the rubber to 39, breaking Tate's record in Anglo–Australian meetings. At one stage Australia were 160 for 7 but their innings was revived by Lindwall, who scored 62 before becoming one of the three entries which read 'c Evans b Trueman'. It was to become a familiar

Hutton, in confident mood, gives England an excellent start at The Oval. He went on to make 82.

A brilliant catch by Edrich to dismiss Archer off Lock's bowling.

jingle in Test cricket, for batsmen who edged Trueman were certain to be the next victim of another of the game's great individuals.

Godfrey Evans's 173 catches and 46 stumpings established a Test record which stood until broken by his successor in the Kent and England sides, Alan Knott. If Blackham was known as the Prince of Wicketkeepers, then Evans was the court jester inasmuch as he not only enjoyed his cricket but was seen to be enjoying it. He was spectacular, and if he could not reach a chance with his feet on the ground, he was quite happy to dive vast distances. Evans was essentially a cheerful character who did much to lift the morale of the team – especially on the long hot days of a tour. Evans was often useful in front of the stumps as well, especially when the situation demanded aggression. On the other hand, as an example of his pugnacity, while one of his two Test centuries came within two runs of arriving before lunch, on the 1946–47 tour, at Adelaide, he remained at the crease for 95 minutes without scoring!

Evans scored a modest 28 at The Oval in 1953, but Hutton (82) erased his disappointment at Headingley, and Bailey added a valuable 64 to edge England into a lead of 31. Australia collapsed in their second innings to the spin of Laker and Lock, who took 4 for 75 and 5 for 45, as a foretaste of things to come in 1956, and no Australian reached 50 as they were shot out for 162, leaving England 132 to win. There was a trip at 24 when Hutton was run out, and May went for 37 with the total 88. But the 'Middlesex twins', Edrich and Compton, saw England home with the Ashes – for the first time in 19 years!

To regain the Ashes in England was one thing; to retain them in Australia was another. Yet in 1954–55, after initial surprises, England confirmed their superiority with conviction. The first surprises were sprung even before the touring party left Tilbury. Laker and Lock were left out in favour of McConnon of Glamorgan and Wardle. Perhaps the greatest surprise was the fact that Frank Tyson was preferred to Trueman. Some

Right: *Up goes the finger of umpire Dai Davies and Jim Laker has Hole l.b.w.*

scandalous stories circulated about Trueman's behaviour on the tour of West Indies which did nothing to endear him to the game's establishment. Yet, Trueman's omission meant that a place was found for the man who was to play a highly significant part in the retention of the Ashes, for Tyson's speed on Australian pitches earned him the nickname 'Typhoon'. He certainly put the Australian batsmen in a whirl.

Not even Tyson's speed, however, could prevent Australia from recording an emphatic victory in the first Test at Brisbane. England suffered two losses in the course of 24 hours which did nothing to improve their chances. Evans went down with influenza on the eve of the match, and his place behind the stumps was taken by Keith Andrew of Northants. Andrew was an extremely talented performer, unfortunate to be capped only twice by his country. But he could not bat as well as Evans, one of the all-time great wicketkeepers.

Andrew's usually safe hands let him down on the first morning of the new series when Morris edged Bedser and the chance was grassed. Morris went on to 153. There was another disaster in store for England: Compton, chasing a ball, fell against the fence and broke a bone in his left hand.

All this happened after Hutton had invited Australia to bat first. England, having selected no slow bowler, and with Bedser below his best, had little variety in the attack, and laboured long and hard as Morris and Harvey put on 202 for the third wicket. The rest joined a run spree which rattled up 601 for 8 before Ian Johnson declared. Colin Cowdrey, on his Test debut, made 40, and Bailey a characteristic 88, but the total was a mere 190. There was greater application in the follow-on, when Edrich scored 88, but the deficit was still an innings and 154 runs.

The second Test, at Sydney, started as the first at Brisbane had ended, with England's batsmen struggling. The obdurate Bailey opened with Hutton but England could muster only 154. Tyson was felled by a ball from Lindwall and if it was in response to such a blow that Tyson summoned up phenomenal pace, then this ball could be said to have decided the series. Tyson did not open the bowling when Australia batted,

Left: *Keith Miller in full flow at The Oval. The batsman is Bailey.*
Below left: *A streaky boundary for Peter May in the final Test.*
Below: *Compton has a narrow escape as the Australians wait to snap up every chance . . . or not, in this case!*

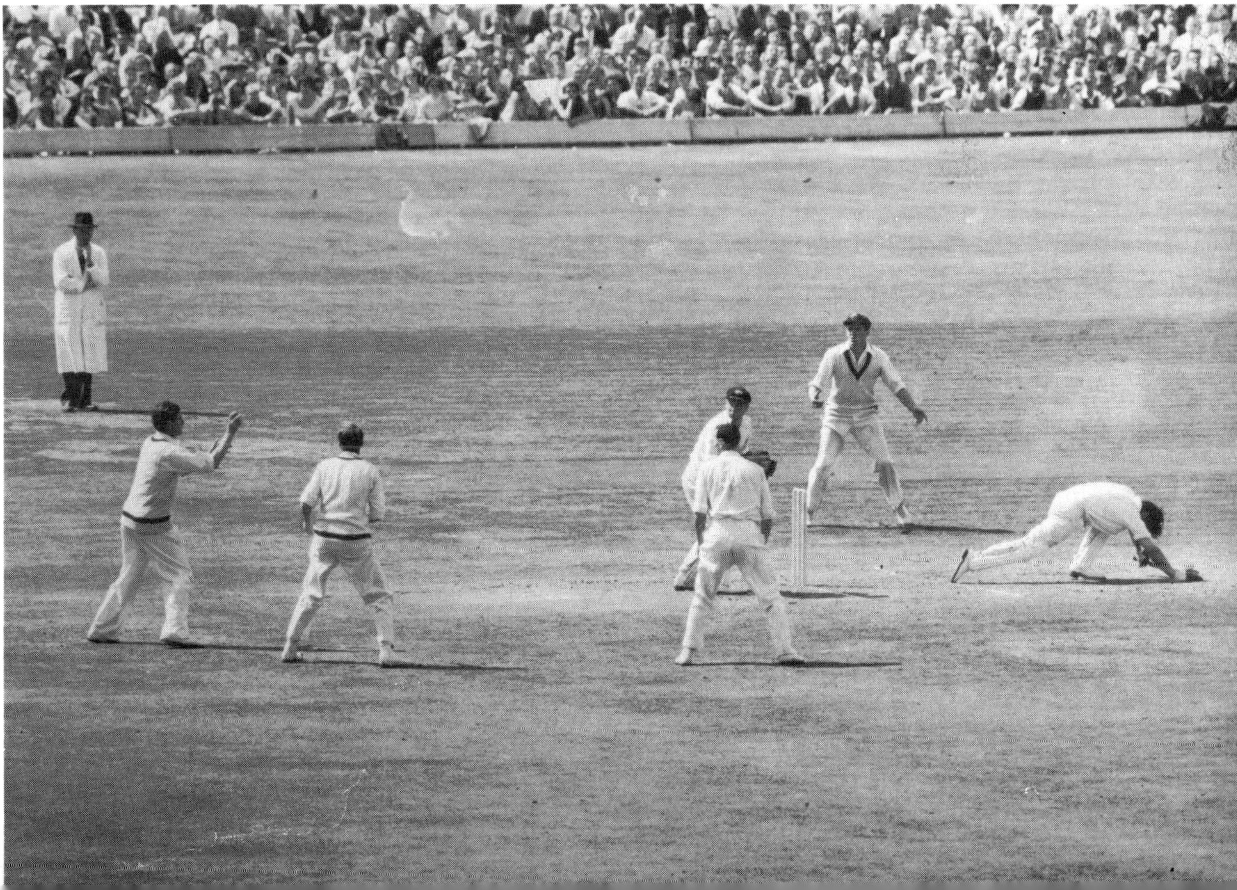

The Ashes regained. A mighty swipe by Compton, off Morris, wins the Oval Test.

The tide of success. Oval fans invade the pitch at the end of the match.

but coming on first change he topped Bailey's 4 for 59 with 4 for 45 – including the wicket of Lindwall. Even so, Australia had a lead of 74 which must have been a source of comfort to Morris, Australia's acting captain, who had put England in.

The satisfaction was short-lived, however, for May scored an imperious century in the second innings, Cowdrey registered his first half-century in Test cricket, and Australia needed 223 to go two-up. Now Tyson had something stronger than a stiff breeze to encourage him, and at great pace, on a true line, picked up six wickets, four of them bowled, for 85. Brian Statham plugged away faithfully into the wind and deserved his three wickets, but neither could account for Harvey, who made a grand 92 not out in Australia's 184. Thus England levelled the series with a 38-run victory. Hutton controlled his resources to great effect and the team had responded in the best possible way.

Arthur Morris survives a difficult chance to May off Bedser, at Brisbane, and goes on to make 153.

The Tyson–Statham partnership forged in Sydney bloomed further in Melbourne in the third Test.

Tyson's career, like his bowling, was irresistibly meteoric. He played in only 17 Tests yet took 76 wickets at less than 19 each. Any judgment about the quickest bowler of all time must be subjective, but few people who saw him at his peak on the 1954–55 tour will ever bother to assess the merits of other candidates. In the Championship he appeared for Northamptonshire, though born in Lancashire in 1930, the same county and year as Statham. Lancashire's misjudgment in letting Tyson go ranks alongside that of Essex, who tried and rejected a young man by the name of Jack Hobbs.

Whereas Tyson came and went, Statham stayed on to forge another great fast-bowling partnership with Trueman. Statham played in 70 Tests and only Trueman and Underwood have taken more than his 252 wickets for England. What is more, he was marginally more economical than Underwood. If the popular image of fast bowlers is one of the flamboyant extrovert, difficult to play and even harder to control, then 'George' Statham was the antithesis of a fast bowler. Quiet and retiring, he was not one for explosive gestures, even when a succession of batsmen played and missed. He was remorselessly accurate off a smooth run and from a loose action which owed much to the fact that he was double-jointed in shoulder and elbow. Statham never seemed to tire and was always willing to find that little bit extra at the end of a long, hot day. It could be said of both his famous partnerships that he was the perfect foil, first to Tyson and then Trueman.

In that third Test of '54–55, it was Tyson who stole the glory, but as the players stood aside to allow him to lead the side in, he made sure that Statham was with him. England, despite a cul-

The young Richie Benaud falls to Alec Bedser – caught Evans for 47 in the Melbourne Test.

Frank Tyson – a fearsome pace intelligently used.

tured maiden century from Cowdrey, had scraped together only 191. Though Statham bowled superbly to capture 5 for 60, Australia climbed to a lead of 40. Victorian wicketkeeper Len Maddocks celebrated his debut with 47 and a ninth-wicket stand of 54 with Johnson.

A splendid 91 from May enabled England to raise 279 in their second innings and set Australia 240 to win. By the fourth evening only two wickets were down for 75, with the pitch playing placidly. Yet by lunch on the fifth day, the game was over, England the winners by 128 runs. Tyson walked off having bowled 6.3 eight-ball overs and taken 6 for 16 in 80 dramatic minutes. It was a magnificent spell, and he finished with 7 for 27; but Statham also served!

The Australians looked forward hopefully to the next encounter, for Adelaide was reputed to be slow and easy. Yet England won by five wickets to claim their first series in Australia since the dark days of 1932–33. Maddocks was again top scorer in Australia's first innings with 69, and again Johnson joined him to add 92 valuable runs.

England took a lead of 18, 341 to 323, and then set up their victory chance by dismissing Australia for 111. Only 94 were needed, but five wickets were down when Evans hit the winning runs.

Tyson and Statham played important roles in Adelaide, but it was Yorkshireman Bob Appleyard who made the major impression. Not only did he take three wickets in each innings, at miserly cost, but each was a prized victim. The medium-pace off-spinner did not enter the first-class game until relatively late, playing his first full season at 27. But three years later, here he was in Australia, helping to win the Ashes. As with Tyson, this tour was to be the high point in a short career. Illness, not injury, prevented Appleyard from maintaining the heights of which he was undoubtedly capable; but Australian pitches gave him the bounce that made his individual style of bowling highly dangerous. He rarely strayed from a length and even at that pace, he could beat the batsmen through the air. Appleyard topped the bowling averages in this series with 11 at just over 20 runs each, and played a valuable part in England's strategy – even if the performances of the quicker bowlers are more readily remembered.

May pulls Johnson for four during the final Test in Sydney.

The Bailey speciality. Forward defence at full stretch.

In the rain-ruined fifth Test in Sydney no play was possible until after lunch on the fourth day of the scheduled six-day match. With the Ashes decided and so much play lost, there was an anti-climactic end to the series, though the final Test was not without its moments of drama as the panicking Australians fought to save it.

Put in, England found runs easy to come by. Graveney graced the proceedings with a fine century, and May, Compton and Bailey weighed in substantially so that Hutton could declare at 371 for 7. The seventh wicket had fallen in strange circumstances. Bailey was 72, the match was safe for England, and Lindwall's tally in Anglo–Australian Tests stood at 99 wickets. A declaration was imminent and Bailey, who had played such a consistently large part in England's successful tour, left a straight ball from Lindwall and was off to shake his hand the moment the bails had been dislodged.

In the spirit of this match Trevor Bailey did what was required. He had a reputation as a dour, defensive batsman, and he unquestionably enjoyed a last-ditch battle more than most. But often the role was forced upon him by failures

Johnny Wardle – a shadow over his great spin-bowling talent.

higher up the order. He did have attacking shots and could use them to great effect, but there was little possibility of using them when a sheet-anchor was urgently required. Bailey's immense value to the sides he played for cannot be measured in mere statistics. He played 61 times for England, scoring 2290 runs at an average touching 30 and taking 132 wickets at a little under 30, to say nothing of 32 catches!

Bailey never cheated on a cricket field, but if the legislators made the rules he would test their legislative ability to the full. At Headingley in 1953 he frustrated Hassett's team not only by occupying the crease for an inordinate length of time, but also slowing the over rate right down with negative bowling. A seemingly incurable problem with his bootlaces was an 'innocent' source of delay.

He had done a superb job on this 1954–55 tour, and his name must rank alongside those of Tyson, Statham, and Hutton on England's roll of honour. Hutton did not score as many runs as expected, but his captaincy was of the highest quality. Having made the declaration in the final Test, he used his bowlers intelligently to bowl the Australians out with a deficit of exactly 150 – despite Colin McDonald's dogged 72. Johnny Wardle was the man of the moment with 5 for 79 and Australia followed on with just under two hours of play left. Although the new ball was seen off for the loss of one wicket, Wardle then initiated a collapse and a win for England became a possibility. McDonald was partnered by Miller long enough to see off England's hopes. However, Hutton and Graveney picked up a wicket each as the last rites were played out.

Though Tyson had taken his haul of wickets to 28 and Statham would up with 18, it was gratifying to see a spinner picking up eight wickets in this final match. Wardle had come into his own and justified his selection as the team's left-arm spinner. A series of newspaper articles towards the end of his career cast a dark shadow over Wardle's memory – a tragedy, for he was an enormously talented cricketer. As a lower-order batsman, he believed the ball should be hit. As a close catcher he was excellent, and could always be relied upon, in the field, to keep the crowd amused without jeopardising his ability. As a left-arm spin bowler he was quite outstanding, as one would expect of a man who regularly captured a hundred wickets in a season.

Wardle defied specific categorisation by being able to produce the orthodox delivery or the wrist-spinner at will, and all with potential threat to the batsman. The degree of control can be gauged by the fact that his 102 Test wickets cost a little over 20 each.

Thus, the 1954–55 series ended with a drawn match, England taking the rubber by a healthy 3–1 margin. Australia were clearly in a period of reconstruction.

11

THE MAY UPRISING

PERHAPS the most significant change in the English camp when the battle lines were next drawn, in 1956, was that, following Len Hutton's retirement from Test cricket, the asterisk on the scorecard had alighted by the name of Peter May. It was a change that left England no weaker in terms of leadership, but it did leave an ominous gap at the top of the batting order. In the first Test, at Trent Bridge, the position was adequately filled by a man making his debut, Peter Richardson.

Richardson was as noted for his practical jokes as his batting, and both were formidable. He would cheerfully instruct the printer to run off several hundred scorecards bearing the name of 'I. Snapham' as the wicketkeeper. He would foist fictitious cricket records on a national newspaper. Yet he introduced himself at the highest level of the game in some style, following a top score of 81 with 73.

England declared at 217 for 8 and Harvey was one of the few to defy Laker and Lock as Australia were hurried out for 148. Richardson and Cowdrey (81) then shared an opening partnership of 151. The second day was completely washed out and a further six hours were lost to the weather, so May declared again, setting Australia a target of 258. They took 86 overs to reach 120 for 3 as Lock and Laker began to assert their influence on the series.

Lord's has not been a happy hunting-ground for England in the history of the Ashes, and the second Test of 1956 was no exception. Their misfortune began when Johnson won the toss for Australia, and ended in a 185-run defeat. It was the first time for eight years that green caps were raised in Test victory on an English field. A side that had lost the art of winning needed a good start. McDonald and Burke accomplished this with a stand of 137, Australia's highest since the war. Harvey failed to score, and the remaining batsmen accomplished little – though one of the two Australian debutants, Ken Mackay, came up with 38. The other, Pat Crawford, had an unhappy match. He opened the bowling with Miller but, in his fifth over, pulled a leg muscle and had to retire. As he could not bowl in the second innings and made no runs his introduction to Test cricket was memorable for all the wrong reasons.

Australia's depleted attack was well served by Miller, who took 10 wickets in a match for the only time in an illustrious Test career. Wicketkeeper Gil Langley also played a major role and set a new world record by accounting for nine victims.

May played the captain's role to perfection with scores of 63 and 53, but he received little support. Trueman (5 for 90) and Bailey (4 for 69) did their best to get England back into the match, and Australia had slumped to 112 for 6 before Benaud joined Mackay. Mackay never surrendered his wicket easily, and took nearly 4½ hours to glean 31 runs, chewing gum all the way. Benaud decided on a more adventurous style, and hit a lively 97, so that England were set 372 to win on a wicket tailor-made for Miller. The end was swift. The last five wickets fell for only 11 runs and Australia won by 185.

Events of the fourth Test at Old Trafford have tended to overshadow what happened in the third Test at Headingley, but Leeds did stage what would otherwise be remembered as one of the more remarkable matches. One of its extraordinary features was the recall of Cyril Washbrook, who was 41 and had not played Test cricket since returning from the 1950–51 tour. Alan Oakman, making his debut, was one of the first three batsmen to fall to the fast-medium Ron Archer, who bowled nine overs on that first morning. His wickets cost three runs and only 17 were on the board when the third wicket fell. Into this crisis the familiar, stocky figure of Washbrook made his way to join his captain. May and Washbrook began cautiously but, gradually their partnership developed to add 187 in just under five hours. This was to swing the destination of the Ashes. By the time the partnership was broken they were safe in cold storage for another three years.

Former England captain Hutton – now retired – greets his old adversary Ian Johnson as the S.S. Himalaya arrives at Tilbury with the 1956 Australians.

May made 101, and became the first English batsman to record five consecutive scores of 50 or more against Australia. Washbrook fell for 98, but, naturally, was afforded a hero's acclaim. Bailey and Evans had an eighth-wicket stand of 53, and when Lindwall wrapped up the tail England were 325.

The third day was lost to rain – which merely postponed the triumphant march of the Surrey spinners, Laker (5 for 58) and Lock (4 for 41). Australia were forced to follow on, 182 runs behind. Batting again, they could not even clear the deficit – despite a gallant 69 from Harvey. Laker took 6 for 55, Lock 3 for 40, and England, who had stumbled into the fray at 17 for 3, emerged victorious by an innings.

The fourth Test at Old Trafford is remembered almost exclusively as Jim Laker's match. But the batsmen's part in England's victory should not be

Gil Langley – A world record nine wickets at Lord's.

Cyril Washbrook, recalled to Test duty at 41 – after a five-year break.

underestimated. Their total of 459 was formidable by any standard, but in the context of this particular match it took on enormous proportions. Richardson, who made 104, subsequently claimed that nobody even recalled him playing in the match, let alone scoring a century! The Reverend David Sheppard also reached three figures, Cowdrey made 80 and England's first three wickets took the score to 288.

Jim Laker's ten wickets in Australia's second innings was a unique Test achievement. He also completed another record as the only man ever to take all 10 wickets in an innings twice in the same season, for he claimed 10 for 88 when Surrey played the tourists. Furthermore, 10 second-innings wickets at Old Trafford followed nine in the first, and his overall 19 for 90 represented the finest figures in Test cricket. Few realise that those 90 runs were spread over 68 overs, so he was not only effective but extremely economical.

Born in Yorkshire, Laker made his Surrey debut in 1946, primarily as a batsman. His best domestic season was 1950, when he took 166 first-class wickets, and he shattered a Test trial at Bradford by taking 8 for 2!

By 1956 Laker had reached his peak and was blessed with pitches that encouraged his ability to give the ball a fiendish twirl. He had an immensely strong spinning finger, strengthened by years of toil, and the ability to propel the ball accurately through the air as well as turn it off the pitch. Anything could happen at the end of a run which appeared so gentle and friendly that venomous turn or cunning deceit came as a most unwelcome surprise.

Everything was right for Jim Laker on those July days in 1956. All the finely-honed skills were at his command, the pitch gave him all the help he needed, and the catches were held as he spun his way into history. Australia started with 48 from McDonald and Burke before Burke became Tony Lock's only victim in the match. From then on it was all Laker. Once the openers had gone no batsman reached double figures. There were four noughts, and there was not a single extra to boost the score beyond 84. Laker finished with 9 for 37.

Compton returns for the Oval Test with a brilliant 94. Here he sweeps a ball from Benaud past Johnson.

Lock, who had wheeled away for 14 overs at the Warwick Road end, took his one wicket for the same number of runs.

In the second innings the openers again offered some resistance, and McDonald survived to gather 89. The rest of the order was again littered with noughts (Mackay and Harvey bagged 'pairs') and, with the last pair together, 170 runs were still needed to make England bat again. Maddocks got his pad between ball and wicket, the umpire's finger went up, and Laker had 10 for 53 off 51.2 overs.

With the Ashes safe and the hysteria of Old Trafford still in the air, it was perhaps inevitable that the final match of the series at The Oval should be something of an anti-climax – especially as the weather wiped out the fourth day and more than 12 hours in all. So far in the rubber the selectors had done pretty well. The men recalled to Test cricket, Washbrook and Sheppard, had performed admirably, and now they looked to Compton, minus his knee-cap, to follow the example. He did not disappoint them. Compton seized the opportunity to contribute a splendid 94 to a distinctly patchy innings. He, May, Sheppard and Richardson accounted for all but nine of England's 247 in a parade that included five noughts. Archer took five wickets and four went to Miller, who went on to score 61 as Australia replied with 202.

In an attempt to manufacture a result, May declared the second innings at 182 for 3, setting Australia 228 to win. A wet wicket had enabled Laker and Lock to share six wickets in the first innings and now the spinners got to work again. Five wickets fell for just 27 before Miller and Benaud saw it out. Laker's seven wickets in the match gave him 46 in the series, and a new record for an England–Australia series.

England did not expect to find conditions anywhere near as favourable on the 1958–59 tour, but such was their variety of talent and their self-confidence that the party embarked in good heart. They were convinced that Laker and Lock were going to torment Australian batsmen again – if a formidable pace attack of Trueman, Statham, Tyson, Loader and Bailey didn't overwhelm them first. Top-class batsmen like May, Cowdrey and Graveney would provide the necessary runs. Furthermore, the Australian selectors were criticised for naming Richie Benaud as captain in preference to the more experienced Harvey.

Everything went according to England's plan right up to the first Test at Brisbane. True, they had already started to experience the injuries which were to dog the tour – Subba Row suffered a broken thumb and would take no part in the series – but the balance looked good.

The first session of play started a series of almost unremitting English disappointments. Australia's opening attack of Meckiff and Davidson, exploiting a green wicket, dismissed England for 134. Australia established a lead of only 52, and no-one had yet scored a half-century. England needed a steadying influence in the second innings, so Bailey was sent in at No. 3. He batted for the next 7½ hours, faced 425 balls, and scored 58. Not a pretty sight, but it did serve a purpose. England scraped together 198, with Graveney (36) the next-highest scorer. A cartoon in an

Right: *May survives an l.b.w. appeal from Lindwall during his partnership with Compton at The Oval.*

Peter Richardson caught behind the wicket by Wally Grout, off Davidson, during England's first innings at Melbourne.

English paper summed up the popular view of Bailey's innings. It showed him lunging forward with massive bat on which were inscribed the statistics of his epic. The caption read: THANK YOU TO TREVOR BAILEY, and then in a smaller setting 'for doing it 12,000 miles from home'. The back-handed gratitude was premature. Australia cruised to eight-wicket victory as Norman O'Neill, playing the first major innings of an exciting Test career, reached a handsome 71 not out.

England won the toss again in Melbourne and, in overcast conditions, May decided to bat. The third over of the match – bowled by Davidson – raised doubts about the wisdom of that decision. Richardson was caught behind by Grout off the first ball; two balls later Watson was bowled; and the next delivery had Graveney lbw, offering no stroke. From a disastrous 7 for 3, however, Bailey and Cowdrey, with 48 and 44, held the fort while the majestic May, apparently playing a different game, composed a delightful century before being beaten for pace by Meckiff, who rifled one beneath an elegantly high backlift.

Such incidents convinced several Englishmen (players and journalists) that there was something distinctly suspect about Ian Meckiff's bowling action. It was not only the delivery but a marked change in pace that attracted suspicion to the well-built, left-arm bowler and, eventually, an Australian umpire, Colin Egar, no-balled him for throwing four times in one over against South Africa in 1963. Right or wrong, Meckiff never played first-class cricket again.

In contrast, Alan Davidson's smoothly-controlled action was above the slightest suspicion. An automatic selection to open for Australia, 'Davo' did not rely on sheer pace for his wickets, though he could certainly make batsmen hurry their strokes. He had the priceless ability to make the ball move late in the air and nip off the seam. At a time of fewer Test matches, Davidson represented his country 44 times and captured 186 wickets –

84 of them in 25 Ashes encounters. He also made 750 of his 1328 Test runs against England, and as a fielder he was equally at home close to the wicket or in the deep.

He had an excellent match at Melbourne in 1958–59, with 6 for 64 in the first innings (Meckiff 3 for 69) as England were put out for 259. The Australians found batting no easier. The exceptional was Harvey who, like May for England, stepped onto an elevated plane. Thanks to his mastery innings of 167, Australia led by 49, while England were grateful to Stathem, whose 7 for 57 reflected a reward often deserved but seldom forthcoming. Yet his efforts were sorely squandered when England were shot out in the second

Davidson juggles with the ball in an attempt to dismiss Graveney in Brisbane.

May falls to Meckiff after scoring a majestic century in the second Test.

innings for a paltry 87 – their lowest score in Australia for 55 years. Meckiff was the chief destroyer with 6 for 38. Australia, needing a mere 39 to go two-up in the series, collected them for the loss of two wickets.

England desperate for a win as they went to Sydney, made only a modest start. Evans was absent with an injured finger, and Roy Swetman, making his Test debut, scored 41 – second only to May's 42 – as England made 219, Benaud 33.4 overs, 5 for 83. In seeking explanations for the reversal of England's fortunes between 1956 and 1958, the Australian captain is worthy of serious attention. Benaud not only brought out the best in players under his command but so enjoyed the captaincy that it brought out his own best form. Though he had done well enough in Test cricket before assuming the captaincy, the appointment had a seemingly dynamic effect on his career. Benaud's secret (though he made no secret of it) was to work hard to maximise the talent he had. Long hours of practice gave him superb control over all the conventional weapons in the leg-spinner's armoury – plus a speciality of his own: the 'flipper', a variation on the top-spinner that hurried the ball onto a batsman.

Benaud had become one of a triumvirate of all-rounders who filled the numbers 6, 7 and 8 berths in the batting order – usually going in between Mackay and Davidson. He scored three Test centuries in a career that brought him 2201 runs,

Cine sequences of cricket history. In the top series Meckiff is bowling the third ball of his only over – his last in Test cricket – during the first Test against South Africa in 1963. His arm bends then straightens up at the top of the arc and in the follow-through. Umpire Egar, at square leg, ruled it a no-ball.
In the bottom sequence, Meckiff's approach is identical. In the third frame his arm bends, but straightens out again for delivery. This time, umpire Egar passed the action as legitimate.

and he became his country's leading wicket-taker with 248. He also held 65 catches, most of them in the gully, where he was quite brilliant. His catch there to dismiss Cowdrey, middling a ball from Mackay, in 1956, is still mentioned with awe at Lord's. He captained Australia in four series and won them all, rescuing the morale of his country's

Ian Meckiff, Australia's controversial fast bowler, in action during the Melbourne Test.

cricket from a trough. He was a positive captain who believed in sensible rather than reckless attacking. His players responded to this progressive mood and Australian cricket, under Benaud, enjoyed a bright renaissance.

When Australia replied in the third Test, Laker and Lock soon got to work, bowling between them 89 overs. Lock finished with 4 for 130 and Laker 59 for 107, but O'Neill hit 77, Davidson 71, and Mackay and Favell each scored fifties to give Australia a lead of 138.

England then sank deeply into trouble at 64 for 3, until Cowdrey joined May in a fourth-wicket stand of 182. This long partnership between two of England's most attractive batsmen was not, however, a feast of strokeplay and delight. It was a slow, rearguard action wherein both put survival against the turning ball before any idea of adventure. By such means, May made 92 and, when England declared at 287 for 7, Cowdrey was undefeated with 100.

Cowdrey, who toured Australia six times, was to score 22 centuries in a distinguished Test career – but few more disciplined than this. He did not have the appearance of an international sportsman, being on the rotund side, but with a bat in his hand he became an artist. From Oxford, where he displayed outstanding promise, he joined Kent and was soon capped by England. Cowdrey's great gift was one of timing, so that an apparently effortless, almost lazy swing of the bat would send the ball racing towards the boundary. Despite his size, Cowdrey was light on his toes and used his feet delightfully when batting. He also had an excellent sense of balance which, combined with fast reflexes and safe hands, made him an excellent first slip. In 114 Tests he took 120 catches.

His intellect moved as fleetly as his physique, and more than one naive reporter filed outrageous copy after covering Cowdrey's late arrival in Australia on a sixth and final trip. Cowdrey, at 42, was flown out as a reinforcement to face the all-conquering Lillee and Thomson. Asked how he felt about facing the blistering pace attack, a thoughtful Colin replied: 'Well, I coped with Gregory and McDonald without too much trouble . . .' Later, when he actually went out to face the *successors* of Gregory and McDonald, he went up to a nonplussed Thomson, 18 years his junior, and said, 'How do you do. My name's Cowdrey, I don't think we've met.'

Richie Benaud joined Australia's ranks purely as a leg-spinner.

Alan Davidson: Eighty-four wickets in Anglo-Australian Tests.

Cowdrey's hundred at Sydney in 1959 took 362 minutes, and was the slowest in Anglo–Australian Tests until Bob Woolmer, his successor in the Kent side, took 34 minutes longer in 1975. May's declaration set Australia a target of 150 on a pitch taking appreciable turn. When Laker took two cheap wickets Benaud gave orders that there should be no mad scramble for runs, and Australia were content with a draw.

England now had to stake all on the last two Tests. In the hope of forcing a result, May sent Australia in at Adelaide – despite the fact that conditions appeared to favour the batsmen. Statham all but bowled McDonald with the first ball of the match – and that was typical of the way fate was to taunt England. Laker had withdrawn with a painful spinning finger, Evans fractured a finger on the first day, and Graveney had to keep wicket. England then ran up against an unhappy umpire.

Gordon Rorke – a questionable action, but he took 3 for 23 in Adelaide.

A strong appeal for a catch against Burke was turned down; so was another against Mackay, who had even started to walk. When Mr McInnes then changed his mind about a run-out, the Englishmen were speechless. McDonald, meanwhile, sublimely unaffected by his first-ball escape and a pulled leg muscle, was on his way to a splendid 170 and Australia to 476.

England's response fell foul of Benaud (5 for 91) and a newcomer to the Australian side, Gordon Rorke, who took 3 for 23. Rorke's action, like that of Meckiff, aroused suspicions, and his enormous 'drag' took him way past the popping crease. Cowdrey scored 84, but England had to follow on 236 behind, and were then bowled out for 270 (Benaud 4 for 82). Australia won by 10 wickets, and after 5½ years the Ashes were back in their keeping.

England had so far won nothing but the toss, and in Melbourne they even lost that. The pitch was well-grassed, the atmosphere humid, and England, having been sent in, were bowled out for 205. Benaud grabbed his quota of 4 for 43. McDonald scored his second successive century for Australia, and although the sixth wicket fell when Australia were only four ahead, Benaud and Grout put on 115 for the seventh, and the lead was 146. When England replied, Bailey, for the second time in the match and in his last Test, fell to Lindwall without a run on the board. Lindwall went on to break Grimmett's Australian record of 216 Test wickets and, despite the effort of Graveney (54) and Cowdrey (46), England managed to leave Australia only 69 to get. Australia's 4-nil triumph was complete. Once more the wheel had turned full circle.

Ted Dexter in some trouble against Burke in the Sydney Test. His partner Cowdrey went on to make a century.

12

LORD TED

THE USUAL sense of continuity from one Test series to the next was weakened between 1959 and 1961 by the withdrawal of familiar faces from both countries. For the first Test at Edgbaston in 1961, Australia fielded seven men who had appeared in the last Test of the 1958–59 series. For England only Cowdrey, Trueman and Dexter made the transition. May was still recovering from the illness contracted in West Indies and Cowdrey was in charge of the England team. Laker and Lock were no longer spinning spells; Illingworth and Allen had replaced them. Pullar and Subba Row opened the innings, Barrington and M. J. K. Smith led the middle-order brigade, and John Murray made his Test debut as wicket-keeper.

England were making steady progress until Mackay ripped through the middle of the innings. Three catches in the space of four balls accounted for Barrington, Smith and Subba Row. Mackay finished with 4 for 57 and England were bundled out for 195. The pitch was blameless, as Australia proved by cruising to 516 for 9. Wally Grout was the only man to score less than 20. Some went considerably further: Harvey hit a characteristic century, O'Neill 82, Simpson 76, Mackay 64, and Lawry 57.

England fought back magnificently for the draw that was their only hope. Dexter and Subba Row dug in for the second wicket, each scoring a century as England pressed on to end the match 401 for 4.

Ted Dexter, in his most imperious mood, reached a delightful 180. All the bowlers were treated with the same lofty disdain that made Dexter's nickname 'Lord Ted' so appropriate. Tall and majestic, Dexter was a spectacularly good batsman who hit the ball very hard with a full flow of the bat, and in some respects parallels could be drawn between Dexter and Keith Miller. Both were so good at the game that they needed a challenge to hold their attention. If Dexter were threatened by conditions or opposition he would rise to the occasion and touch sheer brilliance. If the mood did not take him, his concentration could waver. It was tight as a drum at Edgbaston.

England won the toss at Lord's for the 12th successive time in Tests and the ninth time in 10

Ken Mackay, with 4 for 57, rips a hole in England's first innings at Edgbaston.

The S.S. Himalaya docks again and another talented batch of Australians arrive. Left to right: B. C. Booth, L. F. Kline, R. B. Simpson, N. C. O'Neill, F. M. Misson, R. A. Gaunt, I. W. Quick, A. T. W. Grout, G. D. McKenzie, B. N. Jarman, W. M. Lawry.

matches against Australia. It did them little good, for Davidson produced a blistering 5 for 52. England's best performance came from Subba Row – a modest 48 – and they were all out for 206. Though Statham dismissed McDonald early – his 200th Test wicket – Bill Lawry, in his second Test innings, scored a stubborn 130, and Australia, led by Harvey in Benaud's absence with a shoulder injury, were on the way to a substantial total. Mackay, at No. 8, made 54, and the last two wickets added 102 runs.

Australia introduced another debutant in this match. Graham McKenzie, only 19, was the youngest member of the touring party, yet in the second innings he bowled like an old master to take 5 for 37 off 29 overs. 'Garth' (after a comic-strip character) gains a special place among Australia's pacemen as, for much of his career, he carried the Australian attack on his own shoulders. They were impressively broad shoulders and, furthermore, he knew how to utilise every sinew and muscle in his bowling action. McKenzie was not content to bowl sideways on, but, in his delivery stride, showed some of his back to the batsman. This leverage allowed him to bowl at great speed, yet so smooth was his action that the pace was deceptive.

McKenzie showed his class when the pitches were hard and fast. He could extract rather more bounce than most, and this, combined with a late away-swing, guaranteed the batsmen a torrid time. The records for 100, 150 and 200 Test wickets by an Australian in terms of the age at which they were achieved all fell to McKenzie, and he ended with 246 – just two behind Benaud's Australian record. Grout aided McKenzie at Lord's by catching three for him, bringing up his personal 100 catches as he totalled eight in the match.

Trueman and Statham were in great form when Australia batted for the second time, needing only 69 to win. The pacemen dismissed four batsmen with only 19 on the board and, when the fifth wicket fell, 11 were still required. The burly Burge, though, calmly knocked them off to end England's run of 18 Tests without defeat and to inflict the first failure at home since the 1956 Lord's Test.

At Leeds, Benaud called correctly and on what looked to be a straightforward batting pitch, and took first use of it. Fred Trueman, however, knew a thing or two about the Headingley track. By now he was not just a tearaway fast bowler but, reducing his pace, could bowl penetrative off-cutters. Derbyshire's Les Jackson, clearly one of the best of his type in the country, was recalled to play his second Test 12 years after his first. He took 2 for 57 in the first innings, Trueman 5 for 58, and the last eight Australian wickets fell for 50 after Harvey's defiant 73. Davidson 5 for 63 and McKenzie 3 for 64 ensured that England's first innings did not get out of hand, but Cowdrey played soundly for 93 and, supported by Pullar (53), helped England to a lead of 62.

Fred Trueman – a match-winning spell of 6 for 30 at Headingley.

Graham 'Garth' McKenzie – a devastating debut at Lord's with 5 for 37.

In the second innings, Trueman did even better. Australia at one stage were 99 for 2. Then came dramatic collapse. Only 21 runs were added for the loss of the remaining eight wickets, and Trueman took five of them without conceding a run in a match-winning spell of 6 for 30. England, with an eight-wicket win, squared the rubber.

Lawry proved to be a most obstinate tenant in the fourth Test, at Old Trafford, and was top scorer with 74 as Statham (5 for 53) worked his way through the Australian ranks. England, facing a modest 190, lost a quick wicket, but others built what appeared to be an impregnable lead.

May made 95, Barrington 78, and opener Pullar 63. Even Allen, batting at eight, contributed 42 before Simpson's leg-breaks accounted for the last four wickets at a cost of two runs.

The two second innings could have belonged to another match. England's lead of 177 was erased shortly after the fall of the second wicket. Lawry refused to be evicted until he had scored a century. Half-centuries came from Simpson, O'Neill and Davidson who, in scoring an undefeated 77, hit off-spinner David Allen – on a turning wicket – for 20 in an over. This prompted May to concentrate on a pace attack – which taxed neither Davidson nor McKenzie, who helped him to add 98 for the last wicket. That took Australia to 432 and a testing lead of 255. Though the pitch was taking spin, the target seemed well within England's compass – especially as they reached 150 for 1, with Subba Row and Dexter going well. At that point, Benaud decided to exploit the footmarks by bowling his

Alan Davidson hits David Allen for six – and takes twenty off the over – on the way to an undefeated 77.

The last shot of an all-too-short Test career. Raman Subba Row, caught and bowled Benaud for 137.

leg-breaks from around the wicket. Whether defiant gesture or inspired strategy, this final ploy transformed impending defeat into exciting victory. Dexter was caught behind, Subba Row was bowled, and so was May – round his legs while attempting a sweep. Brian Close played the game he knew best, but holed out to O'Neill. Murray and Allen were taken in the slips by Simpson, and panic overtook planning. England fell under Benaud's spell of 5 for 12 in 4.1 overs, and fainted away – all out 201. If the 1956 Old Trafford Test had been Laker's match, that of 1961 was certainly Benaud's. Despite an inflamed shoulder tendon that was to foreshorten his bowling career, he had taken his side to an improbable 54-run victory.

Though Australia thereby retained the Ashes, the series could still be squared when the sides went to The Oval, but the rain which had dogged the summer damaged the fifth Test beyond redemption. May (71) and Barrington (53) propped up an England innings of 256, and after early setbacks a stand of 123 between O'Neill (117) and Burge (181) saw Australia power on to 494. Allen, Lock and Flavell each suffered an unhappy 'bowler's century'.

Despite the rain-shortened third and fourth days, England still needed some disciplined batting. It was provided by Raman Subba Row, who, with 137, ended his Ashes career as he had begun it, with a fine century. Occupying the crease for 460 minutes, his was a highly creditable performance. He was well supported by Barrington's 83 and, though Mackay bowled 68 overs to take 5 for 121, and Benaud (3 for 113) wheeled away for 51 overs, England reached 370 for 8 – a lead of 132 – to close a series of notable performances. Two in particular are worth mentioning for they are easily overlooked in scanning the bare statistics. Keeping wicket for England, Murray set a new record for a home series by making 18 dismissals, and his counterpart, Grout, claimed 21 for a new Anglo–Australian record.

The next Anglo–Australian encounter, in 1962–63, fell somewhat short of the long and glorious Ashes tradition. The main reason was that the batting of both sides was powerful enough to blunt the opposing attack. Benaud was

Left: *England wicketkeeper Alan Smith catches Bill Lawry for five off Fred Trueman, during the first day's play at Brisbane.*

Dexter, on the way to 99, hit Benaud to the boundary during England's second innings.

still directing the affairs of Australia, Dexter had inherited the England captaincy from May, and if any pair seemed likely to produce a memorable series these were the two. Yet the fire was seldom ignited.

The first Test, at Brisbane, illustrated perfectly the batting strength of the two teams. There was one century, a 99, a 98, and, in all, 14 fifties, which equalled the Anglo–Australian record set at Headingley in 1948. The century came from Brian Booth in Australia's 404, which also provided the first batch of fifties – from Simpson, Mackay and Benaud. Though Dexter, Barrington and Parfitt returned the compliment, Benaud bowled 42 overs to capture 6 for 115 and England trailed by 15.

Lawry (98) continued the run-festival and, with Simpson (71), shared an opening stand of 136. O'Neill and Harvey went past the half-century and Burge was 47 when Benaud declared, leaving England 378 to win at marginally over a run a minute. They began in fine style, Pullar

Garth McKenzie brilliantly caught and bowled by Barry Knight for 4 during Australia's first innings at Brisbane.

(56) and Sheppard (53) putting on 114. Dexter joined in with a dashing 99 but, as wickets began to fall, up went the shutters and, at the end, England, four wickets in hand, were still 100 short.

The runs flowed freely again at Melbourne where, though England ground away with six bowlers, Australia knocked up 316. Despite the loss of both openers for 19, England edged 15 runs into the lead, thanks largely to a third-wicket stand of 175 between Dexter (93) and Cowdrey, who reached 113 to confirm his particular liking for the Melbourne ground. By way of balance, Davidson took 6 for 75 and, in the second Australian innings, Booth scored a century and Trueman took five wickets. It was typical of Booth to score runs when Australia needed them most. Lawry, with 57, was the only other batsman to exceed 17 and England's victory target was a modest 234. Pullar was lost early, but on the last day only two wickets fell – both to run-outs. Sheppard and Dexter made match-winning contributions to a well-paced innings, Sheppard scoring 113 and adding 104 runs with Cowdrey (58 not out) after a stirring partnership of 124 with Dexter.

England's victory in Melbourne was immediately counter-balanced by an Australian success in Sydney. Simpson took 5 for 57 and Davidson 4 for 54 as England lumbered to a first-innings 279. Simpson (91) also shone with the bat before becoming one of Fred Titmus's seven victims. At this stage Titmus was not a prodigious spinner of the ball, but batsmen obligingly hit across the line and perished. A lead of 40, engineered by Barry Shepherd (71 not out), did not look decisive until England, batting again, walked into one of Davidson's most devastating spells. When he took the last of five wickets he was still in only his 11th over and had conceded only 25 runs. The only real English defiance came from an unexpected source. John Murray injured his shoulder as he dived to dismiss Lawry off Coldwell, and Parfitt had taken over the gloves. Now, partly immobilised by the injury, Murray batted for 100 minutes for three runs. In the event, this time-consuming hindrance was to no avail: Australia scored the 65 runs to level the series.

Neil Harvey joined in the Brisbane run-festival but, with this skyed shot off Dexter, departed – caught Statham for 57.

Ted Dexter's party embarks from London Airport for the 1962–63 tour. From the top: F. S. Trueman, E. R. Dexter, F. J. Titmus, L. J. Coldwell, D. A. Allen, J. D. F. Larter, K. F. Barrington, B. R. Knight, J. T. Murray, A. C. Smith, M. C. Cowdrey, R. Illingworth, T. W. Graveney, D. S. Sheppard, A. V. Bedser (assistant manager).

At Adelaide neither captain was going to concede an inch and, after losing two quick wickets, Australia ground on to a total of 393. Harvey made 154, having been dropped for the second Test in succession by Sheppard, and shared a partnership of 194 with O'Neill (100). In reply, England showed vast improvement. Barrington and Dexter made sixties, and Titmus an undefeated 59. Even Trueman, at No. 10, weighed in with 38 as they came within 62 of the Australian total. Second time around Australia pressed on to a lead of 355. Thoughts of a declaration lapsed with Davidson out of the attack (a torn hamstring), and England were allowed only two sessions of play to attempt a win. Having lost the openers for four runs, they settled for a draw, though Ken Barrington embarked on an uncharacteristically swift 132, reaching his century with a six.

As a good professional, Barrington came to realise that he scored more runs when he tempered his enthusiasm for the spectacular. He eliminated shots that offered undue risk and began to bat with all the determination characterised by his jutting jaw. So often he carried the full weight of England's batting, concentrating for hours on end. In all, Barrington scored 20 centuries for England, and in 82 Tests averaged 58.67 to illustrate an outstanding consistency.

In the final Test, at Sydney, Barrington scored

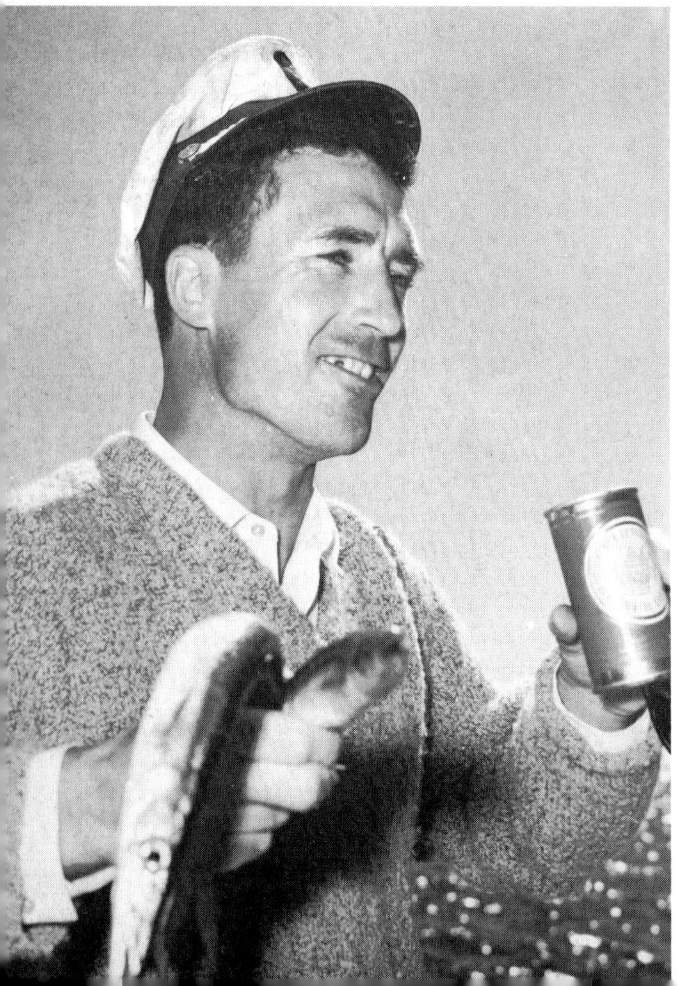

Above: *Harvey pulls Barrington during an innings of 64 at Sydney, Parfitt the substitute wicketkeeper.*

Left: *Fred Titmus relaxes (Fishing and Fosters) between the First and Second Tests.*

another century as England made 321 at a leisurely pace. Australia were no quicker. Burge ground out a century, Titmus took five wickets, and the lead of 28 seemed hardly worth the effort. The match progressed at a funereal pace as Barrington, back in bottom gear, came within six runs of his third successive century. England declared at length, leaving Australia to score 241 runs in as many minutes. It was by no means an unreasonable challenge, but the pitch was taking spin and Allen got to work to reduce the home side to 70 for 4. That, as far as Benaud's men were concerned, was that, and reflecting the tenor of the series; the shutters went up again.

When the Australians next came to England, in 1964, there were big changes. Benaud, Davidson and Mackay were gone, and the captaincy had passed to Bobby Simpson. First impressions were that here was a weak Australian side. In fact, though Simpson led the team in a different style, he was no less effective. And, if this were not the

Above: *Aerial view of the Adelaide Oval during the fourth Test, 1962–63.*

Right: *Ken Barrington hits a six to reach his century during the second innings at Adelaide.*

strongest side to leave Australian shores, they were not to encounter a particularly formidable English team.

England went into the Trent Bridge Test with an experimental opening partnership which was to be upset by injury. Geoffrey Boycott, making his debut, scored a creditable 48, but broke a finger while fielding and missed the second innings. Dexter then promoted himself to open, and the unlikely number two on both occasions was Titmus, who shared in partnerships of 38 and 90. During the first innings he was the beneficiary of an outstanding piece of sportsmanship. Boycott tucked a Hawke delivery away towards mid-on and went for a single. As Titmus responded, the bowler went for the ball and bundled over the batsman, still yards from safety. Corling sent in the return to Grout, who, realising that Hawke had been largely to blame for the collision, refused to remove the bails. Cricket was meant to be played in this spirit, and it was refreshing to

Left: *Fast bowling buddies Fred Trueman (in sun-hat) and Brian Statham share a moment of joy in the Adelaide Test.*

see such sporting goodwill. As a contest, the match was marred by the weather. Only the fourth day was free from interruption, and the third was completely lost.

England declared at 216 for 8, and Australia's reply – 168 – was barely adequate. England's second declaration left Australia to make 242 in 3¼ hours. They had made 40 when rain terminated a damp and dismal match.

If Nottingham felt hard done by the weather, compared with the climate's major innings at Lord's, Trent Bridge had merely given the rain a gentle net. Norman Gifford, the Worcestershire left-arm spinner, making his debut, despaired of ever setting foot on a Test match field. No play was possible on the first day or the second, but, when the match eventually started, England put Australia in and a Saturday crowd enjoyed the bloodcurdling spectacle of Trueman (5 for 48) bowling them out for 176. England's batsmen then played largely supporting roles as John Edrich of Surrey made an excellent 120 in his first Ashes Test. Only two other batsmen in the match reached fifty and, when rain finally triumphed after lunch on the final day, Australia led by 98 with four wickets down.

One of cricket's perpetual fascinations is the way a single action can determine the result of a match just as surely as a goal in soccer, a try in rugby, or a long golf putt sunk. At Headingley in 1964 not only the third Test but the whole series hinged on one decision by Dexter. He had done his bit by scoring 66. So, too, had wicketkeeper Parks, who reached 68 before falling to Hawke (5 for 75). England were out for 268 and on a pitch offering assistance to the spinners, Australia were on the rack at 178 for 7. Titmus and Gifford were causing all sorts of problems and, after Lawry was run out for 78, only Peter Burge stood between a rout and respectability. He was 38 when Dexter summoned Trueman and Flavell to blast out the tail with the new ball. That was the signal for Burge to cut loose and, aided by Hawke and Grout, who each made 37, he rattled up a glorious 160. For seven overs the new ball was dispatched

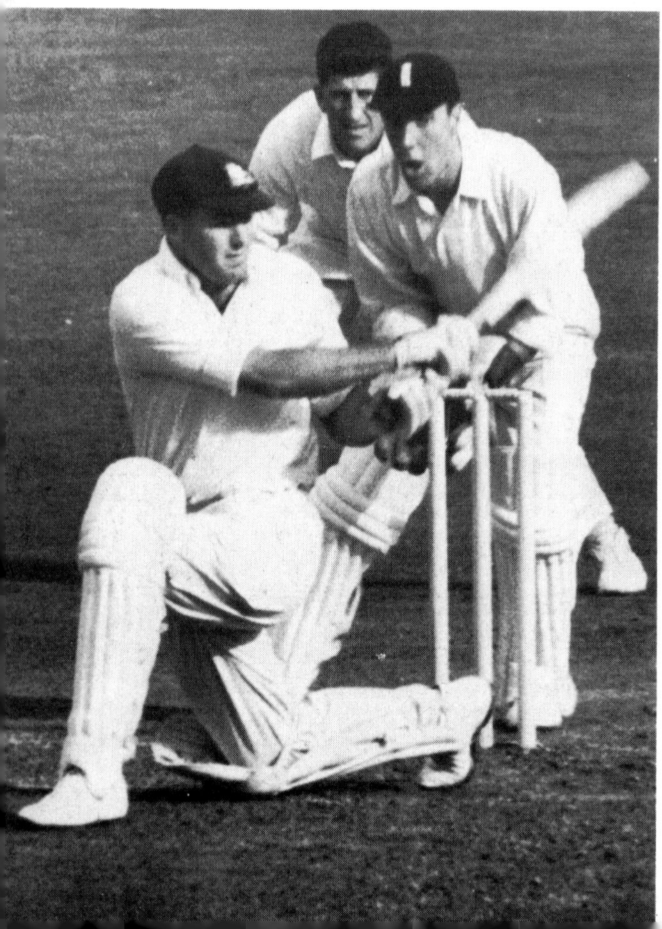

Left: *Peter Burge, who batted 5½ hours for his century in the last Test.*

at a rate of six an over, and when the entertainment was finally concluded, 389 were on the board.

England then scored 229 (Barrington 85) and Australia needed 109 to win. Titmus bowled 27 overs of spin and took 2 for 25, but a target of 109 was too good to miss, and Australia marched to a seven-wicket victory.

Having taken the lead, Australia went to Old Trafford with an almost prescient confidence. They won the toss and batted . . . and went on batting! Lawry and Simpson were the chief generators of a massive 656 for 8 declared. Lawry

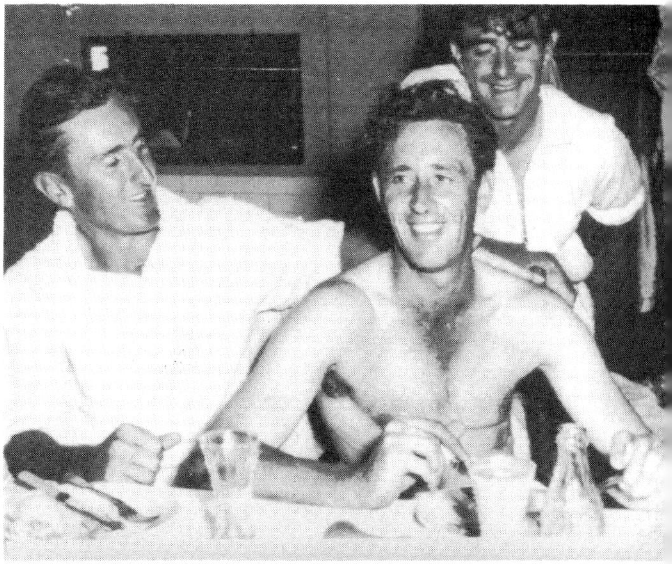

Right: *Dexter and Trueman congratulate Statham on passing Alec Bedser's all-Test record of 236 wickets during the Adelaide match.*

Below: *Brian Booth misses a chance from Boycott, off Neil Hawke, at Trent Bridge.*

Booth – an almost incidental 98 at Old Trafford.

scored 106 and Simpson 311, after which Booth's 98 seemed almost incidental. Bobby Simpson's innings was a particular triumph. Though he had scored 15 fifties in 51 Test innings (average 36), this innings of 311 was his first of three figures. He had got the taste when, in the season preceding the tour, he hit 359 for New South Wales against Queensland. Furthermore, his Old Trafford stand with Lawry was to prove prophetic for, with the same partner, he was soon to put on 382 against West Indies – an opening record for Australia.

Simpson could play all the strokes, but was at pains to execute them without risk, and relied on superb footwork to get into position. He made his first-class debut at the tender age of 16 and worked hard to develop into one of Australia's finest batsmen – as well as arguably cricket's greatest slip fielder. Such batting and fielding ability tended to overshadow the fact that Simpson was also a useful leg-break bowler who claimed 71 Test wickets – albeit somewhat expensively. As a captain he always commanded respect, yet there were times when his leadership mirrored his batting. Safety was the first rule and there was sometimes a lack of imagination and tactical inspiration.

Though Simpson's partnerships with Bill Lawry were prolific, these two never quite caught the public imagination. Lawry lacked the glamour of the great strokemakers. In a distinguished Test career he maintained an average of 47.15 (5234 runs) over 67 matches. Despite a short backlift, Lawry timed his drives well and hooked savagely, yet his prime quality was an

Right: *Bobby Simpson, on his way to a maiden Test century in Manchester, gets a lucky four over the slips off John Price. Keeper Parks, Fred Rumsey and Ken Barrington react despairingly.*

Below: *Simpson, in more confident mood, drives Titmus as he presses on to a magnificent 311.*

Below right: *The 300 milestone – Simpson raises his bat after hitting Price to the boundary.*

1 2 3 4 5 6 7 8 9 10 11 S
TOTAL
Nº 3 201 Nº 2
88
WICKETS 1
LAST PLAYER 106
5 BOWLERS 8
LAST WICKET FELL AT
201
CAUGHT
9 9 OVERS SINCE NEW BALL TAKEN
VISITORS
HOME

Left: *Australia's record-breaking 201 for 1 at Old Trafford, displayed on the scoreboard immediately after Lawry was run out for 106.*

incredible concentration. Time after time he held together a shaky innings and turned potential defeat into a match-winning situation.

England had no option but to go for a matching total at Manchester in '64, and Barrington's 256, incorporating a third-wicket stand of 246 with Dexter (174), took them to 611. Just as Simpson had chosen this match to make his maiden Test century, so Barrington scored his first in England – after nine overseas. Australian off-spinner Tom Veivers got among the records by bowling 95.1 overs during the England innings, 51 of them in a single spell.

In many ways the fifth Test was reminiscent of its predecessors. Personal milestones came and went; the rain came and determined the result. England blundered into seamer Neil Hawke, who took 6 for 47. In a total of 182, Barrington was top scorer with 47, which took him past his 4000 runs in Tests. Australia replied with 379, and four of their wickets fell to Fred Trueman, who thereby went through the tough 300 Test-wicket barrier. He had to work hard for the honour, and conceded 80 runs before claiming a victim. Then, before lunch on the third day, two wickets fell to consecutive balls. Thereafter, Hawke and Veivers batted sensibly against a strange attack. Instead of calling on John Price as Trueman's new-ball partner, Dexter preferred the medium-pace Cartwright. So, too, did the Australian batsmen!

Eventually, however, Hawke edged a ball from Trueman to Cowdrey at slip, and the 300th Test wicket was his.

England's batting showed much more resolution in the second innings. Boycott scored his first Test century, and Cowdrey was 93 at the end of the fourth day. If Lawry and Simpson had shown single-minded dedication for Australia, then, in Geoff Boycott, England had found the perfect answer. Perhaps it was Boycott's almost fanatical pursuit of the ultimate in batsmanship that led to his complexity of character and its subsequent problems. It is inarguable that Boycott has been an outstanding opening batsman for England. As a product of the age in which he reached Test status, Boycott realised that the professional batsman's most valued possession was his wicket. Never would he give it away – it had to be taken from him. And that philosophy, over the years, had served him, and England, splendidly.

Tom Veivers among the records with 95.1 overs at The Oval – 51 in a single spell!

In scoring his undefeated 93 at The Oval Cowdrey passed 5000 runs in Tests, and, at the close, England were 381 for 4. There the game and the series ended, the final day being washed out. Thus this damp postscript concluded a rubber of overall disappointment. And yet the Australians had kept their powder – and the Ashes – dry. Not a bad achievement for a side of 'no-hopers'!

13

NEW FACES

M.J.K. SMITH, an Oxford and England rugby cap, reached another pinnacle in a fine sporting career when he was appointed captain of the MCC team to tour Australia in 1965–66. As a batsman, the tall bespectacled Smith was somewhat susceptible to the fast yorker early in his innings (who isn't?), but, once set, he was both stylish and prolific. Finding the leg-side gaps with unerring accuracy while retaining the essentials of good batting. As captain of the touring party he acted as a splendid ambassador and accomplished the none-too-easy task of satisfying the Australian Press by his approachable and friendly manner.

The saga of the Ashes needed a fillip, and while the strength still lay with the batsmen, the overall quality of play and purpose in this series was undoubtedly raised. On a damp Brisbane day, Lawry opened the batting with Ian Redpath. David Brown duly launched the England attack, and in his first over he joined wicketkeeper Parks and the close field in a confident claim that Lawry had snicked the ball. The appeal was rejected and nearly seven playing hours elapsed before Lawry edged a ball from Higgs, Parks again held it aloft, and the Australian opener was given out – for 166!

By now, the match was into the third scheduled day, for the first day's play was restricted to two hours and the second washed out.

Acting captain Booth's dismissal had left Australia swaying at 125 for 4, but his place at the crease was filled by the 19-year-old Doug Walters, who, in his first Test, shared a stand of 187 with Lawry and went on to make a brilliant 155.

England viewed an Australian total of 443 for 6 with some dismay. Their batting had already been weakened by an injury to Cowdrey, and Eric Russell, his replacement, came into the match with a fractured thumb. Worse, while fielding Russell split his right hand and eventually came in to bat not as an opener but at No. 11. By this time England needed every run they could muster, for leg-spinner Philpott had been among them with 5 for 90. Russell's brave gesture did not prevent them following on 163 behind. By now, there was little time left and Australia's hopes foundered on Boycott's rock-like bat as he made an unbeaten 63.

Injuries forced England changes for the second Test at Melbourne, where Higgs and Brown gave way to Jeff Jones and Barry Knight. The new pace combination did well in claiming seven wickets, but there was plenty of run-scoring. Simpson came back with 59 and Lawry, solid as ever, made 88. Cowper joined the unhappy band who have been dismissed on 99, and Australia reached a comfortable 358. England, however, had a batting line-up packed with runmaking potential. Knight was a genuine all-rounder, and so was Titmus, at nine. Titmus was undefeated with 56, and none of the first seven batsmen scored fewer than 41.

Edrich compiled a five-hour century, Cowdrey scored his usual Melbourne hundred, and England (558) gained a lead of exactly 200.

Australia lost four wickets in clearing the deficit, and could easily have been in trouble. Parks, off the field for part of the fourth day, returned to make a mistake that might have cost England the series. Burge, facing the leg-spin of Barber, was well out of his ground when Parks failed to accept a simple stumping chance. In company with Walters (115), Burge went on to score 120 and, once again, the match was drawn.

At this point in his career Doug Walters must have been wondering what was so allegedly difficult about international cricket. He had gone to the wicket three times and twice come back with a century. Now it was his turn to attract the 'new Bradman' accolade his fellow-Australians were so eager to hand out. Walters always seemed to see the ball early and, when in form, there was a sureness and excitement about his strokes which suggested he was going to be something out of the ordinary. But in England, where the pitch encouraged movement off the seam, his technique was less than secure and he was likely to offer only a brief view of his outstanding ability. He was also suspect against the bouncer – ducking under the ball but leaving his bat aloft like a periscope. In 74 Tests, Walters compiled 15 centuries, and his 5357 runs averaged out at 48.26. As a bowler, he developed the happy knack of coming on to make a vital breakthrough.

In Melbourne, the partnership between Burge and Walters raised 198, and, when Australia were finally dismissed for 426, time had almost elapsed. It was the tenth match in the Ashes series since England's last victory – at Melbourne on the 1962–63 tour. However, the England party had only three days to dwell upon this sobering fact before the start of the third Test in Sydney. Here, they got away to a tremendous start. Openers Boycott and Barber put on 234. Boycott brought a slightly more adventurous spirit on this tour and found an opening partner who needed no encouragement to take the attack to the Australians. Bob Barber, a former Lancashire captain, had now settled in with Warwickshire as a fast-scoring opening bat. The left-hander was ideally suited to the role, for he was one of the few who could refute the saying that nobody likes fast bowling but some show it less than others. Barber relished the challenge, and was capable of destroying an attack of the highest standard. Indeed, there was not much wrong with an Australian attack that included McKenzie and Hawke, but, in Barber and Boycott, they met their match on January 7, 1966. Boycott made 84, but Barber savaged the bowling to reach 185 – his highest score in first-class cricket. Edrich followed with his second successive century, and 303 were on the board before the second wicket fell. The middle order collapsed to Hawke (7 for 105) and

Bob Cowper – failed by one run to score a century in Melbourne.

Grout, who held five catches. Allen, however, 50 not out, topped up the innings to 488.

Perhaps the dour Lawry was bemused by the blitz of Boycott and Barber, for he departed before a run had been scored in the Australian innings. He was one of Parks's five victims, and Brown, back after injury, took 5 for 63, including three in the first over of the second new ball. That collapse left Australia at 221 and Smith had no hesitation in enforcing the follow-on. The introduction of spin saw the innings crumble. Titmus and Allen took four wickets each, and Australia, all out 174, were crushed by an innings.

Cricket can be the cruellest of games for dash-

Grout dismisses Mike Smith with a brilliant diving catch in Sydney.

ing high hopes and reversing fortunes. Such was the case in the fourth Test, at Adelaide, where Mike Smith won the toss again. The partnership that had raised 234 in Sydney now managed only seven as McKenzie embarked on a 6 for 48 assault. It was a pretty fair return for a man who should have lost his place in the side. Having taken 0 for 113 in Sydney, 'Big Garth' was dropped for Adelaide, but when his replacement, Peter Allan, went sick, the selectors gave him another chance. They had reason to smile as England were all out for 241.

The smiles broadened as Lawry and Simpson took revenge for Boycott and Barber's effort in Sydney, putting on 244 – Lawry made 119, Simpson 225 – to rewrite the record books. Although Jeff Jones took six wickets he was one of four England bowlers to concede over 100 runs as Australia reached 516. England needed 275 to make Australia bat again, but Hawke, with 5 for 54, sent them crashing nine runs short. There was some personal satisfaction for Ken Barrington, who added a century to his 60 of the first innings.

In the fifth Test, at Melbourne, England batted first and proceeded solidly to 485 for 9 declared. The highlight of the innings was a century from Barrington, who completed his second successive three-figure score in 2½ hours by hoisting a six over long-on – as Edrich had done in Sydney. Edrich (85) and Parks (89) also contributed their runs briskly – in stark contrast to what was to

Above: *Neil Hawke with Wally Grout, who took four catches in succession off Hawke in Sydney.*

Below: *Cowper is congratulated by Bradman after reaching the first triple-century scored by an Australian in a home series.*

Bill Lawry, Australia's captain and opening bat on the 1968 tour.

come. Lawry scored a century, as he had in Adelaide, and, with Bob Cowper, shared a third-wicket stand of 212. Cowper batted 12 hours and seven minutes to record Australia's longest-ever first-class innings, and his 307 was the first Australian triple-century in a home Test.

Cowper, a left-hander, had little in common with that other Australian triple-centurymaker, Don Bradman. Certainly, nobody downed tools and flocked to a cricket ground simply because Cowper had gone to the crease. Even so, he was a wholehearted player who served Australia well. He averaged 46.84 in 27 Test matches (2061 runs) and hit five centuries.

Cowper's Melbourne marathon shut England out of the series. In their second, curtailed, innings the tourists had moved just 11 runs in front, for the loss of three wickets, when time ran out. The cricket of the '65–66 series seldom reached fever-pitch, but England had proved popular, and interest had been sustained by individual performances and oustanding partnerships. More often than not England offered the more positive approach . . . but the Ashes were safe in Australia.

Bill Lawry led the 1968 tourists against Cowdrey's England, and won the toss for the first Test at Old Trafford, choosing to bat on a pitch as amenable to spin as it had been in 1956. The major difference was that neither side contained a slow bowler of Laker's stature. England's spin attack rested in the hands of 21-year-old Pat Pocock and the less specialised Bob Barber. In Australia's first innings Barber's 11 overs cost 56 runs, though he claimed the wickets of Lawry and Walters, both of whom scored 81. Pocock's 25 overs conceded 77 runs for no wicket as Lawry, in particular, knocked him off a length. Australia's 357, compared with England's 165 in reply, became substantial.

Australia's second-innings batsmen, cushioned by the big lead, could afford to take a more phlegmatic view of the turning ball. And turn it did, as Pocock's 6 for 79 testified, Walters passing 80 again. There was plenty of time for England to score the 413 runs required or, as things transpired, to get themselves bowled out. In fact they made only 253 – despite a courageous 87 not out from Basil D'Oliveira.

The English selectors followed up with an incomprehensible move for the second Test at Lord's. Two of the more successful members of the Manchester team were dropped. D'Oliveira was out and did not appear again until the final encounter at The Oval – and then only as a late replacement. Pocock also disappeared. For this 200th meeting between the two countries the sounder batting of D'Oliveira was sacrificed for the quicker and more penetrative bowling of Barry Knight. Pocock's off-breaks were replaced by the left-arm spin of Derek Underwood. The other change was expected, and Dennis Amiss, who had bagged a 'pair' at Old Trafford, gave way to Colin Milburn. When the Northamptonshire heavyweight made his entry, England had lost Edrich and were 10 for 1. Millburn had scored 16 by lunch, at which time Lord's was hit by a hailstorm which ended play for the day. The white blanket eventually receded and play restarted on a treacherous pitch. It was a suitable

Right: *Basil D'Oliveira – a courageous and undefeated 87 at Old Trafford.*

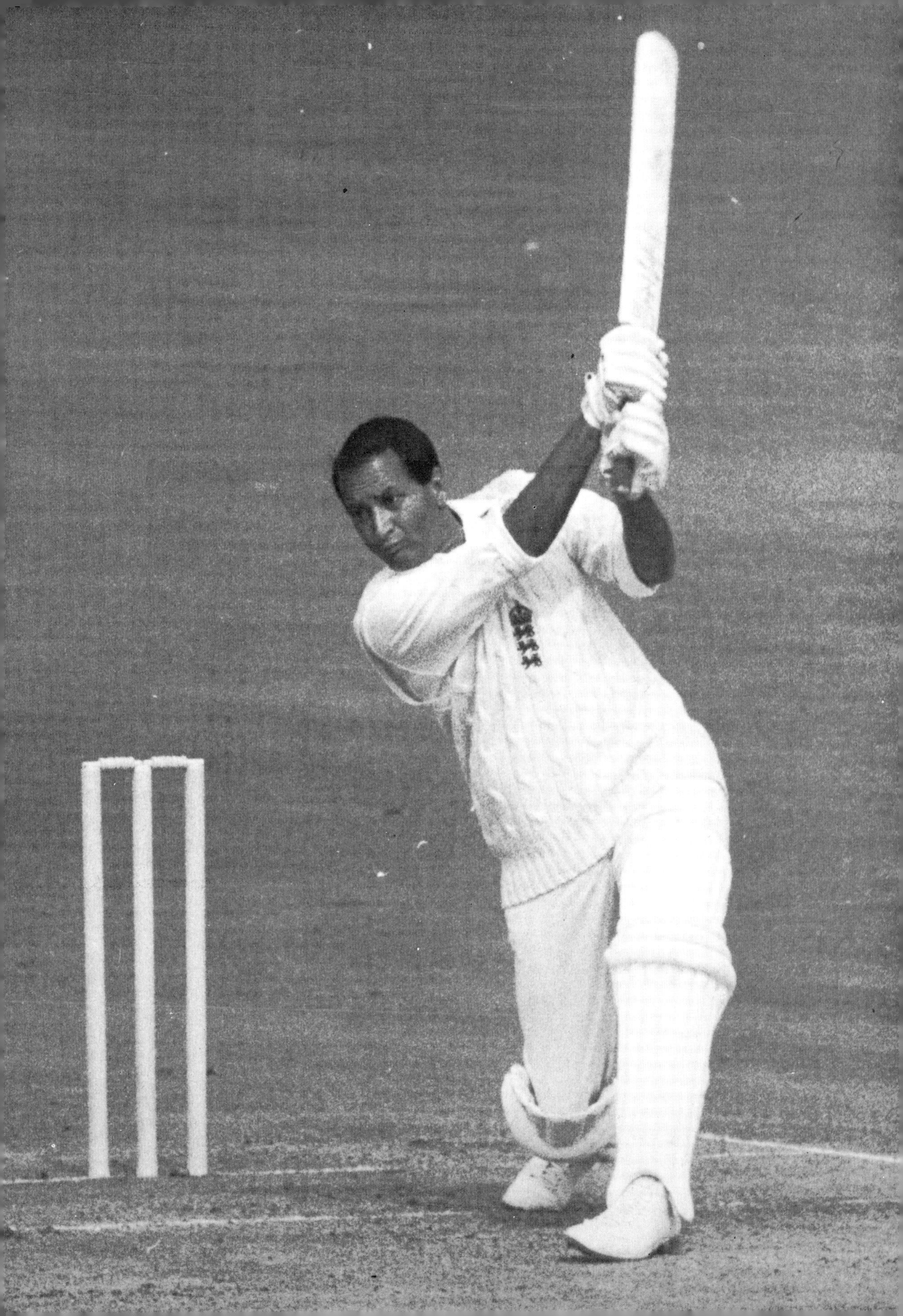

circumstance for Milburn's special talent to come into its own.

There were no half-measures about Milburn. In character and size he was a larger-than-life figure, his best batting weight around 18 stone. When he tried to lose weight, his form suffered, so merry Milburn had to admit to being one of nature's big men. He hit the ball hard and often and, by doing so, attracted big crowds. Only the naive regarded him as a slogger, for his technique was sound. This, allied to his power, was the source of his big-hitting success. The crowds loved his infectious enjoyment of the game. While on his way to an undefeated century against West Indies (Hall and Griffith included), Milburn would begin to tell a joke to the close-fielders, pause to thunder a hook to the boundary, and then convulse his audience with the climax of the tale. The loss on an eye in a motoring accident in 1969 was more than a personal tragedy, for it robbed English cricket of its most exciting player.

Pat Pocock claims the valuable wicket of Doug Walters at Old Trafford – one of his 6 for 79 in the second innings.

Colin Milburn – a barnstorming 83 in his debut at Lord's.

In 1968 Milburn's problem was how to deal with the Australian attack on an unreadable pitch. He solved it by launching a furious assault which took his score to 83. Not only did this prevent the bowlers from making optimum use of the conditions but it gave comfort and inspiration to the other batsmen. The weather continued to interfere and, with time dwindling, England declared at 351 for 7.

The fourth day provided high drama as Australia, tormented by John Snow, Brown and Knight, on a damp pitch, were bowled out for just 78. Brown, making the ball lift menacingly, captured 5 for 42, including a catch to Cowdrey which gave him a record 111 Test catches. Knight took 3 for 16, and Jarman, who came out to bat with a fractured finger, was hit on the same finger

Australia's vice-captain Barry Jarman joined skipper Lawry on the side-lines at Edgbaston.

Alan Connolly – 23 wickets in the series at an average of 25.69.

first ball and promptly retired very hurt. Following on, Australia put up a much better show in reaching 127 for 4 as the match petered out to a draw, Paul Sheahan leaving the field with a rueful smile, having batted 50 minutes . . . for nought.

Despite the dreadful weather, some play had been possible on each of the five days at Lord's. Spectators on the first day at Edgbaston were completely out of luck. Next day, however, Cowdrey, playing in his 100th Test, celebrated by winning the toss and scoring a century – aided by a runner. He also recorded his record 7000th Test run. But, that was the end of the good news, for the injured leg forced him to take no further part in the match. Graveney took over the captaincy and marked his elevation with 96 in an England total of 409.

It was not long before Australia, too, called up their deputy captain. Lawry, having scored six off Snow's first over, broke his little finger. As vice-captain Barry Jarman was out of the side, still nursing the injury he received at Lord's, Graham McKenzie took over, to see his team dismissed for 222. When England declared at 142 for 3, Australia needed 330 to win. At 68 for 1, rain intervened once more, and the draw left Australia one-up with two to play.

A similar result in the fourth Test at Headingley, therefore, would ensure Australia's retention of the Ashes. This fact did not escape Cowper, who batted two hours before lunch for 15. Neither captain had recovered sufficiently to appear, but Jarman was fit enough to lead Australia and Graveney carried on for England. Despite Cowper's initial sleep-walk, Australia reached 315 – a total England seemed unlikely to challenge when, after an opening partnership between Edrich (62) and newcomer Prideaux (64), wickets began to fall at regular intervals. Five went to Alan Connolly. His tally for the series was 23 wickets at 25.69, while McKenzie's 13 cost 45.77.

Connolly, tall and strong, was a *thinking* quick bowler. He swung the ball and delivered cutters at a pace so variable that the batsman could never settle. Not even Connolly, however, could prevent Brown and Underwood from compiling a final

Ray Illingworth – 6 for 87 off 57 overs.

partnership of 61 which left the No. 11 from Kent 45 not out. Australia batted again with a lead of 13 which, despite a wearing wicket, they extended to 325. Illingworth's off-breaks reaped 6 for 87 off 51 overs, with three stumping 'assists' from the incomparable Alan Knott.

Knott's all-round ability as a wicketkeeper/batsman is in the highest class – as his records show. Not only did he overtake the great achievements of Evans – for Kent and England – but at the same time he maintained a batting average over 30. County colleagues can recall entire seasons when Knott took every catch that came his way. A great many were taken standing back, even to medium pace, but Knott calculated he would get more catches standing back to seamers than he would get stumpings standing up. His work close to the wicket was frequently in harness with Underwood – not the easiest bowler in the world to take. Knott did it superbly.

Australia were expected to employ the same (spin) tactics as England attempted to score 326 runs at Headingley in just under five hours. Instead, McKenzie and Connolly bowled 25 and 31 overs respectively to keep England in check. While England only lost four wickets they were 96 runs short of their target at the close of another drawn match.

The Oval Test of 1968 goes down as the match that was won by the crowd. Home support is one thing, and batsmen facing Lillee in front of a 'Lil-lee, Lil-lee' chant, or Willis, surging in on the swelling roar of Headingley, 1981, must have felt the battle to be more than single combat. In the last Test of 1968 the crowd certainly were instrumental – in a non-vocal way – in England's victory.

England's batting in the first innings was patchy, but brilliant individual efforts took them to 494. Edrich confirmed his excellence as a Test player by scoring 164, but equally impressive was the performance of Basil D'Oliveira. Prideaux, injured before the match, had to withdraw, and D'Oliveira, who had been dropped after the first Test, was belatedly recalled. It is arguable that, even then, the ground was being prepared to avoid the position wherein England would be obliged to select him for the tour of South Africa the following winter. D'Oliveira, a Cape Coloured, had come to England to play his cricket away from the restrictive South African set-up, and had forced his way into the England side as an instinctive player of much natural ability. From strong forearms, he punched the ball with great power. He had most of the classical shots and a few peculiar to himself. Ironically, at the end of a career which brought him 2484 Test runs

Right: *Ian Redpath, caught Cowdrey bowled Snow for 67, during Australia's first innings at The Oval.*

Ted Dexter (28) turns to see a bail dislodged by Connolly in England's second innings of the last Test.

at an average of 40.06 (five centuries), D'Oliveira had to learn to play a conventional sweep to satisfy the National Cricket Association examiners on an advanced coaching course!

As a bowler of deceptive pace and swing, 'Dolly' took many valuable Test wickets, and altogether his triumph over the adversity of his background was universally admired, as was his delight at playing for England. When the 'D'Oliveira Affair' followed his selection in the MCC side to tour South Africa, he conducted himself with immense dignity at a time when he could have grabbed headlines and cash with ill-considered statements. He emerged with his reputation not only intact but elevated.

This was the man, then, who scored 158 in that first England innings of the 1968 Oval Test. Lawry replied with a determined 135, and Australia reached 324, avoiding the follow-on. England's rushed second innings of 181 left Australia a target of 352 which, on a turning pitch, constituted a purely academic challenge. Only their ability to force a draw was seriously in question.

Moments before lunch on the final day, with Australia 86 for 5, a violent storm broke and, as The Oval subsided under water, a draw seemed inevitable. That is when crowd-power came to the fore. Volunteers, working like beavers, mopped up the lake and, by 4.45, the ground was adjudged playable. Jarman and Inverarity stubbornly negotiated everything until, with 35 minutes remaining, D'Oliveira bowled Jarman. This opened the breach for Underwood to claim three quick wickets and with just five minutes to go, Inverarity, padding up to the Kent spinner, was lbw, and England had won by 226 runs. Underwood's final haul was a remarkable 7 for 50.

It was on occasions such as this that Derek Underwood justified his nickname 'Deadly'. When the ball is biting and turning, few batsmen in the world can survive his skills. To describe Underwood as a left-arm spinner is to call Big Ben a clock. Underwood is unique at a time when cricket lacks true individuality. Walking flat-footed, he looks anything but an international sportsman. And there is nothing in his approach to the wicket to suggest either mystery or menace. If the action is no more striking than the run, then the delivery certainly is. Unerringly accurate, each ball is subtly varied so that the batsman who loses patience is likely to perish by attacking misguidedly.

No other bowler has taken 100 wickets in his first full season of county cricket at such a young age, for Underwood was only 18 in his debut summer for Kent. At 25, he had collected his 1000th first-class wicket. Yet even as he wheeled away, taking wicket after wicket, the pundits were criticising his method. As he pushed the ball through, the purists demanded that he gave it more air, and brought variety into his attack. The point is that the variation is there, but cunningly subtle, and by pushing it through, he affords the batsman little time for footwork. Under certain conditions, Underwood does give the ball more air, but still the stock ball, darting off a perfect length, is there to test the batsman's concentration. At The Oval in 1968 on a 'deadly' wicket, the Australian batsmen could find no answer and England's victory squared the series at one-match-all.

14

THE 'OKKER' AGE

SEASON 1968 represented something of a watershed in the post-war history of Anglo–Australian Test matches. Up to and including that series the essential character of the Ashes contest had changed little since 1948. Individuals came and went, enlivening the rubbers in which they appeared; playing strengths and fortunes ebbed and flowed. The amateurs, so prolific before the war, gave more ground to the professionals and, by the time the 1970–71 series began, that professionalism was finely honed. The attitudes and behaviour of men who relied on cricket for their livelihood were strongly influencing the pattern of the game. It is arguable that this watershed was more clearly defined in 1977, when Kerry Packer's World Series Cricket appeared, but it could equally well be argued that this development was merely the extension of a metamorphosis that began at the start of the 1970s.

The England captain for the 1970–71 tour was Ray Illingworth, who had now left his native Yorkshire to help vitalise Leicestershire into a major force. In a less obvious way he was doing the same job for England, insisting they played with the same highly professional approach that characterised his own game. In this respect, he was not always in complete agreement with his vice-captain, Cowdrey, or even the tour manager David Clark. Nevertheless, Illingworth's forthright attitudes were vindicated as England overcame all the niggling problems of a touring side and regained the Ashes.

England encountered their first spot of bother in the opening Test at Brisbane. Lawry was caught behind off Snow with the score on 12. Twenty runs later, when Stackpole was on 18, a confident appeal for a run-out was turned down. Stackpole went on to make 207, but the newspapers carried photographs of him a long way out of his ground and the wicket broken. Walters also scored a century and, though Snow and Underwood gradually worked their way through the order, Australia raised a formidable 433.

England replied in fine style to lead by 31 and to justify their inclusion of an extra batsman. It could have been an interesting position had not Lawry, in resolute mood, scored 84 of Australia's second-innings 214. Though Shuttleworth took 5 for 47, no time remained for England to press home their advantage and the match was drawn.

The second Test was staged in Perth – a new location for an Ashes match. England won the toss and batted – having been refused a roller by both groundsman and umpires. Despite this unusual rebuff, the opening batsmen put on 171, Boycott making 70 and Brian Luckhurst 131. England's score of 397 was exceeded by Australia's 440, built round a sixth-wicket stand of 219 by Redpath (171) and Greg Chappell, who marked his first Test appearance with 108. During the next decade, he and brother Ian – grandsons of former captain Vic Richardson – were to assume a dominant place in Australian Test cricket.

The two brothers played contrasting roles in the side. Ian's success as a captain often overshadowed his contributions with the bat. In 75 Tests, Ian Chappell scored 5345 runs at 42.42, with 14 hundreds. He led the side 30 times, winning 15 matches and losing only five. No Australian captain had achieved more victories and only Bradman as many. If Ian Chappell's records are the source of unstinted admiration,

A hard-won wicket for Derek Underwood as Alan Knott snaps up a catch from Paul Sheahan during the Brisbane Test, 1970–71.

the same cannot be said of his attitude to the game. It was he who encouraged some of the less attractive aspects of the modern game and because of his success, he could act with impunity. Tracksuit and training shoes became the team uniform, and not only in the pavilion. Behaviour on the field dipped to a new low. And, while skirmishes with authority are not necessarily wrong, Ian Chappell appeared to take an increasingly sour delight in his 'bad man' image. Nevertheless, in terms of results, his record compared with the best.

If Ian Chappell was a good Test batsman, then younger brother Greg was to become one of the greats. A Test average of more than 50 in as many matches emphasised the quality of this graceful, right-hand batsman. While Ian led the team by dynamic – if not always diplomatic – example, Greg Chappell did not motivate a side in the same way. His batting was often inspiration enough. Tall and elegant, he made it seem a trouble-free art against the best attacks and on the worst pitches. There was seldom any haste in his comprehensive repertoire of strokes. Greg's temperament was perfectly illustrated by that first Test innings in Perth for, when he arrived at the crease, the score stood at 107 for 5. In those circumstances few seasoned old pros would have backed themselves to make a hundred!

Conditions were still good when England batted again and Illingworth, delaying his declaration (Edrich 115 not out), left Australia 145 minutes to score 245. Lawry demonstrated what he thought of the challenge by scoring 38 not out in 32 overs, and the match was drawn.

The third Test, scheduled for Melbourne, went into the record books – alongside those of Old Trafford in 1890 and 1938 – as the only Test matches abandoned without a ball being bowled. All involved England and Australia and each was designated as the third match of the series.

Illingworth again won the toss at Sydney and chose to bat on a good-looking wicket. After Boycott and Luckhurst had opened with 116, spinners Mallett (4 for 40) and Gleeson (4 for 83) pinned England down to 332. Underwood then responded with 4 for 66 as Australia struggled to 236, only Redpath and Walters reaching half-centuries. England now needed to press on. And, for once, the strategy materialised. An excellent 142 not out from Boycott enabled Illingworth to declare with five wickets down and a lead of 415. The rest was up to John Snow, who decided the pitch was made to measure for his particular brand of mayhem.

That was important, for Snow was a man of moods. He could easily become bored with proceedings and graze idly in the outfield, but, when the temperament took him, Snow could suddenly become one of the best and most hostile of bowlers. By alternating between fast and very fast, he had the batsmen in difficulty with their timing; the element of surprise was always there. The lean Snow's powerful action meant that his bouncer did not have to pitch as short as most before rising steeply, and his ability to cut the ball either way could be lethal. In 49 Tests, Snow took 202 wickets at 26.66 each. Had he been selected for as many matches as his ability warranted he might well have passed the 300 mark.

Lawry carried his bat for 60 at Sydney but, of the others, only Stackpole reached double figures as Snow stormed through the side with 7 for 40. Australia could muster only 116 and England took a one-nil lead in the series.

At this point came a broad hint that it was not only the players who were becoming more professional. The authorities, realising that the loss of the third Test would drastically affect the overall takings, hastily arranged a return to Melbourne between Sydney and Adelaide. Manager Clark agreed to the arrangement without consulting the captain or players – who immediately raised the question of extra payment. Eventually they accepted £50 a man (though takings at the gate exceeded £25,000).

Ian Chappell scored his first century against England, and Marsh would certainly have done likewise had not Lawry declared at 493 for 9, with the Australian 'keeper 92.

Though Luckhurst and D'Oliveira scored centuries, England trailed by 101 on first innings, and now Australia should have adopted positive tactics. Lawry, however, was never renowned for adventure and, after creeping to 169 for 4, he set England a target of 271 at more than a run a minute. It was a cheeky invitation, yet the crowd's noisy frustration fell on Boycott and Edrich as they serenely collected 161 runs in playing out time.

Australia introduced an exciting newcomer for the sixth Test, at Adelaide, and, with 5 for 84 for starters, Dennis Lillee served notice that he was about to become a major figure in the annals of the Ashes. On this occasion, Boycott was not one of his victims – and thereby hung a tetchy tale. After yet another century opening partnership with Edrich, Boycott was controversially run out. Believing he had easily made his ground – and doubtless recalling the Stackpole incident in Brisbane – Boycott angrily threw down his bat in dissent. Illingworth said later he believed Boycott was just out, but the incident caused considerable ill-feeling.

Edrich completed his second century of the series and Keith Fletcher chipped in 80 as England ran up a handsome 470. Although Stackpole hit 87 Australia were all out for 235 – at which stage they could have been asked to follow-on. Illingworth decided against it. Snow and Peter Lever had laboured long, and there was the prospect of batting last on a turning pitch. So England went in again and Boycott was 119 not out when Illingworth declared at 233 for 4. Again, a target of 469 in 500 minutes did not whet the Australian appetite. After Lawry went for 21, Stackpole and Ian Chappell put on 202, each scoring a century . . . and another match was drawn, with Australia 328 for 3.

Ashley Mallett, 4 for 40, helped pin England down in Sydney.

Though Lawry had captained Australia in 25 Tests, and won nine of them, there was general dissatisfaction with his cautious approach and the cry went up for a new, more dynamic leader. Lawry's double failure with the bat in the sixth Test was seized on as an excuse to relieve him of the captaincy, though the argument for leaving

Illingworth smartly caught by Redpath off Gleeson, for 41, during the 'rearranged' Test at Melbourne.

Lawry out of the side completely was less convincing. The Australian cause was badly served by his omission from the seventh Test in Sydney. Ken Eastwood, a member of Lawry's Victorian team, was the surprise replacement and Tony Dell, a Hampshire-born Queenslander, became the seventh Australian pace bowler of the series. New captain Ian Chappell put England in, and they were dismissed for 184, spinners Jenner and O'Keeffe taking three wickets each – Australia got away badly, losing four for 66, but were on the way to a sound recovery when, suddenly, the match erupted. Snow bowled a short-pitched ball which struck Jenner on the head. Within seconds an atmosphere had developed that evoked faint memories of the notorious Bodyline tour. Umpire Rowan decided Snow had been guilty of intimidatory bowling. Snow and Illingworth refuted this, and the over was finished without further incident. But, when Snow went down to his position at fine leg, he was greeted by a hail of beer-cans. After a brief altercation with a drunken spectator, Snow returned to the middle where, along with the entire England side, he sat down while the debris was cleared. That done, Illingworth agreed to a resumption, but as Snow reached the boundary, another drunk grabbed his shirt, the bottles flew again, and this time Illingworth took his side off. Having been advised that he could forfeit the match, Illingworth led his men back out when order was restored.

Australia were eventually bowled out for 264 – a lead of 80 – and England, batting much more solidly now, made 302. Illingworth, incidentally, was lbw to Lillee – the first batsman in the match to depart in this way. Indeed, no Australian in the entire series was given out lbw! In the second innings, Australia needed 223 to win and square the series. Snow, having claimed Eastwood for a duck, broke a finger going for a catch on the fence and took no further part in the match. This might have proved significant but Illingworth and Underwood stepped admirably into the breach. Wickets fell with surprising ease and when Fletcher caught Jenner off Underwood, Australia were all out for 160. England had won by 62 runs, the Ashes were won, and England's delighted players chaired their 'professional' captain from the field.

Ian Chappell had gained valuable experience by the next time Australia played an official Test match. Illingworth, 40 on the opening day of the first Test of the 1972 series at Old Trafford, did not need experience but luck, and he got that by winning the toss. Boycott was not so fortunate. Hit by a rising ball from Lillee, he was forced to retire, nursing the same left arm fractured in Australia in 1971. It was Tony Greig's first Test for England and he made his mark with a top-scoring 57 as England reached 249. It was 107 more than Australia could manage against Snow and Geoff Arnold, who took four wickets each. As England extended their lead to 341, Greig took the batting honours again with 62, in defiance of a 6 for 66 spell from Lillee which included three wickets in four balls. Australia made a brave effort to get the runs – especially Marsh, who hit four sixes and nine fours in a typically aggressive

Spectators bombard John Snow with beer cans at Sydney.

The England team chair Illingworth off the field after clinching the series.

Time for champagne. Illingworth celebrates after the sixth Test. A job well done.

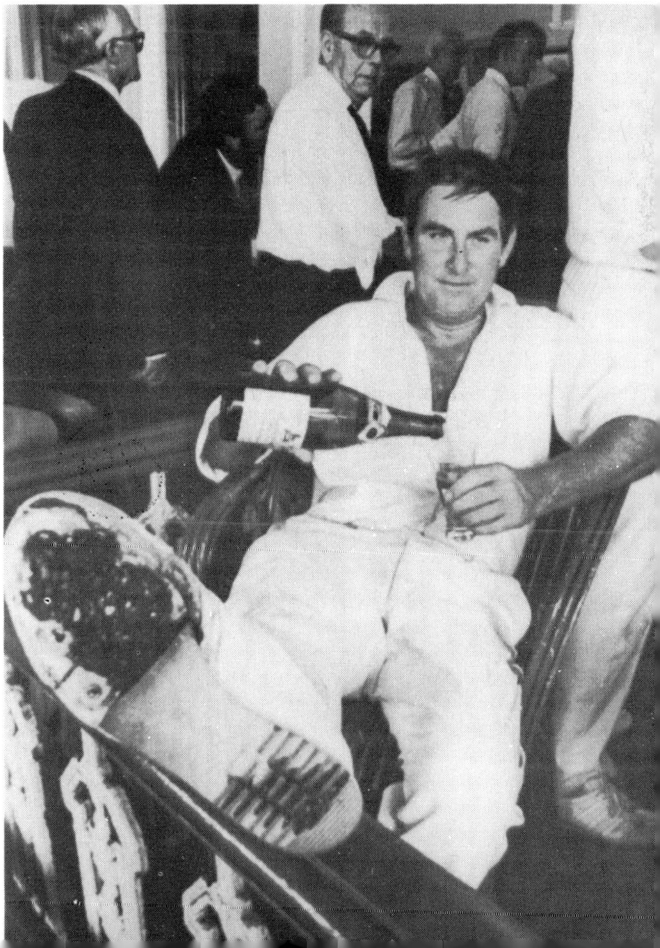

innings of 91. In the second England innings, he had held five catches.

Rodney Marsh is the personification of Australian cricket. Even the English hold a grudging admiration for the man who overcame a host of problems to establish himself as a top-class wicketkeeper. He looked far from that in his first series, when his misjudgments earned him the cruel nickname of 'Iron Gloves'. A powerful, stocky man, Marsh built up his strength by long hours of training and practice, so that he became mobile and seemingly inexhaustible. Marsh believes cricket should be played to the limits, and is one of the most competitive of opponents. He looks the part, with his cap rammed down on his head – almost leaning backwards to see out under the peak. He makes no secret of his emotions on the field. A batsman who plays and misses finds Marsh's head thrown back with an expression of total and painful disbelief. At the same time, he is a fair cricketer. During Derek Randall's potentially match-winning innings in the 1977 Centenary Test, Marsh overruled the umpire and called Randall back because he knew the catch did not carry.

Marsh had a vital part to play at Lord's in the second Test of 1972 – a match dominated by a man making his debut in Test cricket. Bob Massie had a trial with Northamptonshire in 1970, when his three wickets in the 2nd XI cost 55 runs apiece. He now came into an Australian side which needed a quick fillip after England's 89-run victory in Manchester. England immediately lost three wickets, two to Lillee and one to Massie. The middle order provided stability, but no batsman was comfortable against the prodigious swing of Massie, who took 8 for 84 in a sustained effort of 32.5 overs. Greig (54) and Knott (43) helped England to 272, then Snow came back with 5 for 57. But Greg Chappell gave English spectators a glimpse of his greatness with an innings of 131; Marsh and Ian Chappell each scored half-centuries, and Australia took a lead of 36. Notwithstanding its splendour, Greg Chappell's performance was soon to be overshadowed. As in the first innings, Lillee claimed two of the first three England wickets, and Massie the other. Then Massie took seven more to finish with 8 for

Left: *Bob Massie – virtually unplayable as he claimed sixteen wickets in the Lord's Test of 1972.*

53 as England were shot out for 116. Sixteen wickets for 137 runs represented the most devastating debut by any bowler in the history of Test cricket.

Massie had made quite an impact by taking 6 for 27 against the Rest of the World XI in Sydney. But it was at Lord's that his career bloomed like some exotic flower that withers as quickly as it appears. The conditions were perfect for a bowler of his style, but even that did not account for his phenomenal swing. The ball moved so much that Massie was forced to bowl inswingers from around the wicket to the right-hand batsman. Even then, Greig took a guard of middle and off to cover the ball swerving late onto the stumps. Massie never performed such miracles again. In five more Tests he took only 13 wickets. The gift of swing had left him and he played his last first-class game in 1975. But at Lord's in 1972, he bowled Australia into a position where their second-innings 81 for 2 squared the series.

Massie's performance influenced the series far beyond Lord's. When Illingworth won the toss at Trent Bridge its memory was still fresh in the mind, and he decided to ask Australia to bat. But any hopes of skittling Australia were thwarted by a century from Stackpole. Though Snow again took five wickets (and Parfitt held four slip catches) Australia moved into a sound position with 315. Marsh, with five catches, loomed large in England's dismissal for a meagre 189. Australia's second innings of 324 for 4 was founded on an undefeated 170 from Ross Edwards, another Western Australian, who, like Massie, was appearing in his second Test. England were left 9½ hours to score 451 runs – a challenge they were not prepared to accept. Luckhurst (96 – England's highest innings of the series) led the rearguard action as England, 290 for 4, sealed the draw.

At Headingley, a freak pitch awaited the protagonists. On the previous weekend, a heavy storm had poured water down the slope and under the covers. An attack of fuserium fungus had denuded the pitch and now the water prevented the use of a heavy roller. Not surprisingly, the ball turned from the start; yet, although forewarned, Australia elected to bat. They found Underwood a particularly difficult proposition. There are few better wet-wicket wizards, and the Kent man had 4 for 37 in 31 overs as Australia slithered to 146 all out. Ashley Mallett spun back with five wickets and when England had reached only 128 for 7 the likelihood of a lead – let alone a clear one – seemed remote. Illingworth then scored 57 and his partnership with Snow (48) (plus 46 extras!) put England 117 ahead.

Arnold handed a 'pair' to Edwards, and quickly dismissed Ian Chappell to clear the way for another Underwood bonanza of 6 for 45. The match was still only in its third day when England polished off the necessary 21 runs for victory. So, with comparative ease, had Illingworth successfully defended the Ashes he won the year before.

There still remained the fifth Test at The Oval and the chance for Australia to salvage some pride. Lillee took five wickets in both innings – three in four balls in the first – and the Chappell brothers shared a stand of 201, each scoring a century. England, having scored 284 in the first innings (Knott 92), made 356 at their second try, leaving Australia 242 to win. Stackpole led the way with 79 and the series was squared on the last afternoon, four wickets in hand.

When the heat was on the England batsmen during the 1974–75 tour of Australia, it was suggested to Ian Chappell that his relentless use of Lillee, Thomson and Walker was not in the best spirit of the game – especially as their short bowling was responsible for a string of injuries. He politely enquired whether England's five pace bowlers were there to give Australia driving practice off the front foot! It was a poignant question. Yet while five English fast bowlers *did* make the trip, the one paceman who could have made all the difference was watching the tour from the Press-box. John Snow's omission from the party was not entirely a matter of fitness. Whatever the other reasons, captain Mike Denness could not enlist a man who might well have discouraged Lillee and Thomson from dishing out an excessive quota of bouncers.

For all that, as an opening pace attack the credentials of Lillee and Thomson bear comparison with the best. Of the two, Jeff Thomson at his peak – as he was in the 1974–75 season – had the greater pace. His delivery speed touched 100 mph and the effect of his joining the far-from-gentle Lillee shattered the confidence of the English batsmen.

Thomson's action was not in the conventional

mould but, as a means of propelling a cricket ball at a ferocious pace, it was hard to fault and might have been designed by an engineer rather than an artist. His run was considerably shorter than many bowlers of lesser pace and, immediately before delivery, he spread himself like a javelin thrower. The bowling hand was tucked away behind him, giving the batsman no chance to follow it prior to release. The left leg stretched out parallel to the ground and the torso twisted. Then the slinging action unfolded and the ball hurtled on its way.

Thomson's great assets were pace and the bounce he extracted from otherwise lifeless wickets. Lillee, on the other hand, had a more extensive repertoire under perfect control. He too had pace, but could also swing the ball both ways and move it off the pitch. His action was a joy to behold. He began a long run leaning forward as he gathered momentum until, reaching the delivery stride, he adopted a perfect sideways-on position. The arm came over high and his momentum carried him into a perfect followthrough.

Whereas Thomson's shoulder caused problems, Lillee's trouble centred on his back, where he suffered stress fractures that might prematurely have ended his career. He spent many weeks in plaster, even longer to regain his full fitness, and it speaks volumes for his mental and physical resilience that he climbed back to the top and continued to spearhead the Australian attack.

In its heyday, the Thomson–Lillee spearhead was backed by Max Walker, a good-natured fast-medium bowler who always looked as if he should take more wickets than he did. Apparently bowling off the wrong foot (he was nicknamed 'Tanglefoot'), his open-action delivery favoured the inswinger which then cut away off the pitch. In his supporting role Walker came on to deny the batsmen a respite when either Lillee or Thomson was resting. Had half the deliveries played and missed resulted in a wicket, Walker could have re-written the record books.

England encountered this trio for the first time at Brisbane, where the condition of the pitch favoured them. The groundsman, irked by unsolicited advice from the Mayor of Brisbane, Clem Jones, duly handed His Worship the job. The surprising outcome was not how the pitch played but that it was ready at all – especially when a

Ian Redpath, top-scorer with 55 in Australia's first innings at Melbourne.

tropical storm compounded the problems. Though there was uneven bounce throughout, yet the match almost went its full course. Australia batted first and made 309, including a last-wicket partnership of 52 between Thomson and Walker. England's 265 owed much to a century from Greig, who decided to attack. Australia declared their second innings closed at 288 for 5, and England needed 333 for victory, an academic target, for both Amiss and Edrich were batting with hands damaged by Thomson – who proceeded to take 6 for 46. England were all out for 166 – the same margin as Australia's victory.

Though Colin Cowdrey had not played in a Test match for 3½ years, he was the man flown out to reinforce the shattered team. Within four days of arrival he was pressed into action on a very fast Perth pitch. Batting at three, Cowdrey scored 22 of England's 208 – a total pushed into pale perspective by Australia's 481. Edwards and Walters both scored centuries, a feat no Englishman could achieve in either innings. Thomson again was the arch-demon with 5 for 93. Titmus, another veteran, gallantly defied the slings and arrows for a top-scoring 61, but Australia had more than a day to spare when they won by nine wickets.

Only one match in the series of six could be described as evenly-balanced – and the Melbourne Test could hardly have been closer. England were bowled out for 242 but Willis struck back with 5 for 61 and Australia wound up one run behind. It was a good performance by England, who lost Hendrick with a hamstring injury after three overs. In the second innings, England got off to a good start as Amiss (90) and David Lloyd (44) put up 115 for the first wicket. However, Thomson got four wickets – as he had in the first innings – the later batsmen failed, and England were all out for 244. Only three runs spanned the totals of three completed innings, and Australia needed 246 to win. Two early wickets went down; there was a recovery, a collapse and a further recovery as Marsh and Walters came together. When Walters fell, Marsh and Walker went into the last hour of 15 overs needing 55 for victory. Ian Chappell had ordered them to play as they saw fit, and against Greig and Underwood, bowling at leg stump to a six-three onside field, only seven runs came from as many overs. Denness then took the new ball and against a less defensive field the batsmen accelerated until 16 were needed off the last two eight-ball overs. Back came Greig and Underwood and Australia, two wickets in hand, finished eight runs short.

Had England won at Melbourne, the story of the 1973–75 tour could have been very different. As it was, Denness, having played six innings for 65 runs, dropped himself from the side to play in the fourth Test in Sydney. It was a courageous decision and the picture of Denness watching Edrich lead out the side was a sad one – especially as the sacrifice made no difference to the result.

McCosker, opening for Australia with the consistent Redpath, made 80, Greg Chappell 84, and England faced a first-innings total of 405 (Arnold, 5 for 86, reaching his 100 Test wickets). Edrich responded with 50 and Knott put together an enterprising 82, but England fell 110 runs short. Centuries from Redpath and Greg Chappell pushed Australia to 289 for 4 declared and Eng-

Rick McCosker goes down, struck on the head by a fierce drive from John Edrich during England's first innings in Sydney.

In Australia's first innings, Redpath dives for the crease as the wicket is shattered by a sharp return. Arnold looks hopeful, but the umpire turned down the appeal.

Tony Greig (54) has no chance as Rodney Marsh stumps him off Mallett's bowling on the final day of the fourth Test, 1974–75.

land were set a daunting target of 400. Their cause was not helped when the first ball Edrich received from Lillee crashed into his ribs, and he was forced to retire. He returned later in an attempt to play out time but, with just 35 balls remaining, Arnold was caught (Mallett's 100th Test wicket) and the Ashes were back with Australia.

After that Australian victory, Denness returned for Adelaide and it seemed England were about to record their first win of the series. Australia were 84 for 5 in the first innings yet, thanks to an aggressive rally by Walters (55) and Jenner (74), they made 304. Conversely, England – having reached 66 for 2 – were all out for 172. When Australia batted again, Underwood (7 for 113 in the first innings) took his match tally to 11 wickets and the declaration with five wickets down set England 405 to win. It was little comfort that Thomson had damaged his right shoulder playing tennis and was missing. Half the side were out for 76, and the manner of their going sent groans of disbelief throughout the UK. This was the first series from Australia to be extensively televised in England and the edited highlights showed England's players hanging bats outside the off stump or failing to get into line. A

Ian Chappell goes for a big hit at Adelaide off a ball from Underwood. Instead, he gets a top edge and Knott prepares to take the catch.

praiseworthy exception was Alan Knott, who set about the Australian attack for a brilliant 106 not out. He found an ally in Fletcher, who scored 63, but Australia swept to victory by 163 runs.

If England lost that match by failing to capitalise on favourable circumstances, they did not make the same mistake in Melbourne. Peter Lever (6 for 38) bowled magnificently and Australia were all out for 152 – the lowest total of the series. Though Amiss and Cowdrey went quickly, Edrich and Denness settled in against an Australian attack already minus Thomson and now further depleted by the loss of Lillee with a damaged foot. Edrich led the England advance with 70, Denness went on to score 188 – the highest Test innings by an England captain in Australia – and Fletcher made 146. Greig joined in with 89 and England reached a crushing 529. Australia then had 215 up before the second wicket fell. A Greg Chappell century boosted the valiant efforts of openers McCosker (76) and Redpath (83), but the last six wickets failed to add a hundred and England won by an innings and four runs – scant consolation for a 4–1 beating that revived unhappy memories of 1950–51.

Australia, invited to England for the 1975 Prudential World Cup competition, agreed to stay on for a four-match Test series with the Ashes at stake. They finished runners-up to West Indies in cricket's World Cup, and moved on to the first of the conventional Tests at Edgbaston. On the strength of his last-gasp success in Melbourne, Mike Denness retained the England captaincy – but only on a match-to-match basis. In the event, one match was enough to decide his fate.

The weather forecast was for rain at some stage early in the match. Furthermore, the pitch at

Caught Marsh, bowled Lillee. Lloyd falls to a familiar formula during England's first innings in Adelaide.

Edgbaston had seamed all season; so, when Denness won the toss, he consulted his bowlers and decided to put Australia in. When the scoreboard read 186 for 5 the decision seemed justified, but then the lower half of the order took control, and Australia romped to 359. Even worse for Denness, after one over of the England innings a thunderstorm drenched the ground and they were subsequently skittled for 101 – Lillee returning an astonishing 5 for 15 and Walker 5 for 48. In the follow-on, only Fletcher reached 50 and, as Thomson now claimed 5 for 38, Australia triumphed by an innings and 85 runs. Denness was promptly sacked. It was, perhaps, a harsh decision, for he lost only five of 19 matches, and in 28 appearances for England had maintained a creditable batting average of 39.69.

While Denness was cast in a tragic role, his successor, Tony Greig, evoked an aura of triumph – by no means justified. His Test batting average was marginally better than that of Denness, but in 14 appearances as captain he was victorious only three times. Greig was big in every way. A 6ft 7 ins showman, he revelled in the big occasion. He was a compulsorily attacking batsman whose risks were usually sustained by natural ability and aggression. For example, on the 1974–75 tour, rather than shouldering arms or defending, he deliberately played fast, lifting deliveries over the slips. Unfortunately his captaincy followed similar principles – inspiration before policy.

As a bowler Greig had two styles – brisk medium-pace with swing and lift, or a lively off-break. In the field he set new standards of slip-catching. Such were the talents that ultimately persuaded him to turn his back on England and become a prime mover in the development of World Series Cricket.

All that was in the future when the South African-born Sussex player brought his talent and leadership to bear on the second Test at Lord's. He started well. A dashing 96 inspired an England recovery from 49 for 4 to 315. He was nobly assisted by the grey-haired David Steele who, in his first Test, at 33, contributed 50. Greig certainly seemed to have the magic touch as Australia, in reply, slumped to 81 for 7. However,

Left: *The expression says all. Tony Greig, on 96 at Lord's, miscues a ball from Max Walker and Ian Chappell – out of picture – takes the catch.*

Below: *Barry Wood goes, l.b.w. to Lillee for 6 on the first day of the Lord's Test, 1975.*

Above: *Double trouble for Steele and Edrich during a second-innings running mix-up at Lord's. Miraculously, they survived.*

Left: *Rod Marsh is amazed. A ball from Greig misbehaves, he fences at it and . . . appeals for justice as Amiss, the catcher, and Knott, walk forward to congratulate Greig.*

Above: *Characteristic defiance from 'overnight' success David Steele during the second innings, at Lord's.*

Ross Edwards (99) and Lillee (73 not out) rallied the cause until it ended only 47 runs adrift. Edrich then hit a splendid 175 and England's lead was extended to 483. Unfortunately time ran out on an enthralling contest, with Australia 329 for 3 in the fourth innings.

The list of Test cricketers who have influenced matches between England and Australia over the years does not include the name of George Davis, yet it was on behalf of this unwilling guest of Her Majesty's Government that a number of his friends vandalised the Headingley pitch before the final day of the third Test. Davis, convicted for armed robbery, had apparently been looking forward to watching the final hours of the match on the prison television. Like thousands of unquestionably innocent cricket enthusiasts, he was robbed of the chance. It should have been a fascinating day, for newcomer Phil Edmonds had opened up the match by taking 5 for 28 to dismiss Australia for 135. This performance countered a fine effort by Gary Gilmour, a left-arm pace bowler, who took 6 for 85 as England launched the proceedings with a respectable 288. After Australia's batting collapse, Gilmour took three more wickets to help contain England to a second-innings 291. (Steel 92) and a lead of 444.

Rick McCosker (95 not out) and Ian Chappell (62) set the tone of the response and, when the vandals struck, the match was tantalisingly balanced with Australia 220 for 3. In the spontaneous indignation that followed the abandonment, few cared that rain would have interfered anyway, and that Australia had retained the Ashes. In any case, the issue was confirmed at The Oval. England's hopes of victory were buried

under a second-wicket stand of 277 by Ian Chappell (192) and McCosker (127) which lifted Australia to 532 for 9 declared. England fell foul of drizzle and bad light – not to mention Thomson (4 for 50) and Walker (4 for 63) – made only 191 and followed on 341 behind. A marathon 396-minute century by Bob Woolmer helped put England ahead by 197, but – once again – time ran out on Australia.

England's unlikely hero of the series was the quiet, bespectacled Steele. At first appearance he looked far from the saviour knight, but he was a fighter and a sound technician who brought a refreshing stability and defiance to the English batting. Indeed, no-one seemed less concerned by the hostility of Lillee and Thomson, and Steele topped the English averages for the series. His Test career was destined to be short – many would say *too* short – but it was glorious while it lasted.

When Australia and England next met, the Ashes were not at stake. Instead, the contest, in Melbourne, celebrated the Centenary of Test cricket. It was a remarkable occasion which Australia won by 45 runs – the same margin by

Gooch hooks Walker, Thomson ducks. Walters, Greg Chappell and Marsh look on.

Gary Gilmour, 6 for 85 in England's first innings at Headingley, appeals in vain for l.b.w. against Edrich.

which they won the first Test, 100 years before. A more sinister aspect of the Centenary Test lay in the fact that during the match the Packer organisation was busy sowing the seeds of cricket's great divide. By the time the Australians arrived in England the following summer, most were committed to World Series Cricket. Among the English signatories was Tony Greig, who thereby lost the captaincy to Mike Brearley. Consequently, the series was dominated by events in courtrooms and counting houses rather than those on the field of play.

The series began at Lord's to coincide with celebrations for the Queen's Silver Jubilee. England's batsmen, though celebrating the absence of Lillee, quickly discovered, in Len Pascoe, a formidable replacement. Batting first, they had to rely too extensively on Woolmer and Randall, and Australia led by 80 on first innings. Some hours were lost to rain and bad light, but the match was not without drama. Woolmer scored 120 in England's second innings, Greig – the deposed captain – hit 91, and the new incumbent, Mike Brearley, made 49. Though there was no time for Australia to score the 226 they needed to

Phil Edmonds claims Ross Edwards, l.b.w. – one of his five wickets for 28 in Australia's first innings at Headingley.

Mallett strikes, and John Edrich departs – clean bowled in the second innings of the ill-fated Leeds Test.

Above: *Knott improvises. A signal success against Gilmour?*

Left: *John Snow, not always in the mood, but 4 for 66 at Lord's.*

Right: *Ian Chappell hits Edmonds for four on his way to a splendid 192 at The Oval.*

win, they nearly came unstuck in losing six wickets for 114 in the final session.

Lancastrians made much of the fact that, after the dismal London weather, Old Trafford provided five days of uninterrupted play. Australia's first-innings 297 (Walters 88) seemed a safe enough platform until Woolmer, with his second successive century, set England on the way to 437. That proved decisive, for although Greg Chappell played a skipper's part with a century, Underwood claimed six scalps and England clinched a nine-wicket victory before lunch on the fifth day.

Changes were made for the third Test at Trent Bridge as Boycott ended his self-imposed exile and Ian Botham made his debut. Botham began by taking five wickets as the Australian batsmen

GO SEGAS CENT

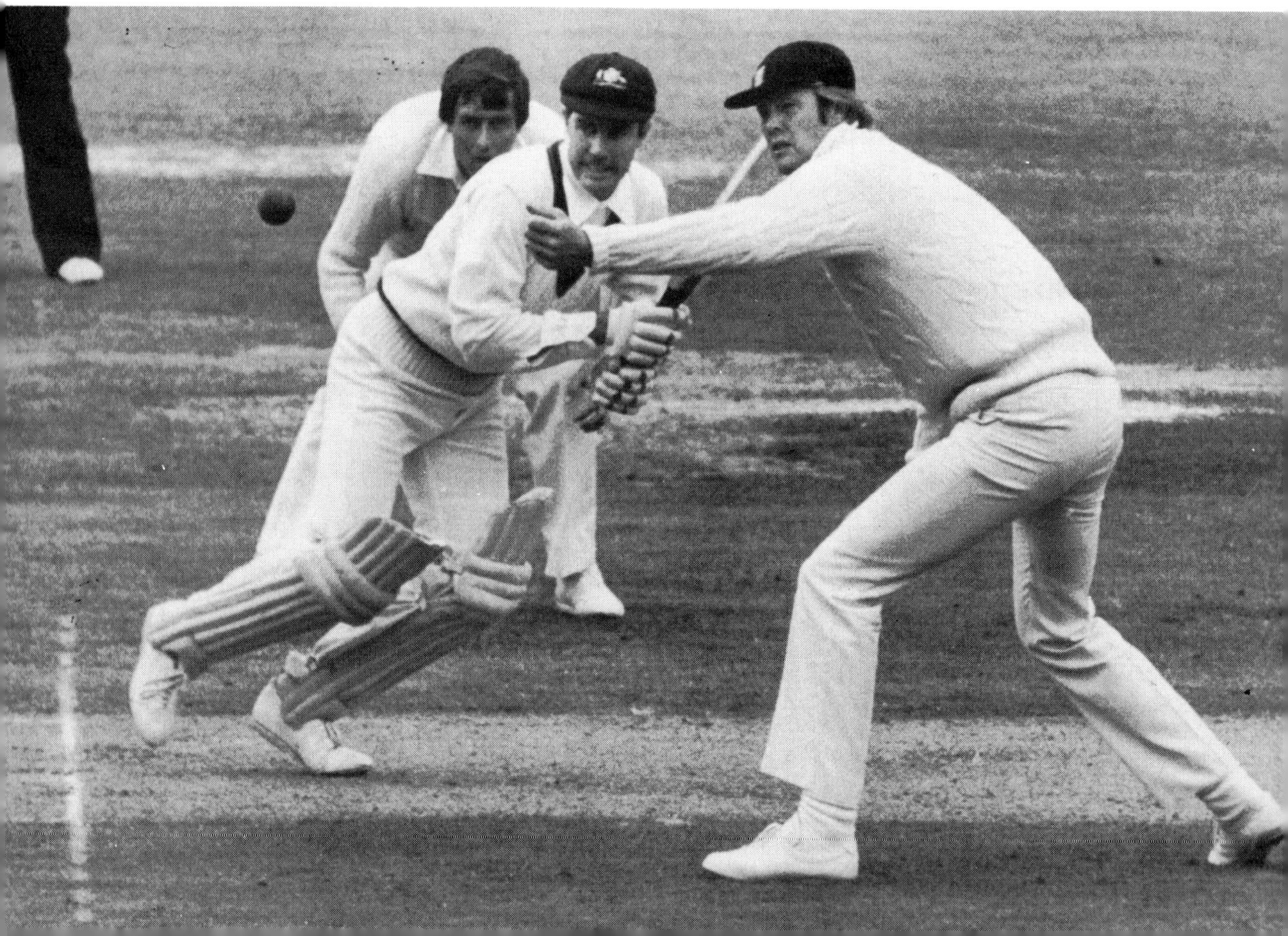

England open the Jubilee Test at Lord's, 1977, and Amiss departs for a duck – bowled by Thomson. Richie Robinson jumps for joy.

failed again, and Boycott, almost inevitably, celebrated his return with a century. It was not, however, a wholly satisfactory occasion for Boycott. He gained no friends by running out the local Nottingham hero, Randall, and subsequently became becalmed. Knott then came to play a bright innings of 135 which inspired even Boycott to re-open his miser's chest. By now, England were in a powerful position. Willis took 5 for 88, which included centurymaker McCosker, and, before long, Randall and Boycott re-united to complete a seven-wicket success.

Australian morale was now beginning to collapse. The team was divided into the pro- and anti-Packer factions, and the Australians, drawn into the chasm, could not concentrate on their game. Brearley had steeled the England team to withstand internal divisions on the subject, and this helped him regain the Ashes at Headingley. Brearley's personal performance was negligible, for he was out before a run had been scored. But, while the captain directed affairs with his customary authority, Boycott was the hero of the hour. On his own domain he scored his 100th hundred, going on to make 191 – to the unconfined joy of his Yorkshire subjects. Australia wilted for 103, Botham taking 5 for 21 in 11 overs, Hendrick, who had taken four wickets, bagged a similar return in the follow-on and Australia were still 85 runs behind when Marsh lofted a catch to extra-cover. Randall accepted it, turned a cartwheel – and England had won back the Ashes.

When a series is decided before the last match, an element of anti-climax is inescapable. This decline of public enthusiasm was further dampened at The Oval by recurring rain. No play was possible on the first day and there were further lengthy breaks. Mike Malone made a cheerful debut by taking five English wickets and sharing a century partnership for Australia's ninth wicket

Above left: *The brothers Chappell, Rod Marsh and Alan Turner show their delight as Barry Wood is bowled by Max Walker at The Oval.*

Left: *There it goes! Greg Chappell clips away a ball from Underwood. Woolmer and Greig keep an eye on it. Chappell went on to score 66, but the Lord's Test was drawn.*

Mick Malone strikes – and Derek Randall falls to a catch by Marsh in England's first innings at The Oval.

with Max Walker. Australia's 385 gave them a lead of 171. England were 57 for 2 when the series came to a cloudy end. There were some who feared that Test cricket was about to suffer a similar fate. . . .

In fact, when the struggle for the Ashes was resumed, at Brisbane in December 1978, there was a considerable dent in traditional concepts. Though England still had the nucleus of their former side, Australia paraded a team of virtual 'rookies'. Certainly none was familiar with the cordite whiff of rivalry between England and Australia. Some were eventually to establish a place in a full-strength Australian XI but, at this point, they were not ready. Furthermore, the inexperienced Graham Yallop, making his debut as captain, was beaten to every trick by England skipper Brearley.

Packer cricket was in direct competition and despite attempts to jazz up the series – parachuting in the coin for the toss, Australian badges on shirts and sweaters, on-the-spot television commentary of the toss, etc – the young Australian team provided a scant counter-attraction to the Packer pyrotechnics.

Though early conditions at Brisbane were likely to favour the bowlers, Yallop chose to bat. It was a disastrous decision, for Australia – almost helpless against Willis, Old and Botham – were all out for 116. Fortunately for Yallop, Australia were spared total ignominy when Rodney Hogg took 6 for 74 in his first Test attempt, to restrict England to 286.

Hogg, who until recently had been unable to command a place in a State side, thereby came to the rescue of Australia's great pace-bowling tradition. In fact, he went further by taking a most creditable 41 wickets in the series at 12.85. That record was achieved in a sequence of short bursts, for an asthmatic condition sapped his stamina and precluded extended spells.

Fired by Hogg's example, Australia mounted a second-innings revival based on a fourth-wicket partnership of 170 between Yallop (102) and Hughes (129). Nobody else made 20, however,

Greig congratulates Underwood, who has just caught and bowled Greg Chappell in Australia's first innings.

and England – required to score 170 – did so for the loss of three wickets.

In the second Test, at Perth, it was movement rather than speed that troubled the batsmen, and Yallop, having won the toss again, cannot have been displeased when England lost three for 41. David Gower, at his fluent and elegant best, then joined Boycott to send the England innings past 300. Again, Hogg was the bowling hero with 5 for 65, but Willis matched him as Australia were bowled out for 190 – only Toohey, with an undefeated 81, looking Test class. Hogg claimed another five wickets when England batted again, but John Lever came back with 4 for 28 and England were home by 166 runs.

Another English victory in Melbourne would have killed off the series – despite the fact that this third Test represented only the halfway mark. Yallop, who had won little but the toss so far, retained his fortune in that respect and batted. At last, England were forced to roll up their sleeves as Australia, inspired by a six-hour century from Graeme Wood, reached 247 for 4. Then, as the six remaining wickets fell for only 11 runs, it seemed Australia had squandered their big chance. If so, Hogg snatched it by taking 5 for 30 as England collapsed for 143. The pitch was proving a batsman's bad dream, its bounce quite unpredictable. Thus, when Australia earned a lead of 282, the prospect of victory loomed large. It was entirely appropriate that the gallant Hogg, with yet another five wickets (for 36), should turn the prospect to the reality of an Australian win by 93 runs.

Now it was England's turn for soul-searching. Brearley's form was atrocious and some considered he should follow the example of Denness and drop himself for the fourth Test in Sydney. However, the quality of his leadership prevailed and he held his place. In the euphoria of the English comebacks in the 1981 series, the one of 1978–79 is easily forgotten. Yet it was then that Brearley learned that games can be won even by sides bowled out for 152 on the first day (Alan Hurst for 28). England were apparently beyond redemption when Australia scored 294 (Rick Darling 91, Allan Border 60 not out). But now it was Derek Randall who changed the course of the match. In the second innings he disciplined himself, keeping his natural instincts in check, concentrating throughout the immense heat to score a magnificent 150. Even so, Australia needed only 205 to win in 265 minutes. It might have been within their reach had not Wood become the fourth Australian opener run out in as many matches – an unforgivable statistic for a struggling side. The wicket was taking turn, and Emburey and Miller fully exploited the Austra-

Yardley, caught Taylor bowled Hendrick as Australia head for another crushing defeat in Perth, 1978–79.

A great scalp for Rodney Hogg. Boycott falls to his first delivery in the fourth Test at Sydney.

lians' weakness against off-spin. Thus, to Yallop's consternation and Brearley's beaming delight, England turned almost certain defeat into a comfortable 93-run victory.

The fifth and sixth Tests were almost formalities for England – though with a little more experience and luck Australia might have reduced the overwhelming margins of defeat. At Adelaide, though England's first innings realised only 169, they went on to win by 205. Australia, five runs short on the first innings, saw the match slipping away with every run Derbyshire's Miller (64) and Taylor (97) added for the seventh wicket. It was a demoralised Australian side that subsequently crumbled for 160 after Wood, once again, had engaged in a run-out pantomime with Darling.

For the final match in Sydney, Darling was dropped in favour of Hilditch – who was promptly run out! Yallop scored a century that stood out like a beacon in a sea of despair, contributing 121 to the total of 198.

England encountered no such problems and, having taken a lead of 110, Graham Gooch making 74, they dismissed Australia again for 143 (Miller 5 for 44). The runs were knocked off for the loss of Boycott, and England ended a triumphant if somewhat unreal tour with a freak margin of five wins to one.

Such dominance over the old enemy was too good to last and, by the time England returned to Australia the following season, the roles had been reversed. A truce between Mr Packer and the Establishment enabled Australia to field a side worthy of the name. To celebrate the cessation of hostilities England joined West Indies in a double tour with one-day and conventional matches thrown into a jumbled fixture list with little to recommend it. Certainly it did not recommend itself to the English authorities, who declined to put the Ashes at stake. Needless to say, Australia's chagrin increased from a gentle simmer to boiling point as they proceeded to win all three Tests. Greg Chappell, in fact, insisted from first to last that, whatever they said at Lord's, the Aussies were playing for the Ashes – and that was it, cobber! Well, *wherever* they were in the meantime, the events of 1981 convinced even the most hard-bitten Okker that those burned-up old bails are back where they belong . . . for the time being.

SUMMARY OF RESULTS

1882	The Oval	Australia won by 7 runs
1882/3	Melbourne	Australia won by 9 wickets
	Melbourne	England won by an innings and 27 runs
	Sydney	England won by 69 runs
1884	Old Trafford	Match Drawn
	Lord's	England won by an innings and 5 runs
	The Oval	Match Drawn
1884/5	Adelaide	England won by 8 wickets
	Melbourne	England won by 10 wickets
	Sydney	Australia won by 6 runs
	Sydney	Australia won by 8 wickets
	Melbourne	England won by an innings and 98 runs
1886	Old Trafford	England won by 4 wickets
	Lord's	England won by an innings and 106 runs
	The Oval	England won by an innings and 217 runs
1886/7	Sydney	England won by 13 runs
	Sydney	England won by 71 runs
1887/8	Sydney	England won by 126 runs
1888	Lord's	Australia won by 61 runs
	The Oval	England won by an innings and 137 runs
	Old Trafford	England won by an innings and 21 runs
1890	Lord's	England won by 7 wickets
	The Oval	England won by 2 wickets
1891/2	Melbourne	Australia won by 54 runs
	Sydney	Australia won by 72 runs
	Adelaide	England won by an innings and 230 runs
1893	Lord's	Match Drawn
	The Oval	England won by an innings and 43 runs
	Old Trafford	Match drawn
1894/5	Sydney	England won by 10 runs
	Melbourne	England won by 94 runs
	Adelaide	Australia won by 382 runs
	Sydney	Australia won by an innings and 147 runs
	Melbourne	England won by 6 wickets.
1896	Lord's	England won by 6 wickets
	Old Trafford	Australia won by 3 wickets
	The Oval	England won by 66 runs
1897/8	Sydney	England won by 9 wickets
	Melbourne	Australia won by an innings and 55 runs
	Adelaide	Australia won by an innings and 13 runs
	Melbourne	Australia won by 8 wickets
	Sydney	Australia won by 6 wickets
1899	Trent Bridge	Match Drawn
	Lord's	Australia won by 10 wickets
	Headingley	Match Drawn
	Old Trafford	match Drawn
	The Oval	Match Drawn
1901/2	Sydney	England won by an innings and 124 runs
	Melbourne	Australia won by 229 runs
	Adelaide	Australia won by 4 wickets
	Sydney	Australia won by 7 wickets
	Melbourne	Australia won by 32 runs
1902	Edgbaston	Match Drawn
	Lord's	Match Drawn
	Sheffield	Australia won by 143 runs
	Old Trafford	Australia won by 3 runs
	The Oval	England won by 1 wicket
1903/4	Sydney	England won by 5 wickets
	Melbourne	England won by 185 runs
	Adelaide	Australia won by 216 runs
	Sydney	England won by 157 runs
	Melbourne	Australia won by 218 runs
1905	Trent Bridge	England won by 213 runs
	Lord's	Match drawn
	Headingley	Match Drawn

	Old Trafford	England won by an innings and 80 runs
	The Oval	Match Drawn
1907/8	Sydney	Australia won by 2 wickets
	Melbourne	England won by 1 wicket
	Adelaide	Australia won by 245 runs
	Melbourne	Australia won by 308 runs
	Sydney	Australia won by 49 runs
1909	Edgbaston	England won by 10 wickets
	Lord's	Australia won by 9 wickets
	Headingley	Australia won by 126 runs
	Old Trafford	Match Drawn
	The Oval	Match Drawn
1911/12	Sydney	Australia won by 146 runs
	Melbourne	England won by 8 wickets
	Adelaide	England won by 7 wickets
	Melbourne	England won by an innings and 225 runs
	Sydney	England won by 70 runs
1912	Lord's	Match Drawn
	Old Trafford	Match Drawn
	The Oval	England won by 244 runs
1920/21	Sydney	Australia won by 377 runs
	Melbourne	Australia won by an innings and 91 runs
	Adelaide	Australia won by 119 runs
	Melbourne	Australia won by 8 wickets
	Sydney	Australia won by 9 wickets
1921	Trent Bridge	Australia won by 10 wickets
	Lord's	Australia won by 8 wickets
	Headingley	Australia won by 219 runs
	Old Trafford	Match Drawn
	The Oval	Match Drawn
1924/5	Sydney	Australia won by 193 runs
	Melbourne	Australia won by 81 runs
	Adelaide	Australia won by 11 runs
	Melbourne	England won by an innings and 29 runs
	Sydney	Australia won by 307 runs
1926	Trent Bridge	Match Drawn
	Lord's	Match Drawn
	Headingley	Match Drawn
	Old Trafford	Match Drawn
	The Oval	England won by 289 runs
1928/9	Brisbane	England won by 675 runs
	Sydney	England won by 8 wickets
	Melbourne	England won by 3 wickets
	Adelaide	England won by 12 runs
	Melbourne	Australia won by 5 wickets
1930	Trent Bridge	England won by 93 runs
	Lord's	Australia won by 7 wickets
	Headingley	Match Drawn
	Old Trafford	Match Drawn
	The Oval	Australia won by an innings and 39 runs
1932/3	Sydney	England won by 10 wickets
	Melbourne	Australia won by 111 runs
	Adelaide	England won by 338 runs
	Brisbane	England won by 6 wickets
	Sydney	England won by 8 wickets
1934	Trent Bridge	Australia won by 238 runs
	Lord's	England won by an innings and 38 runs
	Old Trafford	Match Drawn
	Headingley	Match Drawn
	The Oval	Australia won by 562 runs
1936/7	Brisbane	England won by 322 runs
	Sydney	England won by an innings and 22 runs
	Melbourne	Australia won by 365 runs
	Adelaide	Australia won by 148 runs
	Melbourne	Australia won by an innings and 200 runs
1938	Trent Bridge	Match Drawn
	Lord's	Match Drawn
	Headingley	Australia won by 5 wickets
	The Oval	England won by an innings and 579 runs
1946/7	Brisbane	Australia won by an innings and 332 runs
	Sydney	Australia won by an innings and 33 runs
	Melbourne	Match Drawn
	Adelaide	Match Drawn
	Sydney	Australia won by 5 wickets
1948	Trent Bridge	Australia won by 8 wickets
	Lord's	Australia won by 409 runs
	Old Trafford	Match Drawn
	Headingley	Australia won by 7 wickets
	England	Australia won by an innings and 149 runs
1950/51	Brisbane	Australia won by 70 runs
	Melbourne	Australia won by 28 runs
	Sydney	Australia won by an innings and 13 runs
	Adelaide	Australia won by 274 runs
	Melbourne	England won by 8 wickets
1953	Trent Bridge	Match Drawn
	Lord's	Match Drawn
	Old Trafford	Match Drawn
	Headingley	Match Drawn
	The Oval	England won by 8 wickets
1954/5	Brisbane	Australia won by an innings and 154 runs
	Sydney	England won by 38 runs
	Melbourne	England won by 128 runs
	Adelaide	England won by 5 wickets
	Sydney	Match Drawn
1956	Trent Bridge	Match Drawn
	Lord's	Australia won by 185 runs

	Headingley	England won by an innings and 42 runs
	Old Trafford	England won by an innings and 170 runs
	The Oval	Match Drawn
1958/9	Brisbane	Australia won by 8 wickets
	Melbourne	Australia won by 8 wickets
	Sydney	Match Drawn
	Adelaide	Australia won by 10 wickets
	Melbourne	Australia won by 9 wickets
1961	Edgbaston	Match Drawn
	Lord's	Australia won by 5 wickets
	Headingley	England won by 8 wickets
	Old Trafford	Australia won by 54 runs
	The Oval	Match Drawn
1962/3	Brisbane	Match Drawn
	Melbourne	England won by 7 wickets
	Sydney	Australia won by 8 wickets
	Australia	Match Drawn
	Sydney	Match Drawn
1964	Trent Bridge	Match Drawn
	Lord's	Match Drawn
	Headingley	Australia won by 7 wickets
	Old Trafford	Match Drawn
	The Oval	Match Drawn
1965/6	Brisbane	Match Drawn
	Melbourne	Match Drawn
	Melbourne	Match Drawn
	Sydney	England won by an innings and 93 runs
	Adelaide	Australia won by an innings and 9 runs
	Melbourne	Match Drawn
1968	Old Trafford	Australia won by 159 runs
	Lord's	Match Drawn
	Edgbaston	Match Drawn
	Headingley	Match Drawn
	The Oval	England won by 226 runs
1970/71	Brisbane	Match Drawn
	Perth	Match Drawn
	Sydney	England won by 299 runs
	Melbourne	Match Drawn
	Adelaide	Match Drawn
	Sydney	England won by 62 runs
1972	Old Trafford	England won by 89 runs
	Lord's	Australia won by 8 wickets
	Trent Bridge	Match Drawn
	Headingley	England won by 9 wickets
	The Oval	Australia won by 5 wickets
1974/5	Brisbane	Australia won by 166 runs
	Perth	Australia won by 9 wickets
	Melbourne	Match Drawn
	Sydney	Australia won by 171 runs
	Adelaide	Australia won by 163 runs
	Melbourne	England won by an innings and 4 runs
1975	Edgbaston	Australia won by an innings and 85 runs
	Lord's	Match Drawn
	Headingley	Match Drawn
	The Oval	Match Drawn
1977	Melbourne (Centenary Test).	Australia won by 45 runs
1977	Lords	Match Drawn
	Old Trafford	England won by 9 wickets
	Trent Bridge	England won by 7 wickets
	Headingley	England won by an innings and 85 runs
	The Oval	Match Drawn
1978–79	Brisbane	England won by 7 wickets
	Perth	England won by 166 runs
	Melbourne	Australia won by 93 runs
	Sydney	England won by 93 runs
	Adelaide	England won by 205 runs
	Sydney	England won by 9 wickets
1979–80 (unofficial series)	Perth	Australia won by 138 runs
	Sydney	Australia won by 6 wickets
	Melbourne	Australia won by 8 wickets
1981	Trent Bridge	Australia won by 4 wickets
	Lord's	Match Drawn
	Headingley	England won by 18 runs
	Edgbaston	England won by 29 runs
	The Oval	Match Drawn

INDEX